GOOD NEIGHBORS

GOOD NEIGHBORS

Gentrifying Diversity in Boston's South End

Sylvie Tissot
Translated by David Broder
with Catherine Romatowski

VERSO

London • New York

This edition first published by Verso 2015
Translation © David Broder, Catherine Romatowski 2015
First published as *De bons voisins: Enquête dans un quartier de la bourgeoisie progressiste*
© Éditions Raisons d'Agir, Paris, 2011

1 3 5 7 9 10 8 6 4 2

Verso
UK: 6 Meard Street, London W1F 0EG
US: 20 Jay Street, Suite 1010, Brooklyn, NY 11201
www.versobooks.com

Verso is the imprint of New Left Books

ISBN-13: 978-1-78168-792-5 (HC)
eISBN-13: 978-1-78168-949-3 (US)
eISBN-13: 978-1-78168-950-9 (UK)

British Library Cataloguing in Publication Data
A catalogue record for this book is available from the British Library

Library of Congress Cataloging-in-Publication Data

Tissot, Sylvie.
[De bons voisins. English]
Good neighbors : gentrifying diversity in Boston's South End / Sylvie Tissot ;
translated by David Broder.
pages cm
"First published as De bons voisins: Enqu?te dans un quartier de la bourgeoisie
progressiste, Editions Raisons d'Agir, Paris, 2011."
Includes bibliographical references and index.
ISBN 978-1-78168-792-5 (alk. paper : hbk) — ISBN 978-1-78168-949-3 (ebk.)
— ISBN 978-1-78168-950-9 (ebk.)
1. Middle class—Massachusetts—Boston—Attitudes. 2. Gentrification—
Massachusetts—Boston. 3. Cultural pluralism—Massachusetts—Boston. 4. Cultural
fusion—Massachusetts—Boston. 5. Sociology, Urban—Massachusetts—Boson. 6.
Neighborhoods—Social aspects—Massachusetts—Boston. 7. South End (Boston,
Mass.)—Social conditions. 8. Boston (Mass.)—Social conditions. I. Title.
HN80.B7.T5713 2015
305.5›50974461—dc23
2015004601

Typeset in Electra by Hewer Text UK Ltd, Edinburgh, Scotland
Printed in the US by Maple Press

CONTENTS

Introduction

"Landlords are the real terrorists."

After scribbling these angry words across his storefront window, the manager of the Life Café at New York's Tompkins Square Park slid his keys under the door. Confronted with a steep rise in rent, he had decided to close up for good. This was September 2011, a decade after the World Trade Center attacks. The Life Café was situated in Manhattan's East Village, a neighborhood that had seen accelerated gentrification over the last twenty years. Rising rent, population turnover, the restoration of old apartments and the construction of new housing aimed at high-income professionals: this already-familiar story today extends across New York to Brooklyn, as well as neighborhoods in the eastern parts of London, Paris and Berlin. The words of the Life Café manager, which I happened across in 2011, seemed to bring together all of today's symbols of evil: terrorists and landlords, Al Qaeda and hipsters, bombs and bulldozers. Of course gentrification does not mobilize the same energy at the highest levels of government, nor does local policy make a real attempt to curb it, but gentrification is nevertheless the object of ever more numerous critiques. And in large part for good reasons — ones that the East Village's anti-gentrification movements already understood in 1988, before the police evacuated the occupants of Tompkins Square Park.

Gentrification, the rehabilitation of old and degraded neighborhoods as wealthier households move in, is one of the more flagrant manifestations of the inequalities that mark the early twenty-first century. The phenomenon can hardly go unnoticed: it affects more and more cities, from New York and San Francisco to the capitals of Europe and now South America, as changing lifestyles and the transformation of commerce brutally reorganize public space. Racial minorities and the working class today are relegated ever further into the periphery or, for the very poorest, into the insalubrious interstices of the city. But if concern for this phenomenon is mounting, it's also because part of the middle class, spending an ever-greater portion of its income on housing, is no longer spared from these pressures. The slogan "the right to the city" seems more timely than ever more in the planet's great conurbations.

The arrival of rich homeowners suddenly attracted to long-stigmatized neighborhoods recently roused the anger of the famous director Spike Lee, who grew up in Fort Greene, then a working-class neighborhood in Brooklyn. Incensed by a *New York Times* piece invoking the purportedly positive aspects of gentrification, Lee questioned why improvements of schools, policing and trash collection took place only when white people moved into neighborhoods where the black population had long been deprived of quality services.[1] He also castigated the lack of respect shown by new homeowners claiming to have "discovered" the neighborhood. Like many who have seen the streets where they grew up transformed in recent years, his anger was fed by often unexpected changes, such as the parade of chic dogs, those emblems of gentrification, in Fort Greene Park, or the new names designed to wash away a neighborhood's "ghetto" reputation, as when Washington, DC real estate agents rechristened LeDroit Park with the more elegant "Bloomingdale".

As a consequence, many artists and minorities lament living in cities where alternative counter-cultures and spaces of resistance no longer have any right to that city. Who today can afford to live in Manhattan's SoHo or even the Castro in San Francisco? If fashionable galleries prosper, where do artists and writers have to go to find a decent place to live, where they can write and create? When gay neighborhoods see an influx of ever-wealthier heterosexual families, how can gay and lesbian people maintain protected spaces in societies that remain heteronormative? To be sure, the renewal of these areas no longer takes place to the rhythm of bulldozers and riot police batons, but

---

1 Joe Coscarelli, "Spike Lee's Amazing Rant Against Gentrification: 'We Been Here!,'" *New York*, February 25, 2014.

eviction of tenants asked to leave their homes to give free rein to real estate speculation has not stopped.

Even if we ought to be pleased that criticism of gentrification is multiplying, it remains the case that discussion of the phenomenon mostly takes the form of irony. The figure of the hipster is known to all, and blogs post endless, more-or-less humorous comments on the hipster's habits, the variety of coffee he prefers and the length of his beard. The residents who look on, stunned or incredulous, as these "hipsters" move in next door to them get rather less attention, particularly from journalists, who rarely see rising rent as worth covering. When it comes to gentrification, websites and magazines seem to see gentrification as a kind of board game, where players may choose from several different familial roles: the grandmother (the empty nester rescued from the residential suburbs once her children leave for college); the father (the wealthy banker who owns a brownstone); the mother (the stay-at-home mom pushing her stroller endlessly between the sandbox and the neighborhood cafés); the gay uncle. Or equally, the cousin hipster on his bike, plaid shirt and moustache waving in the wind. Not to forget the baby or babies nestled in the stroller, between the café and the aisles of Whole Foods. And, of course, the dog—the poodle, the Labrador or the chihuahua. When one speaks of gentrification, the black family, the butch lesbian and the Hispanic worker are always absent.

The denunciation of the hipster (in France called the *bobo*, "bourgeois-bohemian") is all the more unsatisfying for in reality it is always a way of saying that one is not, or not completely, "like them." This means of distinguishing oneself betrays a sense of culpability among those who, in looking for housing, must move to ever-poorer, more remote neighborhoods, and in doing so, often unwittingly contribute to transforming these areas. Whether irony or guilt, these sentiments offer few tools for understanding, and ultimately intervening in the urban changes that are taking place.

Novels that take well-known neighborhoods in the process of gentrification as their setting are marked with the same ambivalence. One such work, written by the black novelist Nathan McCall, portrays a tenant about to be kicked out of his apartment on Atlanta's Auburn Avenue, and his white neighbors, who are enthusiastic new homeowners. The author astutely describes the physical and symbolic violence provoked by the latter's lifestyle and naïve quest for adventure, accompanied by a total incomprehension of social distance and racial tensions. The white homeowners ultimately sell their house, while the black tenant is evicted from his apartment. Curiously this did not prevent the novel's publisher from using this *USA Today* quote in the book's back cover: "Against the odds, it offers a glimmer of hope." The writer Adam Langer, meanwhile, has a more developed sense of the happy ending: the black renter on Manhattan's Upper West Side, like McCall's character, watches stupefied as his neighborhood transforms—but ends up marrying the young white woman who was about to buy his apartment.[2] In sum, gentrification may be bad, but no one wants there to be any bad guys in this story. And ultimately, everyone seems resigned to see gentrification as a regrettable but ineluctable phenomenon: nothing can be done to stop it.

Numerous sociological and geographical analyses have been developed over the last twenty years, shedding a different light on this process. The aim of some of these researchers has been to break with individual, often psychologizing, approaches, instead addressing gentrification as a structural phenomenon. Far from the good (or bad) intentions of individuals, instead the logics of capitalism or of the political field explain in large part the urban transformations that these studies examine.[3] Unfortunately these analyses, focusing on macroeconomic phenomena, show little interest in local realities or indeed the variety of different situations, which are not reducible to the logic of real estate investment alone. Moreover, as stimulating as these analyses might be, they are sometimes reappropriated politically, giving rise to a hostility on principle against this homogenized category, "the gentrifiers," who are set up as a new political enemy—as if here, too, we needed a renewed injection of moralizing, and thus of easy dichotomies, when in fact the social sciences offer much more valuable tools. In this book, I suggest an approach that seeks to grasp the particular social relations that exist in these gentrified neighborhoods and the kind of local power that has been constructed there over several decades, and still facilitates the continued arrival of new populations.

---

2   Nathan McCall, *Them*, New York: Atria Books, 2007; Adam Langer, *Ellington Boulevard: A Novel in A-Flat*, New York: Spiegel & Grau, 2008.

3   See for example Neil Smith, *The New Urban Frontier: Gentrification and the Revanchist City*, London: Routledge, 1996. For a presentation and discussion of works on gentrification, see Loretta Lees, Tom Slater and Elvin Wyly, *Gentrification*, New York: Routledge, 2008.

As many works have already described, the urban renewal policies implemented in North American and European city centers since World War II, the deindustrialization that left many spaces vacant in these cities, and the political and social upheavals of the 1960s all promoted unprecedented residential migration to the run-down neighborhoods of rapidly growing cities. The arrival of wealthier populations and the material regeneration of certain sites are the most visible and well-known phenomena. But they are also accompanied by a transformation of local organization, marked by the emergence of a new kind of local elite. The predecessors of those we now term "hipsters" appropriated these areas for themselves in unprecedented fashion, becoming invested not only in public spaces but also in the institutions of local power; and succeeding, more generally, in "setting the tone" for life in the neighborhood. This type of power, whose different facets we will analyze, has the specificity of being built around a watchword previously unknown among the country's upper classes. The gentrifiers who came to live in run-down city-center neighborhoods from the 1960s onward invoked "diversity," a slogan directly inherited from social movements. At that time, those who opposed the bulldozers of urban renewal (redubbed "Negro removal") dreamed—inspired by the essayist Jane Jacobs—of different ways of living in the city, far from the suburban way of life where whites lived exclusively among themselves.

What happened in these now sought-after neighborhoods cannot, then, be reduced solely to the brutal displacement of the preexisting population. Nor is it a simple matter of cohabitation among different populations, whose consequent encounters or avoidance of one another we could thus analyze. This book hypothesizes instead a highly particular manner of taking over space, constructed across several decades. Transformations of the real estate market did encourage this, but we also need to integrate logics beyond just the economic into our understanding of how these spaces are transformed. The newcomers' power is constituted in relation to City Hall as well as the world of civic associations. But more broadly it rests on a particular legitimacy, an order at once moral and cultural, which runs through tastes, lifestyles, the writing of an area's history, a language and an ethos, and which exists not only within the interiors of the newly renovated houses, but is also propagated across the neighborhood's squares, restaurants and local institutions.

So what is the composition of this new elite, whose culture today marks the landscape of so many major cities? Valuing diversity at the neighborhood level, and cosmopolitan in their relationship to the outside world, these white homeowners break with the racial segregation that has marked the history of the United States, and they condemn any overt expression of racism. Their lifestyles are less exclusively based on the family sphere and heterosexual conjugality, marking a further break with the image of the paterfamilias and the woman-as-housewife. They often describe themselves as liberals, even if this means—as they often put it—a combination of social liberalism and fiscal conservatism. Some might say that this liberalism does not count for much, that the interactions among the different social groups living in "mixed" areas are very limited, and that, at best, the benevolence of the richest serves to buy them a clear conscience, and at a bargain price.

This book, though, does not propose to judge whether this local power is democratic or elitist, or to reveal the "truth" of how far these gentrifiers do or do not practice the principles they preach. The book is not about measuring the extent of the proclaimed diversity, but rather about analyzing how mixing across social groups is defined and controlled. Diversity's defenders are as ready to live among black and Hispanic people, and to share certain social spaces with openly gay people, as they are, at the same time, devoted to a very careful organization of this proximity. Having a right to oversee housing projects, while being in favor of "mixed" construction projects; making generous donations to charity associations but intervening in the way aid recipients are managed; favoring the opening of chic and "exotic" restaurants after having forced "disreputable" bars to close down; participating in the renovation of parks, only then to control access to them; inscribing their presence in a history that celebrates the culture of the upper classes and Victorian architecture, but encouraging the opening of studios for penniless artists: all this in the name of a diversity that does not exceed certain limits.

The enthusiasm for diversity ultimately translates into a form of power that operates on a particular combination of inclusion and exclusion. As such, it contrasts with the systematic efforts since the beginning of the twentieth century to deny black people access to residential suburbs, as well as with the establishment of hyper-ghettos after World War II.[4] It involves the recognition

---

4   Douglas Massey and Nancy Denton, *American Apartheid: Segregation and the Making of the Underclass*, Cambridge, MA: Harvard University Press, 1993. Loïc Wacquant, *Urban Outcasts: A Comparative Sociology of Advanced Marginality*, Cambridge: Polity, 2008.

of the right of the poorest populations to live in their neighborhood, and this sometimes implies combating market forces or the most reactionary residents in order to maintain some minimal percentage of public housing units. The people who are most mobilized in neighborhood associations make an effort to educate newcomers, and this is no easy task: the virtues of diversity are far from *self-evident* to US homeowners, whose need to start saving early for their children's education makes them even more sensitive to property values, and for whom urban decline remains closely associated with the figure of the African-American. So practices we see being put in place in the name of diversity must be understood in light of the attitudes of the elites over the centuries and up to the 1960s: virulent anti-Semitism, systematic racial discrimination in the working and consumer worlds, the obsessive fear of living near black people, the extreme violence of racial discourse and the lynchings that long plagued the South, and a strict control of social reproduction by way of family lineage. The spatial rapprochement in the gentrified neighborhoods marks a break with the strict segregation that divided inner-city ghettos from residential suburbs, and today's prevalent gay-friendliness runs counter to the virulent opprobrium to which homosexuality was subjected for centuries. But this tolerance is far from unequivocal because it entails limits on visibility and interactions only in carefully controlled spaces. In the liberal wing of the upper classes, people are never so gay friendly as when they are in the company of wealthy homosexuals, potentially married or perhaps parents, who appear in public parks bearing the new social markers that are their "luxury pets" and their patronage of the new businesses intended for the wealthy, like upscale spas and bakeries.

The continuous influx of the upper middle classes into mixed neighborhoods is the heir to all this history, which this book recounts by way of a study of Boston at the local level. Why this city? In Boston we find a number of the phenomena at the origin of gentrification. It is a former industrial city, hit hard by the Great Depression and rebuilt on the basis of competitive service-sector businesses from the 1960s onward. Its city center, made up of working-class districts, underwent one of the most brutal urban renewal programs in the United States, allowing a wholesale change in the character of neighborhoods like the South End, the subject of this monograph. Despite the differences in US and European political history, on both sides of the Atlantic the protest movements of the 1960s and the demands for "local democracy" resulted in the creation of new sites of power in the world of civic associations, outside of the traditional organization of the political field. The architectural homogeneity of the South End contrasts with the variety of urban forms in other gentrified neighborhoods (though erased by the homogenizing figure of the hipster). While some new Bostonians were "rediscovering" the glory of the nineteenth century's Victorian architecture and seeing the South End as a "historic neighborhood" and no longer a "ghetto," elsewhere, in a relatively smaller portion of the South End, others emphasized the local art scene, transforming former factories into lofts.

Thus in Boston we see a particular strategy for re-elevating the status of the neighborhood. It has taken different forms elsewhere in the United States and Europe, but this symbolic work always constitutes an essential element of the appropriation of gentrifying neighborhoods, indissociable from the material renovation of their dwellings. One last notable specificity is the gentrifiers' inordinate taste for espresso, cappuccino and other drinks considered sophisticated in the United States. It is true that alimentary practices give rise to forms of distinction that vary highly across space. But once again, it is the social meanings of these operations that interest us here; in other words, that the new residents' aversion to African-American "soul food" on the one hand, and on the other, their taste for a tempered exoticism in restaurants, newly opened as the gentrifiers moved in, provide a window onto a carefully fashioned alterity.

Boston's South End presents one more particularity. Like other neighborhoods termed "super-gentrified,"[5] the gentrifiers there have a specific profile. The upper middle classes today form a dominant group: not by their numbers, but politically, socially and symbolically.[6] Across recent decades a particularly

---

5   Loretta Lees, "Super-Gentrification: The Case of Brooklyn Heights, New York City," *Urban Studies* 40: 12, 2003, pp. 2487–509; Tim Butler and Loretta Lees, "Super-Gentrification in Barnsbury, London: Globalization and Gentrifying Global Elites at the Neighbourhood Level," *Transactions of the Institute of British Geographers* 31: 4, 2006, pp. 467–87.

6   This local elite is, indeed, a minority in a neighborhood of 28,000 inhabitants where still today 40 percent of housing is subsidized and where in 2000, a few years before the beginning of this study, black people made up some 25 percent of the population, Hispanics 16 percent and Asians 11.5 percent. In the same year in the South End, the

mobilized elite has emerged from among these new arrivals, one engaged in local civic associations and acting as a voice for the wealthiest households, now the only ones able to purchase property in the neighborhood. In the South End, the story is in some respects over: they won. How did they do it? In describing a new form of power over space, this book's objective is to explain the secrets of their victory. This power has been constructed on four planes, which make up the four main chapters of this book: politics, morality, culture and public space. After the first chapter's description of the particular stakes posed by an ethnographic study among the wealthy, we will see how a local elite was able to emerge in a US working-class neighborhood. As municipal politics made space for "participatory planning" from the 1960s onward, and state interventionism was drastically scaled back in the 1980s, some residents knew how to access the resources necessary to get involved in managing local affairs. But taking power in a mixed neighborhood is not an easy thing. The wealthiest white residents' gradual exertion of control would not have been possible without the alliances and misalliances this sociological inquiry brings to light, and which would be translated through a rallying around the ambiguous watchword of "diversity."

As explained in the third chapter, devoted to the material and symbolic dimension of this local power, a particular authority was constituted on the basis of a moral posture and political progressivism, but also on an ethos that abhorred conflict and prized "good neighborliness." Following this, the fourth chapter turns to the manner by which residents who engaged in the neighborhood's civic associations knew how to transform the South End's architecture into a historical heritage. To do this, they tapped into the most elite resources of respectable upper-class culture, only subsequently promoting a more "bohemian" image—after they first warded off the threat of a massive public housing project.

The fifth chapter, centered on public spaces, continues the description of a kind of power and a way of life closely linked to the control of place. The

average income was $41,590, though $56,814 for whites, $15,878 for blacks, $18,359 for Asians, and $12,415 for Hispanics. It is worth noting that the 2000 census distinguished between six social categories, with Hispanics counted separately. All the data in the rest of the book come—unless otherwise mentioned—from the census or the Boston Redevelopment Authority.

reorganization of the restaurant scene reduced the visibility of working-class sociability and of black and Hispanic people; at the same time, it has allows for the possibility of distinguishing oneself from a snobbery that insists on French gastronomy alone. Public gardens provide a window onto the kind of social relations being established in mixed neighborhoods: the comings and goings of "undesirables" are carefully controlled, though this means less chasing them out than assigning them to subordinate spaces and distancing them from the exclusive microspaces where gay and straight people of high socio-economic standing mix freely.

While describing these singular interactions in detail, the chapters of this book show how a social group constructed itself as a new neighborhood emerged. This South End, invented by a specific group, is not only a perceived and imagined space, but also one that this group has managed to effectuate in an inextricably linked material and symbolic reality: a trendy neighbor-hood of renovated brownstones and chic restaurants, real estate listings and South End Historical Society meetings, a neighborhood that is simultane-ously "mixed" in its population and "Victorian" in its architecture, gay friendly but also dog friendly. Despite all this, the other residents' neighbor-hood has not disappeared, but its people have been rendered almost invisible in public space. Not necessarily adhering to the new regime of diversity, many of these residents, particularly black and Hispanic people, found their claims and their vision for the "real South End" disqualified.

Chapter 1

A Journey into the Liberal Upper Middle Class

In contrast to the many studies devoted to poor neighborhoods, it is relatively rare that sociologists take an interest in those spaces and populations not designated as "problems." Engaging the latter poses specific methodological issues, which I faced from the outset of my study. Visiting luxe apartments renovated by lawyer, consultant or upper management homeowners, I often found myself on large converted rooftop decks overlooking Boston's downtown skyscrapers. Pointed toward this view by my hosts—rather than toward the less affluent southeast section of the neighborhood—I could admire the impressive array of Victorian houses, dotted by the little green patches of gardens and terraces. Yet once I headed back down to the lower floors and neighborhood streets, it was not so easy to find the proper perspective required for this study, the right combination of distance and proximity.

THE DISCOVERY OF THE SOUTH END

The first contact I made in Boston's South End was with the public-private partnership Washington Gateway Main Street in 2004. At that time it was managing the rehabilitation of undeveloped areas around Washington Street together with—I was told—representatives of the neighborhood.[1] One of its

---

1 On the role of this body in the renovation of Washington Street, see Chapter 2,

employees was a member of a neighborhood association organizing a fund-raiser a few days later; she invited me to go along with her. The soirée was held in a small garden behind a Victorian building. The host's house, which had been entirely renovated, had six floors and faced one of the prettiest parts of the South End, Union Park. Guests entered from the garden by way of the kitchen, which occupied a sixty-square-meter mezzanine. I took this opportunity to check out the impressive extended sitting room situated on the floor above. The party confirmed what I had already observed in community meetings organized by the mayor's office: the role played by neighborhood associations, the vast majority of whose members were white homeowners. Having previously been involved in a collaborative research project on "community movements,"[2] I saw that they had lost much of their influence in the South End, notably to the benefit of developers but also the homeowners' associations. I decided to continue my research among these latter groups, thus orienting my project toward a sociology of the upper middle class.

In doing so, I discovered a quite unique neighborhood, which was hard to imagine having ever been a working-class area, or retaining any demographic diversity, as census data showed. I made my first forays into the South End in June 2004, attending neighborhood association meetings and carrying out interviews in the plush homes closest to the city center. Arriving by subway from Cambridge each day, I walked through the streets lined with brownstones, these multistory bricked edifices, and along its principal artery, Tremont Street. As one might expect, my own tastes—those of a white French academic—took me to cafés serving espressos more often than to Dunkin' Donuts. But when I began frequenting bars, cafés and chic restaurants in earnest, it was foremost because that was where my first interviewees wanted to meet. More than ten dollars for a glass of wine—I was staggered by the sums I had to spend in order to initiate and maintain the socializing necessary for my research. And on Washington Street, the consequences of more than five years of renewal carried out in consultation with the "inhabitants" were striking: a new bus line, but above all pricey restaurants and luxe loft

---

plus chapters 4 and 5 on the creation of an "artists district" and the commercial restructuring of this area.

2   Marie-Hélène Bacqué (ed.), *Projet urbain en quartier ancien. La Goutte d'Or, South End*, Paris: PUCA, 2005.

apartments. No longer could I find any traces of Boston's industrial past in the contemporary urban landscape—or if I did, it was only in a vague sense, through a few details on buildings since transformed into lofts. However, it was this past that gave birth to working-class neighborhoods like the South End at the end of the nineteenth century, before they became ghettos in the interwar period.

The South End
The Industrial and Racial History of Boston

Though slightly slower than other major cities, the demographic growth of Boston in the nineteenth century was still impressive: just 25,000 in 1800, the population grew to 560,000 a hundred years later. Formerly a small town whose influence derived from its harbor and maritime trade, Boston now became an industrial city.[3] The South End was one of the city-center neighborhoods that the industrialization and migratory waves of the late nineteenth century transformed into working-class areas. All the same, it had the beginnings of an upper-middle-class neighborhood. In the mid-nineteenth century, the mayor's office launched a building plan around the narrow corridor of land that attached the center of Boston to the rest of the city. Housing developments built in the 1850s and 1860s made for a neighborhood 1.6 square miles in size: the South End. At that time, the Boston nobility already had its home in Beacon Hill. The new neighborhood welcomed a somewhat less prestigious population, drawn from the middle classes connected to trade and industry. However, the urban planning of the area as well as its architecture, similar to that in Beacon Hill, did allow the South End to lay claim to the same kind of elegance. These town-houses known as brownstones were accessed by staircases with wrought-iron railings, and included space on lower floors (with separate entrances) for domestic servants. Rows of brownstones made up streets that widened, in some cases, around little parks: Union Park, Worcester

---

3   Thomas H. O'Connor, *The Hub: Boston Past and Present*, Boston: Northeastern University Press, 2001.

Square and Chester Square. It was here that the wealthiest inhabitants took up residence.

A number of events led to a sharp reversal of the South End's fortunes, especially the financial panic of 1873. Additionally, the 1860s saw the development of a new neighborhood, Back Bay, which spread from the railways bordering the South End as far as the Charles River. A considerable number of South End residents moved to this district, attractively situated at the foot of Beacon Hill and even closer to the city center. The wealthiest South End residents fled to this new neighborhood, and a poorer and more precarious population, in particular immigrants arriving from Europe, replaced them. First came the Irish, fleeing the potato famine then afflicting their home country. Already in 1830, some 9000 Irish had migrated to Boston, the destination city for a major maritime route from Europe. Then came Italians, East European Jews, and some men coming from the rural areas of New England and Quebec, working on the railways and in the factories in the southern and eastern parts of the South End. Beginning in 1866 , in what was an undeniable sign of decline in status for the neighborhood, in a city where the elite was strictly WASP (White Anglo-Saxon Protestant), the Irish began to build the Cathedral of the Holy Cross on the corner of Union Park and Washington Street. In 1901 an elevated train line began circulating along this main artery, where a range of stores and factories were opening for business.

The population grew rapidly, reaching 76,000 inhabitants by 1910. At the same time, an estimated 37,000 people lived in the lodging houses that were springing up in the very heart of the neighborhood. Immigrant families gradually bought the stately mansions formerly belonging to the upper middle class, and redivided the top floors into rentals. Bars proliferated, as well as community centers and charity associations. The South End became the immigrants' gateway to Boston. The Irish were followed by Middle Eastern and Asian populations, and, after World War II, Puerto Ricans. The black population grew continually as immigration flowed from the Caribbean but also from the southern United States, with black Americans coming in search of better working conditions and a less segregated society. This black population included a substantial middle class, which, as a result of the segregation (at once social and spatial) enforced in Boston and environs, could not make its home in the white residential zones expanding out into the suburbs.[4]

Even if migration to Boston was not as extensive as it was to other Northern cities like New York, Baltimore or even Chicago and Detroit — where significant ghettos built up in the interwar period and most of all after World War II — the black population of Boston rose from 23,000 in 1940 to 40,000 in 1950, and in 1960 hit 63,000. Between the two world wars, the South End became Boston's "Harlem": a relatively socioeconomically mixed neighborhood where bars and jazz clubs flourished, as did theaters and casinos. Subsequently, Prohibition spurred the growth of crime, and the Great Depression led to economic decline. Economic sectors like textiles that had made Boston rich in the nineteenth century migrated toward the southern United States. The southeast portion of the South End turned into a vast expanse of abandoned industrial facilities: it was from this fallow ground that loft buildings would spring up at the turn of the next century.

My study thus focuses on the mobilization of the upper middle classes, and more precisely, on the appropriation of a neighborhood and re-establishment of that neighborhood's social status by a very particular group of inhabitants, a local elite that seemed to me to be formed of genuine "notables" who maintained

---

4   Kenneth T. Jackson, *Crabgrass Frontier: The Suburbanization of the United States*, Oxford: Oxford University Press, 1985. On early migration to Boston's suburbs, see Sam B. Warner, *Streetcar Suburbs: The Process of Growth in Boston, 1870–1900*, Cambridge, MA: Harvard University Press, 1962. For many years, in the cities and suburbs of the United States, contracts forbade homeowners from selling their property to black people. These contracts were only declared illegal in 1949, and even then, this did not prevent discrimination against black populations by more covert means. See Douglas Massey and Nancy Denton, *American Apartheid: Segregation and the Making of the Underclass*, Cambridge, MA: Harvard University Press, 1993, pp. 34–8.

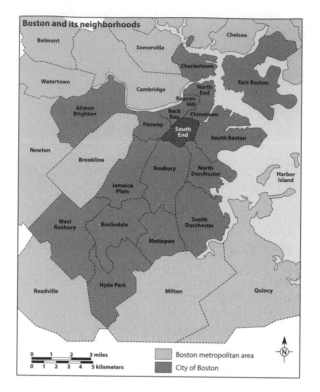

close relationships among themselves. In the South End in 2000, the two employment categories, "management" and "professionals" represented some 56 percent of the South End's population (compared to 43 percent in Boston as a whole), though this does not mean that white upper middle class households made up the majority population of the South End. In 2000, a quarter of households owned their homes, with whites making up just half of the inhabitants (14,048 out of 28,160 total), in contrast to the affluent suburbs which were often 80 percent white, or more. Moreover, one-third of South End households spoke languages other than English, and 23.9 percent of the population lived below the poverty line. Yet—and this was what struck me in my first trips to the South End—it is white property owners who have defined the style of relations prevalent in this neighborhood. They succeeded in imposing their own norms. If Boston's South End had seen some of the kinds of changes common to many of the other areas we term "gentrified" (the upgrading of buildings, population turnover that favored wealthier residents), the South End differs in one particular respect: the hold exerted exclusively by one social group, the broad majority of whose members arrived from the 1960s onward. Here, the businesses that dominate the area serve an overwhelmingly wealthy and white clientele. No groups of young black people gather on the sidewalks like in the Philadelphia Elijah Anderson studied (except the restaurants' valets), but instead Puerto Rican residents are confined to just a handful of blocks; few bohemian bars and cafés like Richard Lloyd described in Chicago, rather inexpensive pizzerias and fast-food places relegated to the margins of the neighborhood, while pricey chic restaurants have been proliferating on its principal arteries since the 1990s. Nor did the gentrification of the area involve a reappraisal of interwar black culture as in Harlem, whose second "renaissance" some have heralded on account of recent transformations. There is no celebration of Beat culture like in New York's Lower East Side, or of working-class and multicultural history as in Paris's Belleville.[5] This phenomenon is a striking one: the appropriation of space, at once social, symbolic and material, has reached a very advanced stage. *Contentive progress rather*

For the purposes of accounting for this singular phenomenon, I was interested in those people who, in connection to the public authorities and the other inhabitants, and making themselves the spokespeople of these latter, managed to establish themselves as a *local* authority. Starting from the contemporary plans for the development of Washington Street, then going back in time to the urban renewal of the 1960s, I rapidly came to see the central role that the civic sector played in the constitution of a recognizable group of elites, as these residents participated directly in the transformation of spaces. It was for this reason that I organized my inquiry around the fifteen neighborhood associations, the South End Historical Society, the park management associations and a parents' association at a neighborhood public

---

5   Elijah Anderson, *Streetwise: Race, Class and Change in an Urban Community*, Chicago: University of Chicago Press, 1990; Lance Freeman, *There Goes the "Hood": Views of Gentrification from the Ground Up*, Philadelphia: Temple University Press, 2006; Richard Lloyd, *Neo-Bohemia: Art and Commerce in the Post-Industrial City*, New York: Routledge, 2006; Christopher Mele, *Selling the Lower East Side*, Minneapolis: University of Minnesota Press, 2000; Monique M. Taylor, *Harlem Between Heaven and Hell*, Minneapolis: University of Minnesota Press, 2002; Patrick Simon, "La société partagée. Relations interethniques et interclasses dans un quartier en rénovation. Belleville, Paris XXe," *Cahiers internationaux de sociologie* 98, 1995, pp. 161–90.

school. With an average of about ten members participating actively in each group, we can estimate that in all, mobilized residents of the neighborhood numbered in the hundreds. Because these mobilized inhabitants contribute directly to defining their group's contours, they offer a particularly propitious context for studying the formation and functioning of the local elite.

A Harvard-affiliated French woman in a chic Boston neighborhood

In total, I conducted seventy-seven interviews, fifty of them with current members of local associations. The vast majority of these were white homeowners from the upper middle class, with incomes of between $100,000 and $400,000 for the richest, members of the employment categories "managers" and "professionals." I attended some twenty meetings and fundraisers organized by neighborhood associations, the dog park group and various charity bodies.[6] I enjoyed an exceedingly warm welcome. Access to research subjects often represents the first challenge in conducting qualitative research among the privileged classes. This was not the case for me, since I was inquiring into their participation in an especially esteemed practice: involvement in civic associations. The neighborhood association soirée I was invited to allowed me to make my first contacts. I also met many people by going to meetings by myself: I would briefly present my research to the person chairing the meeting and ask if I could say a few words to the assembled group at the end. I would then pass around a sign-up sheet, asking for prospective interviewees to leave their phone number and email address. I always received more volunteers than I had time to interview. Along with the prestigious Harvard name (where I was affiliated during several of my trips), the prospect of a French woman coming to study their country, their neighborhood and the civic associations that served as the foundation of their moral engagement sparked, if not immediate sympathy, then at least a widely shared willingness to help me. Many volunteers bent over backwards to accommodate my

---

6   I participated in many other events as well: neighborhood clean-up operations organized by the civic associations each year, fundraisers for local election candidates, organized walks in the South End, meals served in a shelter for homeless women, and finally a fundraiser for a South End youth employment group, as well as preparation meetings the same day.

interview, which was often lengthy (as long as an hour and a half) and sometimes followed by a second interview or additional questions sent by email.
My status as an academic, as well as my capacity, on account of my own
privileged background, to display what they considered to be good manners
(without the discomfort researchers from more modest backgrounds might
feel in similar situations) gave the impression of a similar social status,
prompting them to deploy the great affability of the US upper middle classes:
I was invited to numerous soirées and even dinners organized especially for
me. Without their welcome necessarily implying an invitation for prolonged
contact—the boundary marking of their intimate lives largely remained
firm—this openness facilitated my research among these Bostonians, who
generally were, additionally, Francophiles. The fact that I am white and an
academic was also without doubt an asset, as well as my French nationality.
France, and even more so Paris—a sign of cultural distinction but also a
travel destination for these South End residents—functioned as a shibboleth
that opened doors throughout my study.

This ideal situation, which was disturbed just once with an unfortunate
episode at the South End Historical Society ball,[7] did not prevent a certain
amount of questioning from coming up. These uncertainties were redoubled
as my relationships with the inhabitants of the South End became closer,
leading to more socializing outside of interview settings, a considerable
amount of informal conversations, various soirées, and even some of the
research subjects occasionally letting me stay at their homes. This gradual
immersion, which I had not planned at the outset of my study, can be
explained by many factors: the desire to pursue a geographical and social
adventure by plunging myself into the ethnography, but also the need to go
beyond interviewing in order to understand commitments that perplexed
me. More than difficulties accessing the field of inquiry, it was a mix of incre-
dulity and incomprehension that put the brakes on my research. One day I
was invited to a fundraiser for an important charity association located in the
South End. I arrived at the big downtown hotel where the event took place
and was staggered to see this ritual of upper-middle-class philanthropy: enormous buffets at which hundreds of participants helped themselves, edifying
speeches from those who pulled through difficult situations with the help of

---

7   See the account in Chapter 4.

[handwritten marginalia: capitalist paternalism of charity vs State]

the association, and auctions that raised very considerable sums of money (not least of the offers was a dinner with the mayor, the rights to which were purchased by a real estate developer for $9,000). The spectacle of charity directly clashes with the European statist principles—"la pensée d'Etat"[8]— which strongly tie the programs addressing poverty to the social welfare state, making such conspicuous displays of largesse on the part of the wealthiest individuals particularly shocking and incongruous. My surprise grew further still when I delved into the civic associations of these wealthy residents and became aware of the complex personal networks in which the residents were implicated. I contemplated this strange mélange of moral investment and social exclusion, outward bohemianism and the constant surveillance of their neighbors. I discovered the role that the South End's society dedicated to the study of history plays for the elites in whose homes I found so few books. I was forced to recognize that I did not really understand very much, and it seemed that I would certainly have to take a closer look.

My first "ally" played a crucial role in my study's ethnographic turn.[9] I met this South End resident during a soirée held by the neighborhood association in which she is an active member. She agreed to an interview a few days later, as well as to my contacting her again the following year and then regularly during my subsequent visits to Boston. Having taken a certain pleasure in the game of the interview, she continually offered new contacts. "Do you still interview people?" she asked me once again, having someone particular in mind, even in one of my last stays in the city. For each of my visits she drew up a list of events that might interest me, including the fundraisers that had sparked my curiosity from the start. She kept me up to date with news on the latest restaurant openings, recent events, and gossip and conflicts in the neighborhood.

It quickly became clear to me that (in retrospect, quite logically) this ally occupied a particular position in the milieu that I was studying—at once central and marginal. Central because, as a semi-retiree who had moved to the South End some years earlier, having separated from her husband and left their home in an affluent suburb—buying a duplex in the center of the

---

8   Pierre Bourdieu, *On the State*, Cambridge: Polity Press, 2015.

9   On the role of informants, see William Foot White, *Street Corner Society: The Social Structure of an Italian Slum*, Chicago: University of Chicago Press, 1993.

neighborhood with a small garden—she was involved in many local groups, taking part in all sorts of charity initiatives. Being taken under her wing to private soirées and large social events, I found myself at the heart of my subject group, making contact with those who had played prominent roles in some cases for several decades. Accompanying her through the South End with her, no matter where, always paid off: we would have to stop constantly, each "hi" and "hello" an occasion for me to jot down a few names and email addresses and schedule further interviews. I was introduced—with all the authority of her insistent recommendation—as a French woman "who'd come from Paris" to study "civic engagement" in the South End.

Nevertheless, little by little I came to understand that the diehard activism she engaged in also entailed a more ambivalent position. First, this ardent defender of diversity truly took the idea literally, with a fervor absent among many of the residents who adopted this dominant discourse in a more pro forma manner. This made her a representative of the most progressive wing of the South End's mobilized residents—and if it were not for this, the relations that I developed with her, based on real affinities, would doubtless have been more difficult. The intensity of her engagement also led her to seek out contacts with the most varied array of individuals: whether conservative or radical; Jewish (like herself), Protestant, Catholic or Orthodox; Americans or foreigners from other continents; white or black; heterosexual or gay—even starkly opposing viewpoints did not necessarily imply contradiction in this context, as each offered its own contribution to "diversity." As a French woman coming to study the milieu in which my ally was so active, I could easily find my place in this extended network of friends and acquaintances. Other facets of her personality also made our friendship possible: a certain complicity among women,[10] the great freedom in her personal life, her eccentric personality cutting through the amiable—sometimes even effusive—but rather codified patina that coated most interactions among the liberal upper middle class, and her taste for parties where wine flowed freely (which did not at all undermine her

---

10   The determining role that women played in the group in question, particularly single or divorced women, as well as gay people, also facilitated the contacts that I developed. One can imagine that a researcher arriving alone, as I did, would have faced more difficulties inserting herself in an environment more centered on the family unit.

extreme vigilance against the sale of alcohol in the neighborhood). For me all of this made her eminently likeable.

Handling antipathy

Still, the familiarity that I established with this ally and her circle of friends made me somewhat ill at ease. I was left feeling some duplicity, principally on account of what they inferred as my reasons for pursuing this fieldwork: sympathy toward the civic engagement that I presented as my object of inquiry. This impression was reinforced by the position that I took over a conflict that tore through the neighborhood during my research. I openly declared myself in favor of a controversial project proposed by the Pine Street Inn (PSI), a charitable organization that managed a homeless shelter. The group planned to buy three row houses in the middle of the neighborhood to provide housing for formerly homeless people. When the plans were made public, some residents started a petition demanding that at least two of the three buildings be sold at market value in order to bring in new homeowners and limit the arrival of lower-income tenants; a countermobilization then developed in defense of the project. My position in favor of the PSI was not insincere, since the petition to prevent their purchase did shock me. Nevertheless I said nothing about the distance I also felt from the countermobilization, composed of much more likeable white homeowners who nevertheless wanted to negotiate with the charity over the acceptable level of demographic diversity and the degree of control over the future tenants. In addition to this were misunderstandings that developed with regard to my own political ideas, which I largely left uncorrected. I had been open about my vote for the socialist candidate Ségolène Royal in the second round of the 2007 French presidential elections (while remaining silent on my vote in the first round), and the ensuing parallels drawn between Presidents George W. Bush and Nicolas Sarkozy came to suggest a homology between my supposed sympathy for the Parti Socialiste and the residents' support for Barack Obama. This imagined ideological proximity was far from the truth though, as a number of discussions—particularly on healthcare reform—indicated. Although my subjects were much in favor of the reform implemented by the state of Massachusetts—which kept the large private insurance companies at the center of the system—they expressed strong hostility toward state intervention or indeed any kind of social redistribution.

Still, the fact that I was carrying out my research in the liberal upper middle class had certainly smoothed my entry into the milieu. I only very rarely heard racist comments, and we shared certain causes and sensibilities, such as opposition to the war in Iraq and the policies of George W. Bush. Nonetheless, this did not erase the notable differences separating me from them. The spectacle of their riches and their moral pretensions reinforced my hostility toward certain individuals, such that the fine wines that I had the opportunity to try at various soirées and the gourmet dishes served in the South End's restaurants gradually began to take on a bitter taste. The "outsider" position that I felt blighted, ever more vividly, the pleasure of both these tastings and the human company offered alongside them. I found myself passing most of my time surreptitiously observing the menus, decorations and body language, listening to conversations I participated in only artificially, with the zeal of a researcher advancing her study rather than that of a friend in good company. All this became as morally questionable as it was uncomfortable, in a foreign country where, apart from my escapes to the university campus, this schizophrenic situation became my everyday existence.[11]

Nonetheless the distance I felt from my research subjects did have the virtue of preserving my scruples in the face of the luxuries on offer among them. My personal disinclination toward ostentatious displays of wealth had a similar effect. The fact that I had been raised on the Calvinist-influenced middle-class culture that dominates one side of my family, my own activist commitments, and also the sharp contrast between the two different types of capital my subjects and I possessed—economic on the part of my research subjects, cultural on my side—all undoubtedly served to vaccinate against any complacency on my part. Meanwhile, my distress at circulating in this milieu only grew when, at the same moment, the university reforms reducing state funding started to take place in France. Stories I heard from US administrative staff required to seek out private millionaire benefactors made the spectacle of charity I witnessed in the South End seem like it would become the future of French universities as well. Indeed, all this limited my affective investment in my research subjects and their social project—and in any case my empathy for the individuals involved.

---

11   As well as a six-month stay, I made numerous visits of one to two months, amounting to a total of fourteen and a half months in the field between 2004 and 2010.

But beyond this situation, the deontological question—the instrumentalization and even possible betrayal of my research subjects by an analysis based on their own words—arose, in my eyes, in a particular manner when it came to a privileged group. If sociologists carrying out studies among the working classes feel some anguish about taking up their research subjects' time—often offered so generously—in order to serve the researcher's own professional ends, the concern arises principally from the awareness that the subjects occupy a lower rung of the social ladder than do the researchers. The question of what the researcher "owes" the subject in exchange for the latter's contribution to the former's career is very closely tied to the asymmetrical character of that exchange. The sociology of the upper middle class leads to an entirely different situation: beyond the social relationship being partly inverted, the researcher making use of the generosity of subjects themselves already rich in capital is also less problematic. On top of the combination of economic wealth, home ownership and moral esteem that these subjects already enjoy, is there an obligation to offer, additionally, the satisfaction of having been "understood," or even endorsed, by an academic authority? The exchange between myself and the inhabitants of the South End came to feel even more unequal as I became aware of the way these residents used my presence to secure symbolic rewards. The pleasures of talking about themselves, showing off the interior design details of their carefully renovated homes, and recounting their philanthropic commitments, all for an eager audience, also explained why the research subjects found time for me in their packed schedules, some of them even offering to travel over to Cambridge to meet me on campus.[12]

Finally, the subjects themselves sometimes reminded me of the imbalance in our positions. One inhabitant—otherwise generous and unstintingly giving with his time, describing to me in detail the tenants of the neighborhood and the outcome of the controversy surrounding the Pine Street Inn,

---

12   The value that this symbolic gratification had to these residents became even clearer when, by contrast, a few of my interviewees from the working class or the lower middle classes, asked me instead, and quite directly, for some material benefit in exchange for the interview. Along these lines, a Chinese shopowner and fierce opponent of the dog park thought initially that I was a journalist and asked upfront what I could do to help him. On the gentrifiers' mobilization for the dog park, see Chapter 5.

even delving into his archives in order to find old documents that he thought might be useful to me—suddenly let out a cutting remark when I mentioned where I lived in Paris: "Montreuil? It's a slum!" The look that he gave me when I told him the size of my apartment yanked me instantly from our pleasant lunch in a "French bistro" back to the reality of social domination. The qualms about having occasionally been given housing by certain research subjects melted away when I realized that the amounts I would have paid in rent—which they refused to charge me—were, for them, laughable. And I also found myself thinking that, as I looked after and fed their pets, sometimes three times a day, the respectable academic that I consider myself to be had been relegated to the ranks of one among the lowest-esteemed jobs in US society: dog walkers. Such brutal symbolic displacements in the social hierarchy could only remind me of the discomfort experienced by researchers who moved from studying the working classes to the wealthy, in relation to whom the researchers suddenly found themselves a part of the subordinated group.

Another major difference between studies in a privileged milieu and ones among less advantaged groups relates to concern for the image the study will promote of the populations at hand. In the latter case, concern is largely a fear of reinforcing social stigma.[13] This is clearly not the case for a study regarding the privileged class, particularly in the United States where the legitimacy in accumulating wealth is the object of relatively few criticisms. Is this to say that the desire to question the stigmatization of the lower classes must necessarily echo in a denunciation of the privileged? Without wanting to weigh in on the virtues but also the biases that humanist intentions in sociology can induce, it remains the case that social and political hostility has no place in a scientific project. Indeed it could very well destroy that project.

From this point of view, the ethnographic approach has proven a fruitful one. In its singular combination of physical—and sometimes affective—proximity and scientific distance, it has allowed me to avoid the traps that overly simplistic interpretative frameworks, based strictly on class, tend to fall into, subsuming all practices into economic interest (a framework brandished all the more quickly as it dispenses with the necessity of producing

---

13   Philippe Bourgois, *In Search of Respect: Selling Crack in El Barrio*, Cambridge: Cambridge University Press, 2003.

empirical evidence). In this regard, my friendship with my first ally proved to be very valuable. The connection I developed with her prevented me from following a course that would have been of little value: irony and judgment, whether moral or political. Making sociological virtue out of practical necessity, I was driven to adopt a more comprehensive approach, consisting first and foremost of taking her word and her actions seriously. Accompanying this inhabitant through her personal life, seeing her evolve in her network of friends and acquaintances, was decisive for understanding the values that are organized around "diversity." I could observe firsthand the logics of her commitments and also take account of an "interest in disinterestedness" that went beyond simple economic motives and could lead to valuing the presence of "other" populations in the neighborhood. Above all, it became possible to analyze this cultural touchstone as an essential element of the local power studied in my research and, thus, to grasp the particular relations that prevailed in the neighborhood among the different groups—relations that proved not to be reducible to an unchanging reproduction of social domination.

PROXIMITY TO AND DISTANCE FROM THE RESEARCH SUBJECTS

Although I was able to juggle contradictory feelings and keep reasonably in check the qualms I had about benefiting from the welcome and the generosity provided by the research subjects, the divided position the research context required of me remained difficult. In this situation, I decided, relatively explicitly, to seek out other interlocutors. Moved by the desire not to always be obliged to keep my ideas or even judgments to myself, but rather to express them; and genuinely seeking to make friends in this foreign country, I reoriented my study in a manner that proved distinctly fruitful. This reorientation moreover converged with a gradual reformulation of my object of inquiry.

Reconstructing old struggles

An interview conducted with a resident I had come across at a fundraiser played a central role in this reformulation of my research objectives. His wife had been the one to introduce me to him, explaining that I absolutely must interview this "pioneer" who had arrived at the beginning of the 1970s. The ensuing interview quickly turned to the courage and social convictions of the first gentrifiers, the distance that he feels toward newer arrivals, the sense of community that motivates him and his financially disinterested outlook (he left a career as a consultant in order to devote himself to a less lucrative activity). Was it that having interviewed so many of these much-discussed "new" residents—from whom I felt so distant, despite my gradual integration into their ranks—I was glad to hear a different tune? Whatever the reason, it was the case that he succeeded in leading me by the nose through a mythical account of "pioneers" who had always defended diversity, but who were now confronted with the recent and unfortunate arrival of far more selfish yuppies. It was with some anger and no small amount of pique that a few months after that interview, I found his name listed among the members of a small local committee close to the South End Historical Society, where in 1974 the most conservative members of the community gathered to mobilize against low-income housing, to the point of bringing lawsuits against the organizations that were building these projects. It was then that I fully understood the importance of historical research for resisting the biases generated by the reconstruction of the past in interviews.[14]

A remark in my fieldwork diary clearly summarized my state of mind at the time: "That guy really took me for a ride." This supposed pioneer who assumed so many risks in order to live in a mixed neighborhood instead proved to have been one of the residents most hostile to the black and Hispanic movements of the day. All the same, my misadventure did at least have the merit of smashing apart the mythical narrative of the early gentrifiers on which my initial framework had been partly based. Indeed, all of this converged to push me toward analyzing the attitude and practices of the mobilized white homeowners of the South End in relation to the length of their residence in the neighborhood, their political ideas and their socioeconomic status. Thanks to a well-coordinated homology, I had been alternating between representatives of the "counterculture," like those analyzed by

---

14   This work has used the archives of the mayor's office (principally those of the Boston Redevelopment Authority) as well as the Historical Society of the South End. In addition to these, I also accessed the personal archives of my second ally as well as the chair of her neighborhood association (see below). On the role of this local committee, see Chapter 4.

Elijah Anderson, and the wealthiest new inhabitants—from artists to managers, from the most progressive to those most hostile to cohabiting in the space of the South End.[15] This dichotomy between yesteryear's valiant defenders of diversity and today's terrible yuppies was, however, a trap, directly intended to ensnare the researcher. Indeed, I came to understand that the group's celebration of itself by way of trumpeting its defense of diversity—and the accompanying condemnation of those who didn't know how to appreciate it—was as pronounced as my interlocutors were reticent about the struggles of the 1960s and '70s against low-income housing and working-class bars. All this encouraged me to turn to other sociological reference points. Norbert Elias's study at Winston Parva, in which he analyzed seniority in conjunction with the construction of an integrated, respectable group. This model inspired my project examining the genesis of a local elite, and the conflicts that made that elite possible. Especially useful was the work of Jean-Noël Retière, who analyzed the way an aristocracy of the working class succeeded in taking hold of a French city thanks to the biases in interpersonal relationships and local networks. What he referred to, following others, as "autochthonous capital"—designating the resources that an aristocracy built up at the expense of a less "respectable" segment of the working classes— struck me as fruitful for analyzing the upper middle class.[16] Indeed, this notion allows us to bring to light the systematic erasure of the other groups, a process through which the new local elite built its own emergence. I discovered that the story of the South End that research subjects spun for me effectively papered over the process of primitive accumulation of a certain type of capital, built on the basis of a sharply autochthonous relationship to their less affluent neighbors, from the 1960s through the present day.

Having thus reformulated my research object to focus on these residents and the processes by which they established themselves, a different vision of the gentrification process emerged. It occurred to me that in the struggles occasioned by the appropriation of this working-class neighborhood, those particularly conservative residents were also involved—far from the likeable

---

15   Anderson, *Streetwise*.

16   Norbert Elias, *The Established and the Outsiders: A Sociological Enquiry into Community Problems*, London: SAGE, 1994; Jean-Noël Retière, *Identités ouvrières. Histoire sociale d'un fief ouvrier en Bretagne, 1909–1990*, Paris: L'Harmattan, 1994.

hippies, hardened leftists and penniless artists typically envisioned as a neighborhood's first gentrifiers. This ultimately allowed me to analyze the defense of diversity in all its complexity: the task at hand was thus not only a question of evaluating how diversity was translated into practice (including the limits of that implementation), but also of understanding the genesis of this discourse. That genesis itself drew as much on the social upheaval of the youth movement emerging from the middle class in the 1960s as it did from the violent backlash against the black civil rights movement. All this served to clarify the distinctive traits of a segment of the upper middle class that was increasingly interesting to me—one that, though considering itself liberal, had roots in a rather more complex political history.

Taking my distance from the residents who had instituted themselves as the legitimate representatives of the neighborhood provided a breath of fresh air as well as a real step forward in my research. While I continued my interviews and observations among the upper middle class, I also met a social worker, a high school teacher, a public administration lawyer, a librarian, an artist living in economic precarity, a nurse, a ruined real estate developer and an unemployed former bank manager. It was through this shift of focus that I met my second ally. The home address of this older activist (now approximately sixty years old) constituted the first sign of her position relative to the group in question. She lived near the public hospital and Massachusetts Avenue, the street that marks the beginning of the black neighborhood of Roxbury—fairly far from the chic part of Union Park where my first ally lived. The secretary of the advisory board during the urban renewal of the late 1960s, long active in her neighborhood association and thus having engaged in many local battles, she had an address book just as full as my first ally's, but tethered to a quite different period. Most of the members of today's neighborhood association were unknown to her. She had little affinity for the soirées organized around the life of the neighborhood associations, and, as a cat owner, expressed a pronounced aversion to dogs, whose numbers had increased considerably in the neighborhood through gentrification. Unlike my previous ally, who enthused vivaciously about the South End, this second ally looked on the transformations of the neighborhood with consternation, although not without a certain sense of humor. Herself white but close to the black leaders Mel and Joyce King, and a resolute radical, she spoke in a lightly ironic tone about the liberals' "good intentions," and wanted to preserve, despite the absence of collective engagement today, some sense of the revolt that came out of the 1960s.

A geographical decentering

My second ally considerably expanded my vision of the South End. One Sunday morning in June, spent touring Boston with her, my parents and my niece, was particularly instructive. After showing us around a neighborhood whose human richness she enjoyed pointing out at least as much as its architecture, she paused to take stock of the people that we had come across. We had first walked past the terrace cafes of Tremont Street during the Sunday brunch hour: here the impression of homogeneity was the most striking, the summer weekends when the restaurants were full and the terraces teeming with people. Then we stopped at a church with a black congregation, which would soon be sold to a developer and transformed into apartments; interested, we stayed to see the service. Except for the congregants of this church, the only people of color that we ran into were two older women who were perceptibly disturbed—precisely the kind of people, my second ally remarked, that the yuppies detest.

The presence of homeless people and individuals affected by mental illnesses has marked the urban landscape of the South End, much like other major US cities since the late 1970s. It was at that time that many psychiatric hospitals closed, even before the dismantling of social programs in the Reagan years. In Boston, the physical appearance and incoherent speech of these individuals clashes with the first impression of social homogeneity that dominates the South End. The Asian women seen on trash-collection days were likewise part of the population situated at the opposite end of the social ladder from the gentrifiers. The evening before the garbage trucks come, they sweep around the neighborhood to open trash bags left on the ground and take out the cans that can be exchanged for five cents in some supermarkets.[17] For many white and well-off inhabitants, the "different" and "problematic" character of these nonwhite women of very modest means is reinforced by the association between their activity and trash. And even though their passage

---

17   On the people who gather cans in New York, see Mitchell Duneier, *Sidewalk*, New York: Farrar, Straus and Giroux, 2001, p. 152. On the homeless, see Christopher Jencks, *The Homeless*, Cambridge, MA: Harvard University Press, 1994.

through the day is a furtive one, the enormous carts they use to gather their haul, bigger than the women themselves, make them particularly visible. Their status is one of the recurring questions discussed by the members of the neighborhood association.[18]

Understanding the problems posed, in the eyes of my research subjects, by a diversity that they otherwise champion, is crucial to analyzing the efforts they make to organize and control it. Taking the time to walk around the neighborhood and explore its nooks and crannies more systematically, I noticed not only the ambling of the old Chinese women but also the park benches occupied for the length of the day by sometimes-drunken homeless people, often having passed through the shelter situated in the far northeastern corner of the neighborhood. I thus discovered the still-visible and daily presence of the "undesirables," and with each stay, my impression that white homeowners exercised a uniform control over public spaces diminished. Staying in different parts of the South End proved instructive: moving from the area surrounding Union Park down to the far south of the neighborhood near the hospital and Massachusetts Avenue, the number of panhandlers and vagrants steadily increased. Switching from Foodies, a chic South End supermarket with a well-stocked gourmet food display (but where residents of the low-income development, Cathedral, also shopped) to the Tropical Food supermarket in Roxbury, I cut my grocery bill in half. I also observed the sharp boundary marked by Massachusetts Avenue. Only one of the street's famous jazz clubs is left, the last testament to the glory days between the two world wars, when the South End music scene rivaled the Harlem Renaissance. As soon as I was on the other side of Massachusetts Avenue, I began to come across establishments characteristic of working-class areas, such as the Western Union office that many immigrants frequented to send remittances abroad. Black people started to make up the majority of the people I passed in the street.

---

18   The local paper frequently echoes this concern. In an article in the *South End News* of August 2, 2007, evoking the malfunctions in the organization of the South End's garbage collection, the can collectors and rodents are characterized as sharing the same affinity for trash: "Improperly bagged garbage, sometimes in shopping bags or cardboard boxes, can spill out. Garbage put out on the street too early can sit for hours over night, attracting rats and people looking for recyclables."

Little by little I came to see the microsegregations and the subtle incursions of gentrification. Next to cafés and restaurants where economic barriers made for pronounced exclusivity, the neighborhood's small groceries became increasingly rare.[19] That said, in the east toward Chinatown, not far from the homeless shelter, a pawnshop still stood adjacent to a Dunkin' Donuts, near a pizzeria and an inexpensive hairdresser. This section is now the only part of the South End that still has such barbershops, typical of working-class neighborhoods. But today you can have your hair cut at Dessange, which has opened up shop on Tremont Street just below the South End's chicest development of loft apartments, the "Atelier." The contrast between Tremont and Washington Street is constantly diminishing, and I could see this process under way even in the 2000s. Along the latter artery, a particularly pricey sushi restaurant has opened, as have two grooming "salons" for dogs. Just off Massachusetts Avenue, and next to a frequently-packed tapas restaurant, another children's clothing store has opened, Kiwi Baby, drawing in young upper-middle-class parents with $500 high chairs and strollers that cost more than $1,000 each.

The parks proved to be the most mixed spaces in the South End, though they themselves contain differentiated subspaces: Peters Park, where the dog run is located, or Blackstone Square bordering Washington Street a few blocks to the south. In this garden, where lawns and benches encircle a central fountain, we find side-by-side the clients of the nearby Salvation Army and the Asian residents of the adjacent retirement home, but also well-off homeowners who come to walk their dogs, and mothers pushing strollers. A gay man of modest background told me that he preferred to come to Blackstone Square with his dog rather than go to Peters Park, where he feels people are particularly snobbish. But the spatial coexistence in Blackstone Square is organized on the basis of differentiated temporalities. Although, as this man's example demonstrated, the social divisions based on class, race and sexual orientation did not always line up with one another, passing through the park I was still often struck by the sharp opposition between two groups. The poorest people lingering on the benches, sometimes all day

---

19   These observations are also connected to the period in which the study took place, concluding with the 2009 crisis in the housing and financial markets and later the economy at large. In the South End this translated into some of the new restaurants and stores closing down.

long, contrasted with the frequent but briefer use gentrifier dog-owners, whether gay or straight, made of the park's lawns on weekends and evenings after work. On one side cigarettes and alcohol circulated; on the other, dogs, leashes, balls (and the bizarre plastic instruments used to throw them), and coffees and fizzy drinks in takeout containers. On the other side of the street, in Franklin Square Park bordering the Cathedral housing project, even the shade of the great oaks—particularly pleasant in the summer— only rarely drew white residents to sit on its benches or walk their dogs across its lawns.

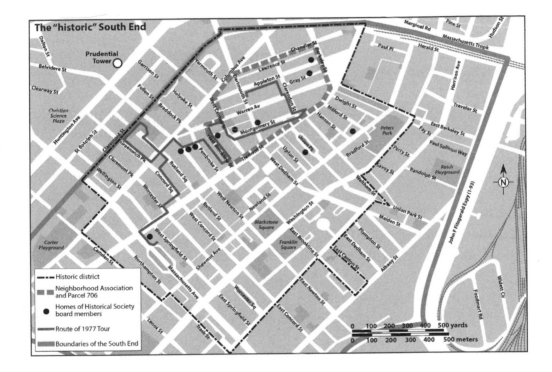

A historical perspective

As my study progressed, I also ventured into the Cathedral and Villa Victoria developments, which "white people only walked [through] . . . when they were heading somewhere else."[20] (See map p. 155.) My second ally introduced

---

20   Mario Small, *Villa Victoria: The Transformation of Social Capital in a Boston Barrio*, Chicago: University of Chicago Press, 2004, p. 121.

me to the neighborhood's longest-standing residents, who were from diverse backgrounds. She herself—though the half-owner of her town house, bought in the middle of the 1970s—was in a precarious economic situation, exacerbated by the onerous health care costs experienced by many Americans. Although I did not carry out a specific study on residents who were nonwhite and/or of modest social backgrounds, I did seize on opportunities to conduct interviews with some of them: the black building superintendant who lived in a shelter and whom I met by chance at a neighborhood association meeting, a Congolese refugee living in the same shelter and a Chinese shop owner from the Castle Square development. In order to understand the emergence of a local elite and its grip on the area, it was clearly necessary to identify the local power relations that had made this possible. I chose to look at the period from the 1960s to '80s, restoring the history of the black and Hispanic tenants' struggles to the analysis of this genesis, and moreover analyzing the role of the fairly singular subgroup composed of owners of lodging houses—residents of more modest means who were nonetheless solid allies of the new, wealthier arrivals up until the 1980s. As for the more recent period, a number of accounts, in particular the valuable work of Mario Small, have attested to the silence of the "other" inhabitants, despite the symbolic violence that they experience. It would require a separate study to examine the variety of perspectives among these residents, as well as their more subtle forms of resistance.

I had an immediate and strong friendship with my second ally, as well as with the co-owner of her town house, where I stayed several times. A retired black lawyer who was very active in the Democratic Party and until recently in her neighborhood association, she too opened up new horizons to me. Thanks to these two women I widened my study threefold: toward different corners of the neighborhood, toward the margins of the subject group (by way of those who had left or distanced themselves from it), and finally toward periods of the neighborhood's history where I could trace the group's exact emergence. Along with her contacts, my second ally's archives were of great value, especially since my attempts to get hold of the documents conserved by two neighborhood associations ended in failure. The person who controlled one of the two associations' archives considered me suspect because of my friendship with my first ally as well as my open support for the Pine Street Inn project. But thanks to my new informant, I could consult the archives of the former chair of her neighborhood association, the owner of several lodging houses. We picked up more than a dozen cartons of documents from the homes of some former residents of the South End, now living in a small town elsewhere in the state. This woman had, indeed, conserved an incredible number of documents: reports, studies, maps, meeting notes from the Boston city planning agency, press clippings, letters, reflections and testimonies on her participation in the renovation of the neighborhood.

As for my second ally, her collection was oriented toward the activist groups whose disappearance she mourned. Nevertheless her archives also provided information about the people who interested me most of all: the "pioneers" celebrated by the press from the mid-1960s, but who were subsequently eclipsed, in the social upheaval of the 1960s and '70s, by activists, marked by afros and flared blue jeans. I discovered that some of the pioneers were dedicated to supporting these activists, which illuminated for me the divisions that existed among these "new inhabitants." Along with her press clippings, in which I occasionally came across the names of residents still active today, my ally also had a collection of newsletters from the advisory board set up by the mayor's office in 1968, whose members were elected. This included information on the constituency boundaries and the list of candidates. Having devoted herself to a book project combining the history of the South End with her own autobiography, my ally's work as a historian drove her to build up a more exhaustive collection than that to which her political attachments alone had taken her. Gradually, she began conserving every trace of the past, in tandem with her growing aversion toward the present day in the South End.

Thanks to this ally, I plunged into the neighborhood's history. While the social movements and countercultures of the 1960s and 1970s are today largely absent from the official history of the South End, she helped me to feel something of the vigor of this activist past, in which she herself had participated through her collective engagement as well as through her life choices, oriented toward local sociability and travel rather than the stability of a professional career. Ultimately, we did not always agree in our analyses of the neighborhood's history, but that's to be expected. Her perspective was indissociable from her commitment to a South End that has now disappeared, and her glorification of the past and tendency to blame "young people" did not resonate with me. Above all, her nostalgia for the South End of old, which in her view, existed free from any dynamics of social distinction (class or otherwise), contrasted with the sociological lens that led me to analyze the divisions of the past as well as those of the present. The differences I sought to identify among the white homeowners did not interest her either, while for me it was important to analyze the full range of complexity in the activism conducted by progressive residents like my first ally, for example, or in the admission of the "old" residents to the group of new elites.

Crossing the Atlantic does not wipe away—far from it—the analytical frameworks and lines of questioning the sociologist developed at home, which inform her perspective out in the field. This research concerned a group of mobilized residents who, in seeking to establish boundaries at once symbolic and spatial—those that define the rehabilitated South End, giving it a new and positive signification—also trace the boundaries separating those residents from other groups. This line of inquiry was an extension of my work on those who, from the top of the social hierarchy, have invented new ways of managing impoverished neighborhoods.[21] This redefinition of urban policy has taken place in a context common to both France and the United States: the challenge to the triumphalist modern urban planning prevalent after the Second World War, at the same time that 1960s critique questioned not only the city's professional planners, but also its social and racial structure. In these contexts, the same question arises: how have the upper classes transformed themselves as they sought to transform the city?

---

21   Sylvie Tissot, L'État et les quartiers. Genèse d'une catégorie de l'action publique, Paris: Seuil, 2007.

Chapter 2

The Birth of a Local Elite in a Working-Class Neighborhood

At the end of World War II, the construction of major housing developments on the peripheries of Europe's major cities rapidly transformed the urban landscape. Meanwhile in the United States, the federal government financed the expansion of residential suburbs. On both sides of the Atlantic, elites rallied around a project of rebuilding the modern city on a rational and scientific basis monopolized by public authorities and specialists. Large-scale projects led to the demolition of entire sections of long-standing neighborhoods. However, as the three decades of postwar growth drew to a close, this interventionist moment was radically challenged, and the hegemony of the functionalist doctrines that had reigned among architects and city planners was shaken. Canadian author Jane Jacobs's pamphlet *The Death and Life of Great American Cities*, published in 1961, crystallized the growing resistance to urban renewal's bulldozers and the rationalism that New York city planner Robert Moses embodied.[1] Manhattan's Greenwich Village, as well as Boston's West End—which municipal experts considered simply slums—would soon be described as having the traits of villages, rich in their maze of streets, countless businesses and social density. This increasingly powerful critical mood translated into the promotion of resident participation, as opposed to

---

1 Jane Jacobs, *The Death and Life of Great American Cities*, New York: Random House, 1961.

authoritarian state interventionism; of the mixing of social groups in each area, as opposed to differentiation among neighborhoods; and the regeneration of old city centers as an alternative to demolition. Such arguments informed the urban reforms of the 1970s and the following decades, through which resident participation became politically as well as administratively self-evident.

In many countries, recognition of the benefits of neighborhood committees and other resident assemblies led to these bodies gaining specific power. Indeed, public authorities in both Europe and the USA used surprisingly similar language in establishing local democracy as an imperative, particularly in working-class neighborhoods, thus seeming to incorporate the demands of the activists of the 1960s and 1970s who had attacked the violence of state power then engaged in large-scale demolition and construction projects.[2]

Such activist movements were particularly powerful in Boston's South End, a neighborhood designated for demolition as part of the urban renewal of the 1950s. Through their struggles against City Hall and its planners to ensure that financial interests did not prevail over the interests of the poorest — particularly, poor black residents — these movements called for profound social transformations. Many works addressing this period note the ultimate failure of urban renewal's critics to realize their demands or point to the institutionalization of the community movements that came out of these protests, which largely lost their oppositional force.[3] Nonetheless, these failures cannot be understood independently of the victory of the group which did triumph in these struggles. Many of the neighborhoods saved from demolition — for which everyone then advocated the merits of "rehabilitation" — experienced little-studied mobilizations by white homeowners — some of whom were involved in the leftist protest movements, while others took much more conservative stances. The South End, where urban renewal was particularly brutal and opposition to it particularly vehement, offers a terrain of inquiry

---

2   Norman and Susan Fainstein, *Urban Political Movements: The Search for Power by Minority Groups in American Cities*, Englewood Cliffs, NJ: Prentice-Hall, 1974.

3   John H. Mollenkopf, *The Contested City*, Princeton: Princeton University Press, 1983; Gordon Rabrenovic, *Community Builders: A Tale of Neighborhood Mobilization in Two Cities*, Philadelphia: Temple University Press, 1996.

for illuminating this lesser-known component of urban struggles. This neighborhood escaped wholesale demolition in the 1960s. Yet it was the upper-middle-class households that appropriated the structures initially dedicated to democratic engagement: namely the neighborhood associations, the basis on which a local authority established itself.

THE TRIUMPH OF RESIDENT PARTICIPATION . . .

Like urban struggles in Europe, US protests against urban renewal were heavily marked by the activism of the 1960s: the civil rights movement, which began in the most segregationist states in the mid-1950s before expanding northward, and the new consciousness and radicalism in a growing section of youth on account of the Vietnam War. What did this urban renewal—criticized as "urban removal" or even "negro removal"—consist of? Financed by the federal government, it entailed a profound reorganization of the urban landscape. Working-class neighborhoods disappeared while displaced black populations were relegated to peripheral ghettos. The famous West End of Boston, object of a study by Herbert Gans, was totally razed to the ground and replaced by luxury homes.[4] Among all the programs implemented in the great American cities, Boston's was distinguished by the reach of its urban planning. Urban renewal completely restructured the inner city; this meant the destruction of thousands of homes and forced thousands of residents of central districts out into peripheral areas.[5] These transformations and the protests that they provoked were the source of an unprecedented opening up of municipal politics, which certain elements of the protest movement as well as their watchwords now entered. In the South End, which was condemned to demolition, black and Hispanic activists, white radicals—or even just residents sensitive to the mood of protest in the air at that time—and conservative homeowners made common cause against the public authorities in order to block the destruction of their neighborhood. But they would soon clash among themselves, for control of the new political opportunity.

---

4   Herbert J. Gans, *The Urban Villagers. Group and Class in the Life of Italian-Americans*, New York: Free Press of Glencoe, 1962.

5   Thomas H. O'Connor, *Building a New Boston: Politics and Urban Renewal, 1950–1970*, Boston: Northeastern University Press, 1993.

1968 and the battle over urban renewal

The center of Boston, particularly its business center, came out of World War II in a run-down state. The construction of an extensive highway network and the guarantees offered to households buying properties on the periphery provoked a migratory movement similar to that affecting the whole country, indeed one which took on unprecedented dimensions in the wake of 1945: "suburbaniza-tion." The great cities of the United States were increasingly characterized by a spatial organization opposing the periphery to the center (though some upper-middle-class pockets did hold out in the inner cities). And this trend became stronger at the same time that the categories for understanding urban space solidified: as "white flight" accelerated, a contrast developed between the slums and the suburbs, which became the symbol of middle-class belonging. Boston was not spared this change, though a part of the city's upper class remained in Back Bay and Beacon Hill.[6] The population sharply declined in the 1950s, from 801,000 to 697,000, while in the same period the suburban population rose from 2 to 3 million. In 1970, 16 percent of Boston residents were people of color, as opposed to just 6 percent for the metropolitan area as a whole.[7]

From the immediate postwar period onward, urban renewal policy began seeking to eliminate neighborhoods that it identified as slums, which had suffered the ravages of the Great Depression and white flight to the suburbs. To this end, the federal government took recourse to expropriations, demoli-tion and selling off land to private developers charged with reconstructing these areas. Such was the plan for Boston's city center. In order to implement this policy, in 1957 City Hall created a body that would allow it to make forceful interventions, namely the paramunicipal Boston Redevelopment Authority (BRA). This body took charge of the demolition of the West End. With some 500 employees and more than 100 million dollars to spend in the 1965–79 period, the BRA enjoyed considerable freedom of action. The theater district, known for its "rash of saloons, all-night restaurants, dime

---

6   In 1894, 45.1 percent of upper-class families in the Boston area lived in Back Bay. In 1929, the percentage was 32.5 percent, and despite the Great Depression and the expansion of residential districts like Brookline, in 1943 it stood at 18.8 percent (Betty Farrell, *Elite Families: Class and Power in Nineteenth-Century Boston*, Albany: SUNY Press, 1993, pp. 29–30).

7   Mollenkopf, *The Contested City*.

museums, penny arcades, pawnshops, and pool rooms,"[8] was the first target of demolition at the beginning of the 1950s. Dozens of houses were razed to the ground, and the number of streets fell from twenty-two to just six. On the land now cleared of its old apartment blocks—as well as its strip clubs—a new City Hall was built. But the promotion of a new Boston also required the enhancement of the surrounding neighborhoods, such as the West End, the South End and Charlestown, which were densely packed with migrant populations, not far from the city elite and its political and cultural institutions.

The South End
A "skid row"

From the end of the nineteenth century there was an increasingly sharp division in Boston between inner-city housing and the detached houses that made up the rapidly-expanding suburbs. After World War II, the city center—small in its land area[9]—comprised traditional elite areas like Back Bay and Beacon Hill as well as run-down areas like the North End, West End and South End. These latter took on the epithet "skid row." Indeed, at the beginning of the 1960s, the city planning agency's reports on the South End characterized it in the terms typically applied to neighborhoods condemned to demolition: an insalubrious district, populated by single men, prostitutes, migrants, the destitute, the sick, gangsters and above all the alcoholics who packed its taverns and sleazy bars. Just like the West End, which was razed to the ground in 1955, it was a "slum area." City planners commonly summarized the neighborhood's situation with a cutting quip: the South End had 5 percent of Boston's population and 95 percent of its problems. Not only did the neighborhood's population fall by half in twenty years—from 57,218 in 1950 to 22,775 in 1970—but the white section of the population, the large majority of them Italians

---

8   J. Anthony Lukas, *Common Ground: A Turbulent Decade in the Lives of Three American Families*, New York: Vintage Books, 1985, p. 195.

9   To be precise, 1.50 square miles versus 5.65 square miles for its New York equivalent.

and Irish, fell from 74 percent in 1950 to 60 percent in 1970, replaced by a black population that was quickly growing. As of 1970, 80 percent of apartments in the neighborhood had been built before 1900, 22 percent were described as dilapidated and 43 percent in need of major repairs.[10] One northeastern part of the neighborhood, called New York Streets, was razed in 1954, leading to the expulsion of 931 families and 125 businesses. Hundreds of residents had to leave Castle Square, another part of the neighborhood that was also demolished.

The year 1968 would mark a turning point in urban renewal. In the very year that Democratic mayor Kevin White was elected, he faced mounting protests. In this city with its numerous universities attracting students from all over the country, the movement against the Vietnam War was particularly powerful. Cambridge was at boiling point and across the river black activists occupied Boston University's administration offices in 1968. In 1969 the mobilization of students under threat of being sent to Vietnam led to a 100,000-strong demonstration. At the same time, Boston—which had been in the vanguard of the abolitionist movement and then the struggle against Jim Crow—was affected by the civil rights movement's shift to the North. In this sense it was like many northern cities. Up to that point, students had set off from the Massachusetts capital in order to participate in the marches in Mississippi and Alabama, carrying on the tradition of the anti-slavery movement; now local activists drew attention to the discrimination that had always functioned in the North on the basis of a subtler but no less real segregation.[11]

Visiting Boston in 1965, Martin Luther King highlighted the parallels between the Northern situation and that in the South. He pointed to the housing question, in particular the barriers to black people moving into white or mixed neighborhoods or getting mortgages, discriminatory practices in the workplace, as well as segregation in the school and university system. Black people coming from the South in search of the "promised land" found

10   Mollenkopf, *The Contested City.*

11   Steven F. Lawson, *Running for Freedom: Civil Rights and Black Politics in America since 1941*, Philadelphia: Temple University Press, 1991; Mark R. Schneider, *Boston Confronts Jim Crow, 1890–1920*, Boston: Northeastern University Press, 1997.

something quite different from the "cradle of freedom" that this famous New England city has become in official histories. For Boston, the activist movements that developed across the 1960s began in the two black neighborhoods: the South End and Roxbury.

Tension mounted in these two neighborhoods after Martin Luther King's death. On 26 April 1968, black and Puerto Rican demonstrators organized a protest in a parking lot in the South End, not far from the city center, demanding the construction of public housing. The previous year, in 1967, residents had set up a group called CAUSE (Community Assembly for a Unified South End), whose black leader Mel King would make his mark on activist life in the South End and Boston in general across several decades. CAUSE demanded an expansion of the community advisory structures that City Hall had initially put in place, and immediately after the "Tent City" protest (so named after the tents erected on the parking lot) called for the election of a new planning committee that would "meet people's needs instead of property needs." The living conditions of the black population in the South End fed discontent. After the adoption of the plan for urban renewal in 1965, road repairs and the installation of street lighting had fallen behind schedule; no progress was made in the construction of subsidized housing for the displaced, and the number of apartments available to the poorest began to decline— between 1960 and 1969, the number of housing units for low-income tenants fell from 14,012 to 7,277.[12] Real estate prices continued to increase, as did rents. Contrary to City Hall's promises, as of January 1968 only five hundred families had been rehoused, and only twenty-five of them in the rehabilitated dwellings in the South End.

Long before it became a "gay district" and then a gentrified neighborhood known for its "diversity," the South End was distinguished by its abundance of activist activity. This has today largely been forgotten, even if black community leaders Mel and Joyce King have become renowned historical figures. Mel King's father was a shipyard worker from the West Indies and secretary of a union local; his mother was a housewife who was very active in the parish and in women's groups.[13] Having earned a master's degree in 1952, he

---

12   O'Connor, *Building a New Boston*, p. 232.

13   Mel King, *Chain of Change: Struggle Against Black Community Development*, Boston: South End Press, 1981.

married Joyce, whose working-class parents had migrated from the US South. She too was a college graduate and had a very early consciousness of the civil rights movement on account of her mother's subscriptions to black newspapers and her sister's membership in the NAACP (National Association for the Advancement of Colored People). It was first Mel King's career, and subsequently his activist engagement, that channeled his interests toward the South End. He taught for a year before being appointed director of a youth employment program in a South End community center. His social-work engagement, his reputation, as well as the esteem that he earned in the neighborhood, all built support for the rhetoric that he now made his own. In conjunction with the catchphrase "Black Power," this discourse sought to orient black Americans' revolt toward constructing institutions and organizations of their own. Thus they rejected the local political system that had up to that point made room for black people only in subaltern roles. Strongly critical of a sham integration, Mel and Joyce represented a generation bearing a more radical discourse (in 1968, they were forty and thirty-eight years old, respectively). They joined the Urban League, which soon became the New Urban League. Mel King became this organization's leader at the same time as new activist groups were also emerging. The growth in the black population in the Northern cities added to the weight of this consituency, which had benefited from economic growth and improved living conditions in the post-war years.[14] All this allowed black people to believe that they might achieve what they, unlike Irish immigrants, had always been denied: local political bastions of their own.

The social movements in the South End were not, however, limited to the black population. Hispanics, whose numbers were growing in the Northern cities,[15] swelled activist ranks. Numerous Puerto Ricans, employed in Boston's factories after arriving from the rural world, participated in the April 1968 Tent City demonstration. Simultaneously denouncing unsanitary housing conditions, they protested against the evictions forced by urban renewal demolition. These movements brought together a convergence of radical activists,

---

14   In the 1940s, the number of black people living outside of the US South grew from 2.36 to 4.6 million. It doubled again by the end of the 1960s.

15   The Hispanic population of the South End rose from to 1 to 7 percent between 1960 and 1970.

churchgoers, and also intellectuals, notably including whites. In the South End, as elsewhere in the country, left-wing Jews also joined the struggles. Alternative currents like Saul Alinsky's movement—in which social workers active in rent battles in the South End took a keen interest—also fed into the wave of activism in the late 1960s. Many churches proved an important base of support. These struggles also benefited from support coming from outside the neighborhood, such as those city planners who stood up against the "federal bulldozer." Urban Planning Aid, a research group created by MIT (Massachusetts Institute of Technology) students and professors in 1966, aimed to place its expertise at the service of "communities." Financed by a program of President Johnson's War on Poverty, this body encouraged the intersection of the city planning milieu— which up to that point had been convinced of the virtues of urban renewal—and activist movements. They joined in a common struggle against the planned extension of the highway network to Boston, crossing the South End. In 1967, Urban Planning Aid published a document, prepared for CAUSE, which showed the disastrous impact of urban renewal on housing for the poorest populations. Other professional categories were also influenced by protest movements, especially health care.[16] Doctors in the South End came together to found a community health center in 1969. Opening its board up to patients and residents, this center's objective was to work for the neighborhood's communities. It became an important meeting space for ethnic-minority activists and certain members of the white middle classes, particularly those who were now beginning to move into the neighborhood.

This activist movement immediately took a stand against the urban renewal program, demolitions and the eviction of tenants—especially black residents. This set a particular tone for local politics, local civic life and the forms that gentrification would take in the South End. Indeed, many boycott campaigns were launched in the mid-1960s targeting companies and banks accused of racial discrimination, albeit unsuccessfully. The local NAACP also campaigned against the segregation that was then prevalent in the city's schools, again unsuccessfully.[17] And after the Tent City demonstration,

16   Lily M. Hoffman, *The Politics of Knowledge: Activist Movements in Medecine and Planning*, Albany, NY: SUNY, 1989.

17   Ronald P. Formisano, *Boston Against Busing: Race, Class and Ethnicity in the 1960s and 1970s*, Chapel Hill: University of Carolina Press, 1991. On three

activists mounted a fervid struggle against the Mindick brothers, owners of forty-four dilapidated blocks in the South End, in which a poverty-stricken population was housed in deplorable conditions. Six black and Puerto Rican families squatted on one of these blocks, which had recently been renovated and was meant to be rented to new tenants, and each day they dumped their garbage in front of one of the brothers' homes. Demonstrations were also organized in front of the synagogue. The episode in which dead rats were deposited outside the bar mitzvah of the son of one of the Mindick brothers also made a deep impression. Ultimately, the landlords were forced to make repairs, supply trashcans and locks, and install a satisfactory heating and hot water system.

An activist group created in 1973, South End for South Enders, took a stand against another South End landlord, Mark Goldweitz, opposing his massive rent hikes. A pamphlet published at the time targeted him as embodying "exploitative landlords, land speculators and the like, who are intent by their investments and attitudes to make the South End another home exclusively for the upper middle class or the wealthy." The document listed the fifty-six buildings Goldweitz owned and detailed the loans that the banks— that had refused to serve black neighborhoods like the South End—had made to him; it was signed by two state representatives (including Mel King, elected to the Massachusetts legislature that same year), nine members of the community advisory body set up in 1968, eleven members of the health center, eight representatives of the Puerto Rican activist association, the pastor of a supportive church, and twelve members of a now-defunct neighborhood association located beyond Massachusetts Avenue, i.e. in the part of the South End near Roxbury. The list of names and groups offers a snapshot of the activist landscape of the time and of its strength, in contrast to the predominance of white homeowners thirty years on.

At the end of the 1960s, activist life was thus structured by personal confrontations, illegal actions like occupations, attacks on the power of money, and antagonism between the residents who declared themselves "the people" or the "real" residents on the one hand, and the estate agents and the South End Historical Society on the other. The radical movement that

---

occasions—1961, 1963 and 1965—Mel King tried and failed to get elected to the body in charge of the city's public schools.

developed in the South End also had a strong media presence, including producing its own paper, the *People's South End News*. At this point, toward the end of the 1960s, the movement was organized around three principal structures: a tenants' association (South End Tenants' Council), the Puerto Rican association (Emergency Tenants' Council)—both later becoming community development corporations—and CAUSE. These groups shuffled the deck of local civic activity such as the public authorities had found it (and begun to reorganize it) at the beginning of the decade—indeed, it now shifted sharply to the left. Activists denounced South End charity organizations' institutional ties, and accused the philanthropic foundations financed by wealthy families of maintaining the subordination of the populations that they purported to help. Under the influence of some of its most politicized staff, the South End community center—formerly an ally of City Hall— began little by little to become the platform for a variety of local organizations. But paradoxically, while City Hall was thus forced to take a more open approach, this ultimately served a quite different set of residents.

Participation and the neighborhood: A political and urban refounding

Such was the balance of forces in May 1969 when the Boston Redevelopment Authority (BRA) decided to suspend its demolition and rehousing operations in the South End, putting in place a new community advisory body called the South End Project Area Committee (SEPAC). Why this retreat, breaking with its long-standing indifference toward "ghettos" like the South End? First, more and more voices were speaking out about the destruction of the West End ten years earlier. The activist researchers at MIT who were study-ing these population displacements called for another kind of planning.[18] The demolition of the West End had come to symbolize the disaster of "slum clearance," and this served to mobilize activists in the South End. The South End also presented particularly decisive stakes in the plans for the new Boston. The electoral boundaries had been fixed to prevent the growth in the black population from leading to the emergence of a new political power,

---

18   This was called "advocacy planning." Chester Hartman, *Between Eminence and Notoriety: Four Decades of Radical Urban Planning*, New Brunswick, NJ: Centre for Urban Policy Research, 2002.

and in 1960 this gerrymandering caused the splintering of the South End into multiple constituencies. Yet the black protests at the moment that the civil rights movement reached its apex propelled the South End onto the political stage. Boston mayor Kevin White was all the more sensitive to this because he was one of the progressive mayors following in the wake of JFK— and like John Lindsay in New York, Carl Stokes in Cleveland and Joseph Alioto in San Francisco, he was committed to implementing a modern municipal government, an enlightened administration that took racial questions seriously. On April 9, 1969, a meeting in Boston organized by the Black United Front rallied some 5,000 people; its organizers demanded the transfer of white businesses to black ownership and the hiring of black teachers. The pressure exerted on the Democratic Party to join the civil rights struggle in order to win black votes from the Republicans had never been so strong. Signaling his desire to get closer to the "neighborhoods," particularly the black districts, the mayor of Boston made a public outing down Blue Hill Avenue, the main artery of Roxbury, where he stopped to shoot hoops on the basketball court. He promised to renovate the neighborhood's Franklin Square park and to appoint black people to official posts.

City Hall's engagements in favor of "resident participation" were not only linked to the need to organize urban renewal more "democratically" in response to the opposition that it faced. It was also part of the postwar effort to recast the city's municipal and political apparatus. More specifically, the recourse to community advisory boards constituted an important dimension of the modernizing effort, which mayor Kevin White became the symbol of after 1968. From the outset, the regeneration of the inner city was also a reform of municipal politics, which ever since the turn of the century had rested on the political machine attached to the Democratic Party.

This local system based on an all-powerful political apparatus had been shaken up in the 1949 municipal elections, and from then onward the subsequent mayors—John Collins and above all Kevin White in 1968—committed themselves to cementing a new alliance bringing together "downtown business elites, ambitious political leaders seeking to modernize urban politics, middle class, good government reform groups, the professional city planners to whom they turned for advice, a powerful new stratum of public administrators, and private development interests, including developers, lenders, builders and the construction trades."[19] These actors threw themselves into the regeneration of the city center, which City Hall had traditionally left abandoned, instead being preoccupied by the redistribution of goods and services in its political bastions closer to the periphery, such as South Boston and Dorchester. The South End now came to the center of its attention.

The need to enter "the rehabilitation planning game" –to take the title of Langley Keyes's work[20]–but also the wider desire to recast a political apparatus that rested on patronage and the exclusion of the poorest districts and populations–particularly black ones–gave rise to ambivalent strategies. City Hall renounced exclusive control of planning as well as the wholesale demolition of poor neighborhoods, now negotiating with local groups about the fate of the land it was acquiring. It launched massive construction programs building housing for low-income residents. Thus it erected a large number of blocks in the South End, on a scale similar to that of other projects in the city:[21] 499 homes in Castle Square (in the demolished area), 508 in Cathedral and 204 in Villa Victoria, today inhabited by a largely Asian, Hispanic and black population, as well as many elderly people. These construction efforts made their mark on the neighborhood's social composition as well as its urban form. Mostly made up of brownstones–brick town houses, which are sought-after today–the South End also comprises large public housing blocks breaking the pattern of the small tree-lined streets set out in the nineteenth century. Nonetheless, at the same time that City Hall encouraged the construction of public housing, it also tried to identify and prioritize residents likely to support its urban renewal project, notably recent arrivals in the South End more open to its "enlightened progressivism" than radical activists.

---

19   Mollenkopf, *The Contested City*, p. 141.

20   Langley Keyes, *The Rehabilitation Planning Game: A Study in the Diversity of Neighborhood*, Cambridge, MA: MIT Press, 1969.

21   For example, the Mission Hill Project in Roxbury (1952), the Bromley Heath Project in Jamaica Plain (1954), the Franklin Field Project in Dorchester (1954) and the enormous Columbia Point complex in South Boston (1954). Laurence J. Vale, *From the Puritans to the Projects: Public Housing and Public Neighbors*, Cambridge, MA: Harvard University Press, 2000. In 1978 the BRA counted 4,316 homes built or rehabilitated for modest or low-income households within the frame of the South End renovation program.

Who were these new residents? The press noting their arrival characterized them in terms that had already appeared in other US cities, particularly
New York and Washington DC: these were "pioneers" or "urbanites" engaged
in the "rebirth" of run-down neighborhoods, like Manhattan's Greenwich
Village. In Boston, a population of young professionals began to move into
the South End, even if this phenomenon was relatively limited. After the
construction of the Prudential Tower was completed in 1964, the neighborhood's geographic and symbolic place in the city began to change. The tower,
inspired by Le Corbusier's modernist school, was a fifty-two-story building on
the border of Back Bay and the South End, and its construction was considered a symbol of the transformation of the old dilapidated city into a "New
Boston." The building of the "Pru" equally had the effect of "extending downtown a mile to the south"[22] — that is, toward the South End. This location now
became a more attractive potential home for young professionals, whose
numbers sharply increased following the postwar transformation of the city.
Hit hard by the Great Depression, Boston gradually emerged from economic
crisis in the 1950s thanks to the development of a high-tech economy. And as
in American society as a whole, young graduates formed a growing sector of
the Boston population: "White-collar professional and technical workers
grew from 33,476 in 1960 to 51,977 in 1980, while blue-collar workers shrank
from 52,175 to 17,320. Real median income also rose by a third."[23]

The construction of offices in the city center accelerated, strengthening the
demand for local housing beyond the small, already-occupied neighborhoods
of Back Bay and Beacon Hill. The South End at this time offered both proximity to the city center and very low prices — in the 1960s it was possible to buy an
entire town house for between $5,000 and $20,000, depending on the state of
the building. Among the new residents there was a mix of singles and newly
married couples arriving from other central districts and the student hubs of
Cambridge and Fenway. There was a local influx of some significance: in
1980, 80 percent of the neighborhood's new arrivals came from elsewhere in
the Boston metro area. This helps explain why between 1960 and 1970 the
median income in the South End rose from $4,542 to $6,122, and the proportion of professionals and technicians increased by 10 percent. In the same

---

22   Lukas, *Common Ground*, p. 168.
23   Mollenkopf, *The Contested City*, pp. 204–5.

period, the percentage of owner-occupied homes went from 7.6 to 11.3 percent and among these there were already upper-class households moving into the South End.[24] City Hall, keen to see the emergence of the "New Boston," and thus to renovate the neighborhoods surrounding the city center, instantly took a favorable view of this migratory movement as young white households from the middle and upper classes moved into the area. This promised not only an increased tax base but also a far-from-negligible pool of voters. The support that City Hall thus gave to owners renovating their houses first took the form of technical and financial advice. One provision of the 1965 plan allowed people to take out twenty-year mortgages at extremely low rates; and it was above all the new homeowners who would benefit from this. This was a remarkable decision at a time when the South End was still subject to "redlining"—a then-widespread practice in the banking system demarcating the generally poor, black and inner-city neighborhoods considered too risky to invest in.

In Boston as in many US and European cities, the 1960s revolt thus forced the public authorities to negotiate with residents. This new terrain of negotiation encouraged the flowering of the South End's civic scene. But the extent of federal subsidies and territorial reorganizations fed political struggles to define and control the coming transformations. The 1965 plan provided for nothing less than the rehabilitation of 3,000 buildings and the construction of over 3,000 private residences, 300 dwellings earmarked for public housing, 500 for retired people, three new schools and seven kindergartens, as well as the renovation of parks, streets, street lighting and sewage systems. The state of conflict that characterized the 1960s and 1970s gave particular virulence to the battles that not only pitted local movements against City Hall, but also set these movements against each other. The South End's new white homeowners did emerge in a dominant position, endowed with extensive and lasting powers, but only at the end of several decades of struggle.

––––––––––––––

24   Lukas, *Common Ground*. According to a study carried out in the early 1970s, out of the forty-three recent arrivals interviewed, nine were lawyers, eight architects, seven university professors, five engineers and four city planners. More than half of them had come from other Boston neighborhoods, and more than three-quarters of them in order to buy a home. Alan Herman Rappaport, "From Skid Row to Brownstone Chic: Neighborhood Revitalization in the South End of Boston, a Case," thesis, Harvard University, 1975.

. . . FOR WHICH RESIDENTS?

That a group of rich white residents would succeed in consolidating power in this context was far from certain at the outset, as we can see in the contrast between today's homogeneity and the civic landscape of the early 1960s. Indeed, in those days there was a great degree of diversity among the associations, some of which had already existed for a number of years. Certainly, there were already some recently arrived white homeowners who bought—often for a few thousand dollars—an entire town house, renting out two or three stories. But they existed side by side with an altogether different owner profile: black, Lebanese, Syrian, Québécois, Irish and Chinese landlords, whose tenants came from the same countries they had. These tenants were often workers living in rooms equipped only with a sink, sometimes the more stably employed, or families covering a whole floor. Some of the owners had been renting out these properties for decades. How did the neighborhood associations develop into what today is a relatively cohesive milieu, which, whatever its continuing internal conflicts, is mostly made up of white homeowners?

Organizing community input

Once the BRA, the body charged with urban renewal, had dismissed the idea of totally demolishing the South End, its director promised to implement "planning with people." But with which people, in a neighborhood that displayed such demographic diversity and was home to countless religious, community and social institutions? "Unlike other Boston neighborhoods, where one particular ethnic group dominated—the Irish, the Italians—the South End had no single group to exert political clout," the Boston historian Thomas O'Connor explained.[25] Kevin White used to compare the South End to the Balkans. The churches, reflecting the neighborhood's ethnic diversity, include Episcopalian, Lutheran, Methodist, Black Methodist Episcopalian, Syrian Orthodox and Greek Orthodox denominations. In addition to these were several gospel groups, and of course the Catholic churches of this city of Irish immigrants—the South End's immense Cathedral of the Holy Cross stands out on the urban landscape, not far from the equally imposing Church of the Immaculate Conception belonging to the Boston

---

25   O'Connor, *Building a New Boston*, p. 226.

College Jesuits. Meanwhile, the shop owners and industrialists of the neighborhood's eastern section were organized in the South End business association, whereas the black middle classes, excluded from the rest of the city, here had their own churches, cultural institutions and political networks. In addition to these populations, City Hall's support rests on the presence of an important group of lodging- and boarding-house owners and on the gradual arrival of white homeowners. These South End residents, convinced of urban renewal's value-creating promise, came together in the neighborhood associations. The new homeowners were, indeed, more liable to meet there than in the churches, which formed strong and segregated sites of community belonging.[26] They also participate in the traditional organizations of the white educated class, like historical societies and the League of Women Voters. However, with the exception of the South End Historical Society, these organizations had little presence in the South End, in contrast to the residential districts on the city outskirts where local branches of the Lions, the Kiwanis and the Junior Chamber of Commerce were established.[27] White homeowners' engagement was concentrated in the neighborhood associations, where they only gradually conquered a hegemonic position.

During the elaboration of the urban renewal plan in the first half of the 1960s, City Hall first made contact with the neighborhood's community center, which emerged from the "settlement houses" movement of the late nineteenth century.[28] In connection with this community center, a first

---

26   The churches, or at least those that have not yet been sold to property developers, today draw a large number of former parishioners who make a weekly return to the South End each Sunday.

27   Founded in 1920, the League of Women Voters, long composed of housewives, has the goal of encouraging women's participation in the political system through its educational activity. On the civic life of the new suburbs, see Herbert J. Gans, *The Levittowners: Ways of Life and Politics in a New Suburban Community*, New York: Pantheon Books, 1967.

28   In this period, Boston like Chicago before it saw the development of settlement houses in its working-class districts, in which the wives of the wealthy bourgeoisie and subsequently young graduates engaged in an on-the-ground fight against the ills of industrial society. Robert Halpern, *Rebuilding the Inner City: A History of Neighborhood Initiatives to Address Poverty in the United States*, New York: Columbia University Press,

community advisory structure was established in which Peter Whitaker,[29] a homeowner who moved into the South End in 1959, played a leading role.

The Ancestor of the "Pioneers"

An employee of Boston's very powerful Unitarian Church, Peter Whitaker lived next to Union Park and was chair of the neighborhood association. By the time he arrived in the district, almost all of the town houses constructed around the park in the 1850s and 1860s had been turned into lodging houses, but the area nonetheless still enjoyed a certain respectability. Langley Keyes described it at the end of the 1960s as "a residential area with stores, restaurants, and clubs catering to the resident Syrian population . . . The cafés are not hangouts for Skid Row people or prostitutes but resemble the 'local pub' of British tradition."[30] Like a few other residents arriving before him, Whitaker bought a house whose renovation he undertook himself. But he was also part of another migratory wave happening at the same time: the arrival of gays attracted by the proximity of the inner-city bars. Married, and father to three adopted children, he kept his sexual orientation a secret, as was the general rule up until the 1970s.

Whitaker's role was an important one, since already in the early 1960s he was a dependable interlocutor with the municipal authorities. And as a member of the body that brought together the seventeen neighborhood associations existing at that time, he worked to develop a network of civic associations within a district that he had promoted among his acquaintances. From 1965 he produced a news bulletin called *New South End* and participated in the first ten-member community advisory board.

1995; Sarah Deutsch, *Women and the City: Gender, Space and Power in Boston, 1870–1940*, Oxford: Oxford University Press, 2000.

29   All the names of South End residents have here been changed, with the exception of the activist leaders Mel and Joyce King, the estate agent Betty Gibson and Colin and Joan Diver.

30   Keyes, *The Rehabilitation Planning Game*, p. 44.

Still, in that period another figure symbolized the first efforts to encourage the "renaissance" of the South End even more so than Peter Whitaker: Brian Hanson. Hanson's profile shows that the group of "gentrifiers" emerged on the basis of a great heterogeneity, not least the alliances between "new" and "old" residents that made their own mark on this still-forming group. Having been born and raised in the neighborhood, Brian Hanson chaired the body that brought together all the associations.

The Local Ally of the "Pioneers"

Brian Hanson lived in West Canton Street, an address close to the city center popular among the new arrivals with whom he quickly began to establish contacts. However, his profile considerably distinguished him from them. Born in 1933 to an Irish family with seven children, he belonged to the more stable layer of the neighborhood's working class: after graduating from college, he joined the army, then was hired by a large dairy company. His social status was strengthened by his ties to the Catholic Church—his father having been active in the Holy Cross parish—and his involvement in networks supporting the Irish Republican cause. While Hanson was far from WASP—his wife, of Lebanese descent, was also a Catholic—this did not stop him from becoming a renowned figure, even today, and one of the privileged interlocutors with the local authorities.

The manner in which he engaged in the civic sphere, subsequently converting his social capital into a post at City Hall, shows how he was able to serve as an ally to certain among the neighborhood's pre-existing inhabitants. Hanson and his wife were members of the first community advisory boards during the period of urban renewal, and they based their activities on their deep local roots and their very early engagement with the issue of security. This was a matter of great importance to new homeowners, but other middle-class inhabitants were also sensitive to it, as were the lodging-house owners concerned for their neighborhood's reputation. Brian Hanson organized a patrol for the street on which he lived. His local engagement (he was a member of the community center board) and involvement in municipal affairs (he was a candidate to the state legislature in 1967) rested on his ecumenical approach—indeed, his support for the Irish cause was not widely known. All this made Brian an interlocutor whom the new homeowners respected. Avoiding any criticism of the police, he promoted public safety campaigns and in 1985 was appointed director of a Neighborhood Crime Watch program for the Boston Police Department. Upon his death in 2009, the local paper dedicated an obituary to this "legend of the neighborhood."

Beyond the question of safety, Brian Hanson exhibited a profile similar to that of certain local lodging-house owners, though a number of them were women. In the 1970s these latter were active in neighborhood associations as well as municipal community advisory boards, the neighborhood town halls and even the group that mobilized against bar closures. Such was the case of Louise Fitzpatrick, the former president of my second ally's neighborhood association, and whose valuable archives I was able to put to good use.[31]

Many documents show City Hall's efforts to support the local milieu of civic associations. In 1962, the first body liaising with the South End decided to extend its domain and therefore invited the existing associations to come under its wing. A pamphlet that the BRA published in 1963 explicitly called on residents to join it.[32] Many documents produced by this same agency counted the number of associations: sixteen or seventeen (in 1966, other lists spoke of twenty, a sign that these structures, their organization and their links to the mayor's office were far from settled). The documents retracing the preparation of the plan that was finally put into effect in 1965 describe a large number of meetings. A two-page text entitled "Strong Community Support Expected for Proposed South End Renewal," published on August 19, 1965,

31   On the lodging-house owners and Louise Fitzpatrick, see Chapter 3.

32   "Urban Renewal will affect every South End resident. All are urged to take an active interest now by joining any of the sixteen neighborhood organizations or one of the following organizations which represent particular interests". "The future of the South End must be planned on a sound basis and in a manner which the people of the area agree is good. This involves many meetings with neighborhood associations and other interested groups."

spoke of "155 separate meetings of different organizations, neighborhood associations, church groups and the like," whereas in February 1966 in the *New South End*, Peter Whitaker expressed "relief" in "think[ing] that we won't have to wait much longer to see some of the new streets and buildings and parks and schools for which South Enders have worked so hard."

The neighborhood associations became official representative bodies sanctioning City Hall's decisions. The modernization initiative led by Mayor Kevin White's office strengthened these links, as it picked up on the idea of "neighborhoods": already in 1967 the theme of his campaign was no longer the "New Boston" but the both modest and modern "city of neighborhoods." Once in office, he created the neighborhood mayor's offices—"little city halls"—for the purposes of allowing residents to express their grievances and drawing them closer to the administration. The mayor set up a specific department, the Office of Public Service, made up of four services and represented by four agents across fourteen neighborhoods.

This "neighborhoods"-oriented policy, along with "local input," was conceived as a response to the civil rights movement in Boston. It simultaneously served to build and strengthen an electoral base, pulling in not only black voters but also the section of the liberal white middle classes who had stayed in the city rather than moved to the suburbs. This group, together with black and Italian voters, thus made up the coalition that cemented Kevin White's victory in the 1967 election as well as in the years to come.[33] The white middle classes represented a valuable electorate, perceived as a counterpower in a South End where social struggles were mounting. At the same time, resistance against the civil rights movement hardened among the Irish working-class neighborhoods, despite the mayor's efforts (as well as those of presidents Kennedy and Johnson at the national level) not to alienate this important component of the Democratic electorate. The white backlash took on considerable proportions in Boston, where it was represented by the charismatic leader Louise Hicks, a candidate whom Kevin White defeated at the 1967 municipal elections.

---

33   Ronald P. Formisano and Constance K. Burns, *Boston, 1700–1980: The Evolution of Urban Politics*, Westport, CT: Greenwood Press, 1984; Martha Wagner Weinberg, "Boston's Kevin White, a Mayor who Survives," *Political Science Quarterly* 96: 1 (1981), pp. 87–106.

The coordinated organization of the South End civic milieu, through neighborhood associations, "little City Halls" and community advisory boards, was thus of crucial importance for the mayor. He could signal his social convictions and at the same time encourage the collective mobilization of young liberal households. And he established an institutionalized dialogue with local actors through the medium of these structures. From the beginning of community advisory structure in 1962, BRA employees provided them with technical support, and over the following decade this policy gave rise to a more expansive network composed of residents keen to engage in such collaboration, utilizing resources provided by the mayor's office. These were young graduates who had recently moved to the South End and who were attracted by White's modern, socially-engaged style.[34] Beyond providing symbolic legitimation, the opening up of municipal affairs in the context of urban renewal created professional opportunities for those inhabitants who had constructed a network of mutual acquaintances in the neighborhood. Moreover, the overlap among the roles that the many different members of the White administration were meant to play only served to strengthen such connections. And activism supporting the mayor went hand in hand with employment opportunities at City Hall.[35] The networks established both within the framework of urban renewal and through the intermediary of the "little city halls" allowed the mayor to attach himself to solid bases of support. Such was the case of a resident who arrived in the South End in 1967 and led Kevin White's campaign there in 1976, before being appointed head of the neighborhood mayor's office and ultimately obtaining a post at the BRA. We will later find him at the source of a parents' association at a public school in the South End. The recomposition of the political apparatus under Kevin White thus consolidated an emerging network as well as serving the imperatives of urban renewal. The election committee that White organized in 1975 included, among others, Peter Whitaker and Brian Hanson, long-standing

34   "Before Kevin White the only agency that had people with college degrees on the staff was the BRA. All that changed under White. The liberals knew that there was a new managerial class all throughout the government." (Formisano and Burns, *Boston 1700–1980*, p. 221).

35   Formisano and Burns, *Boston, 1700–1980*; Tilo Schabert, *Boston Politics: The Creativity of Power*, New York: W. de Gruyter, 1989.

figures in the civic sector who will reappear throughout the coming chapters. Another participant was the "pioneer" mentioned in the first chapter who was less concerned by "diversity" in this period than he would later have me believe when I interviewed him.

Mixed programs in the South End

The civic association scene in the South End was marked by hard-fought political struggles from 1968 onward, often revolving around the use of the land made available by the city's land acquisition during its urban renewal drive. During this period, white homeowners were effectively integrated into the management of the renovation process: indeed, active neighborhood association members made their presence felt in SEPAC, the advisory body created by the mayor's office in 1968. In this regard they were helped by the way in which SEPAC elections were conceived, namely on the basis of four-teen electoral districts more or less following the boundaries of the fifteen neighborhood associations. SEPAC comprised twenty-five white homeown-ers—thirteen of them having participated in the first consultation process—together with eight black and two Puerto Rican members. This body became the legitimate interlocutor of the public authorities.[36] It was closely linked to the neighborhood associations but also to the South End Historical Society, whose members occupied several positions in SEPAC.[37]

For the city's planning agency, the mobilized white owners made up a pressure group that could sometimes be difficult to manage. After all, they were impatient to see the South End freed of the stigmas associated with a working-class neighborhood—the lack of infrastructure and services, disrepu-table bars and drunks crowding the sidewalks—and to replace them with the amenities and social markers characteristic of upper-middle-class neighbor-hoods: brick sidewalks, street lamps in a period style similar to those in Beacon Hill, and restaurants more attractive than the cafeterias frequented

---

36   Mollenkopf, *The Contested City*, p. 192.

37   Created in 1966 and bringing together conservative white homeowners as well as many estate agents, the South End Historical Society organized discussions and visits to old houses, wrote pamphlets, made inventories, and above all fought for the South End to be recognized by City Hall as a "historic district." On its role in the recharacterization of the neighborhood, see Chapter 4.

by the lodging houses' tenants. Yet despite the pressure that they continuously exerted on the BRA, the new homeowners also came to be extremely valuable allies. Not only did the BRA see their arrival as a motor of change, but when they organized in associations, they constituted a counterpower to the activist forces who, in the context of the first riots (like in Los Angeles in 1965, or Chicago and Harlem in 1968), seemed impossible to control.

Even so, in the South End, the period inaugurated by 1968 was a very uncertain one. The inward migration of "pioneers" was to remain modest in scale across the 1960s and 1970s, and there were also other migration flows, such as that of the residents displaced by the demolition of the West End. During these two decades the black population thus remained a constant 39 percent of the population of this neighborhood, while in some areas of particular concentration it even increased. The Hispanic population rose from 1 to 7 percent and the Chinese from 2 to 13 percent across the 1960s, while the white population fell due to the departure of low-income renters. Up to the 1980s, when urban renewal reached its conclusion, the South End was distinguished from other districts by its state of decay.[38] The 1973 elections were a defeat for the owners—both the new arrivals and those who ran lodging houses. These latter were pushed out of SEPAC in favor of activist groups emerging from the black and Puerto Rican community.[39] In January 1974, this body adopted a motion by seventeen votes against three, demanding that any new construction project be at least 25 percent composed of low-income housing. The declaration—which was clearly hostile to the new arrivals, the landlords and the developers—asserted the rights of the poorest residents. During the years that followed, up to the completion of the urban renewal project in 1979 and its own dissolution in 1981, SEPAC turned into

---

38   For a long time it had a higher percentage of overcrowded dwellings and of homes without their own toilets than any other neighborhood. In 1970 the number of dwellings without one or more sanitary amenities made up 23 percent of the total, while 12.3 percent were overcrowded. By comparison, the respective percentages for the older but upper-class Back Bay–Beacon Hill stood at 13 percent and 3.6 percent, and even for another working-class district like South Boston, 6 percent and 9 percent.

39   Deborah A. Auger, "The Politics of Revitalization in Gentrifying Neighborhoods. The Case of Boston's South End," *Journal of the American Planning Association* 45 (October 1979), pp. 515–22.

a bullhorn for these low-income South Enders, whatever their own internal divisions.

This did not stop the white homeowners strengthening their grip on the neighborhood associations in the late 1970s and into the 1980s. The period beginning in the early 1980s thus saw them play a considerable role, to the point of winning a quasi-hegemonic position on the civic terrain. The launch of a mixed housing program in 1988 played a crucial role in this. The program was born of the BRA's decision to develop sixty-eight parcels of land it had acquired during the urban renewal process. The regeneration of the South End had increased the potential profitability of property investments, and at the end of the 1980s the pieces of land under BRA control were greatly coveted. The progress of gentrification considerably increased prices, contributing to population turnover. The increase in the average income is telling: in 1960 the median stood at $4,542 in the South End, versus $7,206 in the city as a whole; no other neighborhood except part of Roxbury was so poor. Ten years later, in 1970, there was still a significant gap ($6,122 in the South End and $9,133 in Boston), but gradually the South End's place in the spatial hierarchy was transformed. It was no longer "the" black district of Boston, as it had been right at the beginning of urban renewal when it took in almost half of the city's nonwhites. In 1980, the black populations of Roxbury, North Dorchester and Mattapan (more on the outskirts and in the south of the neighborhood, where many of those displaced by urban renewal had moved) were proportionally higher than the South End's. The Boston Bank Urban Renewal Group, a program established in 1968 to help low-income black residents purchase homes, included the South End but also covered Dorchester, Jamaica Plain, and above all, Roxbury. It was to this latter district that many residents moving out of the South End and other neighborhoods went to make their homes.[40]

Boston's economic development in this period was spectacular, feeding the demand for city-center housing. While the 1970s were marked by economic depression, and industrial decline increased working-class unemployment, the 1980s saw the accelerated growth of new sectors creating jobs

---

40   On the transformation of Roxbury, formerly a suburb composed of Jewish and Irish residents, see Gerald H. Gamm, *Urban Exodus: Why the Jews Left Boston and the Catholics Stayed*, Cambridge, MA: Harvard University Press, 1999.

in finance, insurance, real estate, health and education. After thirty years of demographic decline—the number of Boston inhabitants had fallen from 801,444 in 1950 to 562,994 in 1980—the population went back up to 620,000 in 1985. With the exception of the early 1990s crash, this economic expansion went hand in hand with an unprecedented property boom.[41] Kevin White's final term in the early 1980s saw the construction of thirteen skyscrapers. Boston now had the fourth highest rent of any US city, and was in second place in terms of the cost of living. Its socio-demographic structure changed, following developments on a national scale: the working-class segment of the population did not disappear but was considerably reduced, in exchange for a more skilled population working in service sectors.[42] Boston took its place as one of the country's most "dynamic" cities, while others that had once been major economic centers—like Detroit, the "Motor City"—plunged into depression.

The South End appeared all the more attractive as a residential setting due to the $135 million of federal funding invested in urban renewal, which by the end of the 1970s had allowed the complete renovation of the neighborhood's infrastructure. The sidewalks were rebuilt, street lighting was installed, trees were planted, the city's public library opened a local branch, and certain among its restaurants began to attract a better-off clientele. While 4,000 subsidized dwellings were built—allowing a poorer population to stay in the area, particularly retirees—any overall assessment of urban renewal shows a clear transformation of the neighborhood toward a wealthier population. Above all, one of the symbols of urban decay—the elevated subway line passing along Washington Street—was torn down in 1987, creating considerable development opportunities. Up to that point, the sight of the train as well as the noise it made added to the degradation of a once-vibrant artery that had been hit hard by industrial decline and the buying-up of parcels of land then left undeveloped by the BRA.

---

41   "With its economy taking off, the price of housing rose faster in Boston between 1980 and 1990 than in any other city." Barry Bluestone and Mary Huff Stevenson, *The Boston Renaissance: Race, Space and Economic Change in an American Metropolis*, New York: Russell Sage Foundation, 2000, p. 6.

42   As early as 1980, while the percentage of workers and farmers had fallen steeply, white-collar employees made up more than half the US workforce.

The price increases in Boston in general and the South End in particular brought new investors onto the scene. They were no longer the young professionals who, up until the late 1970s, had been able to afford whole houses thanks to the income they could collect from renting out two or three floors. From the 1980s, demand never stopped growing and developers flooded into the South End. The price of a house soon hit a million dollars. The conversion of entire houses into apartments that could be sold separately offered sizeable profits, and a singular market came into being—the condominiums, whose numbers exploded in the 1980s.[43] The rate of conversion was particularly rapid in the South End due to the stock of lodging houses, which as of 1960 were home to some 33 percent of the population. For the landlords who did not live in the neighborhood and were incapable of guaranteeing the upkeep of their properties,[44] the price that the developers offered them was a godsend.

At the end of the 1980s, when the mayor's office decided to develop the vacant parcels of land acquired during the urban renewal process, it faced a considerable task: in 1990 the land that it possessed was estimated at 27 acres, that is, 5 percent of the South End's area. This tells us something of the extent of the potential profits and socio-demographic changes that such development could entail. The 1988 plan showed the new priorities that prevailed at the federal level, but also the new power relations in the neighborhood itself. It marked the end of the massive public housing programs of the last two decades, which had led to the construction of large apartment blocks. Yet, echoing the "new orthodoxy of city planning,"[45] it did introduce the principle of "diversity." While the BRA looked favorably on the development of condos, which considerably expanded the property tax base and encouraged the arrival of middle-class residents, White's successor as mayor in 1984 did commit to building dwellings for the poorest. Indeed, the

---

43   The number of condominiums in Boston grew from 4,500 in 1980 to 34,575 in 1990.

44   As of 1964, this was some 55 percent of lodging house owners—that is, 923 individuals. Among these establishments, 12.8 percent were "in need of major repair." Keyes, *The Rehabilitation Planning Game*, p. 42.

45   Susan Fainstein, "Cities and Diversity: Should We Want It? Can We Plan for It?," *Urban Affairs Review* 41: 1 (2005), pp. 3–19.

associations championing public housing—which were also represented beyond the South End by two black members of the Massachusetts state legislature, Mel King (elected in 1973) and Byron Rushing (elected in 1982)—had demanded this. From the second half of the 1970s, SEPAC rallied activists and social agencies around a rhetoric targeting what now came to be called "gentrification." Its newspaper propounded the cause of low-income residents, and up until the beginning of the 1980s, it was a bull-horn for evicted tenants' struggles. This cause was now institutionalized within the so-called "community" structures working with the public author-ities, in the form of community development corporations (CDCs). The association that Puerto Rican activists had set up in the 1960s transformed into a CDC, guiding the construction of Villa Victoria. As for the Tent City development—whose name came from the parking lot demonstration of 1968—black activists here also created a CDC, and—after some eighteen years of mobilizations and financial initiatives—secured the construction of 270 dwellings to be rented to households of various income levels. Another CDC also emerging from a tenants' mobilization at the end of the 1960s, the Tenant Development Corporation, worked in close collaboration with the BRA in the framework of the 1988 plan. Constituting a "form of third sector between the market and the state," the CDCs could be described as local enterprises run by residents.[46] Their growing professionalization never-theless blunted their initially activist approach, and encouraged their adoption of the dominant city planning discourse. At the same time, white liberal residents, opposed to their conservative neighbors from the South End Historical Society and sometimes fighting side by side with black and Hispanic activists, rallied to the principle of "diversity" in housing construc-tion.[47] The alliance between these homeowners and organizations like the CDCs expressed the now rather widely accepted rejection of the ravages of modern urbanism—with its destroyed neighborhoods, highways disfiguring cities, bleak suburbs, and commercial centers stretching out to the

---

46   M.-H. Bacqué, "Associations 'communautaires' et gestion de la pauvreté," *Actes de la recherche en sciences sociales* 160 (2005), pp. 46–66.

47   In the early 1960s many of these had opposed, together with the community center and CAUSE, the plan for a highway crossing the South End. Some also fought for the upkeep of the community gardens—see Chapter 5.

periphery—and the preference for "mixed" units helping the poorest populations access housing, rather than building huge projects.

The compromise sealed in the 1988 construction program appeared advantageous to the activists insofar as City Hall made it a rule that any new residential construction would include at least 10 percent dwellings for low- or middle-income households. It organized the division of units in the South End's new buildings according to the formula of one-third so-called affordable housing, one-third at controlled prices, and one-third at the market rate but with the option to buy. "In total, six operations were carried out, amounting to some 307 dwellings."[48] While the balance of forces apparently seemed favorable to liberal groups, the homeowners who were most hostile to public housing—and who were deeply embedded in community advisory structures—remained vigilant. The composition of the group constituted at the moment of the 1988 program, as described in the BRA documents, is revealing. White homeowners made up around a third of its members, and among them, half were overtly hostile to public housing. The makeup of this list also demonstrates the sharp decline in oppositional movements, replaced by activists who had not taken part in the struggles of the 1960s, but, had, instead, arrived in the neighborhood more recently or come from wealthier backgrounds.

Commercial development in the South End

The transformations of the city and the 1988 program accelerated the socio-demographic reconfiguration of the South End. From 1980 to 1990 the population rose from 27,125 to 28,891 inhabitants, and the percentage of whites grew from 39.3 percent to 44.5 percent, before reaching 50 percent in 2000, while the black proportion of the population fell from 40.8 percent to 34.2 percent to 25 percent. As for Hispanics, they formed 12.7 percent of the population in 1980, 16 percent in 1990 and 11.5 percent in 2000. The income gap between the South End and Boston as a whole fell considerably: in 1980 the mean income was $10,845 for the South End, as compared to $12,530 for the city in general.

In the mid-1990s, the civic scene leaned further toward the white homeowner group, marking a third phase in the history of postwar urban policy. After the renovation of the neighborhood from the mid-1960s to late 1970s,

---

48   Bacqué, "Associations 'communautaires' et gestion de la pauvreté."

based on the demolition of buildings and the installation of new services and infrastructure, and after the 1980s land sales for the development of mixed housing programs, came the mid-1990s and the era of commercial development. This development concerned the part of the South End that had become abandoned industrial sites. In 1993 Thomas Menino was elected mayor in the context of brutal cutbacks in federal subsidies. In so-called "entrepreneurial cities," mayors now gave priority to commercial development.[49] The plan for the regeneration of Washington Street was formed in this context, unfolding at a moment when this most-neglected part of the South End was sharpening financial appetites. The demolition of the elevated train line in 1987, the gradual selling-off of land controlled by the BRA and the construction of many new buildings on the old vacant plots had already begun the transformation of this great artery.

That said, in the mid-1990s gentrification was only slowly breaking down the boundary that Tremont Street represented. At that time, Washington Street—situated two blocks to the east, and where many of the friends of my first ally today live—was for many residents still a street on which one did not travel. This mental boundary was materialized by the architectural division that Washington Street demarcated, with the expanse of industrial wasteland, the imposing Cathedral public housing development, the no-less-imposing Cathedral of the Holy Cross—but so, too, the immense city hospital complex. Many abandoned buildings were home to a particularly impoverished population, while artists occupied a former shoe factory. The Pine Street Inn homeless shelter was not far away either. However, there were also multiple forces encouraging the renovation of Washington Street. This suited not only City Hall's strategies but also the financial interests generated by the real estate boom that was then exploding in Boston.

In the phase that began in 1995, engagement in favor of diversity in the South End's development had not disappeared, but it took "recourse to private intervention to finance the mandatory quota of accessible housing" in homeownership programs.[50] The extent of the land under City Hall's

49   Dennis R. Judd and Paul P. Kantor, *The Politics of Urban America: A Reader*, Boston: Allyn and Bacon, 1998.

50   Marie-Hélène Bacqué (ed.), *Projet urbain en quartier ancien. La Goutte d'Or, South End*, Paris: PUCA, 2005, p. 45.

ownership allowed it to remain in charge of the situation, engaging in a managed partnership with the neighborhood associations and the real estate developers, to the detriment of the CDCs. There was a strong selective element to who could be recognized as the legitimate representatives of the community, fed by the vitality of the homeowners' associations. In 1995 members of the neighborhood association located on Washington Street protested to City Hall over the delays in the organization of the bus route meant to replace the elevated railway. In 1997 a workgroup set up a semipublic program that was later to become Washington Gateway Main Street, financed by a federal program supporting the rehabilitation of old neighborhoods' main thoroughfares through commercial development. City Hall closely controlled its activity. Particularly active among these residents was a figure who provided a rather typical example of the 1990s arrivals. His age and professional category look rather different to the young households generally imagined to make up the "gentrifier" group. Instead, he was one of the upper-middle-class early retirees who, after raising their kids in the secure comfort of the towns on the periphery of the city, moved to the South End in search of an urban lifestyle and a more invigorated sociability. He was one of the first residents that I interviewed. I was particularly surprised by the rational, controlled, explicitly "apolitical" tone of what he had to say, since I had still imagined the neighborhood associations to be part of a more or less activist community. He came to our meeting with a notebook and pen in his pocket. Having retired from his engineering job, he left the suburbs in 1992 to move into a renovated building on Washington Street with his wife. After participating in the launch of Washington Gateway, he became part of its board and supported its initiatives.

Washington Gateway members' overlapping participation in neighborhood associations translated into a crushing majority of well-off white residents in its ranks.[51] Some shopowners were invited, but no black or Puerto Rican activists nor any CDC representatives were involved. This limiting of the official "community" to homeowners was not City Hall's decision alone. Particularly active members of the neighborhood associations had also ensured this outcome (some of the members pursuing careers at the BRA, via Washington

---

51   Karl Seidman, *Revitalizing Commerce for American Cities: A Practitioner's Guide to Urban Main Street Programs*, Washington: Fannie Mae Foundation, 2004, pp. 82–3.

Gateway). The chair of this body, who was my first contact in the neighborhood, illustrates the overlapping interests of the real estate sector, the civic scene and City Hall. A lawyer who enjoys local authority due to her long-standing residence in the neighborhood, she was an active member of the Union Park Neighborhood Association in the 1980s and became its president in 1992 before being appointed to the leadership of Washington Gateway. Her husband, a developer, made his fortune in the condo market. The position that she obtained provided recognition of both a residential and professional career. Her involvement in the neighborhood association earned her the legitimacy necessary to assume the leadership of an organization that—though largely guided by City Hall and subject to commercial interests—needed to appear to emanate from the "neighborhood." That is indeed what its website claims. Centered on commercial and housing developments, this body offers her the means for strengthening her already extensive web of contacts. In close collaboration with the BRA, she participates in selecting which developers should be sold the plots surrounding Washington Street. She also takes part in the distribution of subsidies to entrepreneurs who want to renovate or open a business. The economic interests at stake are enormous, and these ultimately dominate the regeneration effort, prioritizing luxury developments on Washington Street. Receiving a limited degree of outside support, Washington Gateway works in close collaboration with the BRA on the basis of private financing coming from foundations, businesses and private donations, notably those of homeowners' associations and in particular real estate developers. In 2005 this paramunicipal body backed $520 million of investment, $400 million of this coming from the private sector.[52]

The renovation of Washington Street was an important moment in the physical and symbolic appropriation of the South End and the consolidation of a local elite. The marking of public space by the transformation of businesses and the arrival of new restaurants designed for a well-off clientele, but also the renovation of Peters Park and the creation of the dog park—itself a reserved space—went hand in hand with the new narrower definition now attributed to "community." With Washington Gateway we can clearly see the process by which the middle class was gradually pushed

---

52   Chris Orchard, "Washington Gateway Wins National Award," *South End News*, May 12, 2005.

out of the neighborhood associations in favor of the upper middle class that today forms the majority of their membership. The selection of the home-owners invited to represent the community became an ever-harsher process, as a member of its board learned at his own expense. This high school teacher bought a home in the South End in 2001, a so-called "affordable" apartment in a mixed housing initiative. He is a friend of my first ally, but my second ally also held him in high esteem. When he dared to criticize the direction that this paramunicipal body was taking, he was met with a fierce reaction. He ended up having to leave, and when he recounted the dispar-aging remarks that he had heard about the mixed developments, there was a clear bitterness in his voice. In particular, he didn't care for the comments on the troublesome behavior of the owners of subsidized units, himself being part of this group. Thus we see how the boundaries of the gentrifier group shifted, as socioeconomic exclusion—with the in-group defined as the nonsubsidized owners—strengthened.

The imposition of a more managerial register also accelerated the transfor-mation of the South End associations' profile, which followed the same tendency that prevailed in the large national organizations: having previously relied on a large membership base, from the 1970s onward they fell back on a small number of supporters well-versed in fundraising and lobbying tech-niques.[53] Efficient professionalism replaced the amateurism of the activists of yesteryear. The professional register that established itself in the neighborhood associations also prevailed in the South End, a change facilitated by the nego-tiations of the urban renewal period. The competencies of architects, city planners, lawyers and lobbyists now asserted their authority, substituting a technocratic approach for the more informal and contested register that had reigned in the 1960s and 1970s. While today some associations meet in large meeting halls where wine and cheese are passed around, for a long time it was boarding-house owners' kitchens that served as the venues. One 1970s member of a branch of the Democratic Party liked to recall the meetings that often continued long into the night with the help of a few bottles of wine and the

---

53   Robert Wuthnow, *Loose Connections: Joining Together in America's Fragmented Communities*, Cambridge, MA: Harvard University Press, 1998; Theda Skocpol, *Diminished Democracy: From Membership to Management in American Civil Life*, Norman, OK: University of Oklahoma Press, 2003.

amorous liaisons that punctuated the activists' socializing.[54] SEPAC or BRA representatives for their part remember the sometimes-violent clashes to which some negotiations led. The former SEPAC president told me, for example, of one representative of the Hispanic community who, fearing that he would not be given a grant, demonstrated his anger by placing a revolver on the table.

The 1990s marked a turning point in the imposition of a more rationalized city management, encouraged by the advance of electronic media. Websites and e-mail lists provided an opportunity for those who had mastered these techniques (generally the most well-off residents) to introduce new rules. At the end of the 1990s two residents who had known each other since their graduate training in management proceeded to make major changes to their association. "We had some ideas of how to formalize things," one of them, now its president, told me. An active member of another group recounted how the "old" members opposed the creation of a webpage, which, in his view, "brought it into the twenty-first century." The degree of rationalization nevertheless varies from association to association, and their level of activity is often uneven, as the less frequently updated sites demonstrate. In the case of the better organized associations, a board of ten to thirty members meets each month. Contrary to other associations without membership records and email lists, the largest among these is made up of some 300 people. The president or vice president prepares the agenda and draws up the minutes. All these documents are then uploaded to the website. Subcommittees deal with particular subjects. The meetings follow strict procedures. The order of questions and the time allotted to them, generally between ten and twenty minutes, are set down in advance. Out of the fifteen meetings that I attended, none finished more than ten minutes late. These changes have very much contributed to the exclusion of less well-off residents, as Richie O'Brien, an "old" resident discussed in the next chapter, suggests:

> The uneducated people tend to be very loud and talkative. Even though they were not fighting, they tended to get more excited . . . But some of the new people moving in, they were quite taken aback by them . . . Somebody would get up and say: wait a minute, you're not going to do that, that's not

---

54 Of course, this has not all disappeared, but the occasions when a joint might be passed round at the end of a meeting are less in evidence today.

right [raising his voice], instead of saying [adopting a more polite tone], Mr. Chairman, may I, you know . . . That was difficult, and at one time, we had this system called *Robert's Rules of Order*. It's a booklet, a rule book for meetings. Mr. Chairman, may I . . . blah, blah, blah. That kind of things. One time, we had to use that because it became so out of hand. Everybody tried to say . . . Well, there were so many terrible issues, everything was volatile. Now, it's very quiet.

Still today, civic association networks are of some importance in the South End, particularly around the community center and the multiple charity associations based there since the end of the nineteenth century. The community center's programs are still directed toward the poorer populations in the neighborhood. The 1990s also marked a consolidation of the local elite at the same time as accelerating population turnover, due to the rehabilitation of Washington Street and the economic boom the city experienced in the 1980s. The proportion of managers and professionals rose from 43 percent to 56 percent in the 1990s. And while the nonwhite population of Boston rose from 37 percent to 42 percent between 1990 and 2000, it fell in the South End, going from 71 percent to 53 percent in this period. At the very moment when Boston was becoming more cosmopolitan, and without socio-spatial segregation easing as a result, a neighborhood was developing within it in which the white population was constantly on the rise, and above all gaining influence. This was the South End, which nonetheless became the emblem of mixed and multicultural districts.

A NEIGHBORHOOD ELITE

If an elite was constituted over the decades thanks to the renewal of the neighborhood, then what were its powers once this process was completed in practice? One of the interviews I carried out for my study was instructive in this regard. This resident, who looked after real estate issues for his neighborhood association, commented as follows on his negotiations with the developers and public authorities:

It turns out, there is a bunch of us who have been on the other side, and who are perfectly able to do all the numbers, all the professional stuff, so we can make it difficult . . . As I said to somebody recently in a meeting, you don't have to negotiate with us. But if you check around, you're going to find out that if you take that stand to us repeatedly, we are doing our best to make it more difficult. You're going to make it difficult for us, we're going to make it difficult for you.

This interview, during which my interlocutor spoke at length on his career, illustrated the profile and the diversity of the networks allowing for such interventions. Born in 1944 and holding a PhD, he began his career at a university before turning toward politics, first in the federal administration in Washington, then working for mayor Kevin White after he was elected in 1968. He later became a real estate developer and then a consultant, all the while holding responsibilities in his neighborhood association. He moved to the South End in 1997, buying a multistory house in one of its most sought-after areas, near the city centre. He earns $200,000 a year. He and his wife, a lawyer, dine at restaurants several times a week. He normally votes Democrat, even if he admits having a few conservative leanings. Questioned about the South End and his reasons for moving there, he explained this to me, delightedly expounding the theme of diversity: "It's a small community of very different people . . . People are different, age-wise, racially, ethnically, they are different educationally, they are different economically, with regard to their sexual orientation."

These homeowners' engagement in the public affairs of the South End brings us back to the role of the civic sector in social policies and to the tradition of local benevolent engagement that is so strong in the United States.[55] All the same, this resident's invocation of his right to oversee the management of the neighborhood, particularly as regards the appropriation and use of land, is a direct result of the negotiations that took place during the urban renewal drive of the 1960s and 1970s. This interventionism became ever stronger with the rise in the gentrifiers' socio-economic status and the fall of the activist movements. Today, each and every construction project, whether a private development or a public initiative, must be presented to the neighborhood

---

55   Theda Skocpol, *Protecting Soldiers and Mothers: The Political Origins of Social Policy in the United States*, Cambridge, MA: Belknap Press of Harvard University Press, 1992.

associations and approved by them. Their role also involves overseeing commercial activities: the arrival of a new business, the change in a restaurant's license, changing hours of operation or even the installation of terraces require their prior agreement. While the municipal services are, in principle, bound by the associations' votes, contacts with the mayor can allow a developer or a restaurateur to bypass this. But as the former developer explains, this does not save them from having to go through a sometimes-lengthy process of negotiating with the association, which can prove to be a considerable nuisance.

The associations' grip on the neighborhood translates into control over restaurant activities, strengthened by the organizing of fundraisers as rites of the civic sector. On these occasions, members ritually ask restaurants to offer a free dinner—which is then offered as a raffle prize—and a system of gift and rewards is thus established. The associations' power over City Hall encourages restaurants to go along with this, and in any case their members make up a clientele whom these restaurants want to court. The meetings planning these events are often almost-unchanging rituals. The fact that the same schedule, the same addresses, and the same list of tasks are reused for each fundraiser (or for each examination of restaurants' licensing applications) reveals their latent function: it is a way for a group of residents to reaffirm their presence and their influence by way of routinized practices.

The privileged relations thus established are at odds with the attitudes that the restaurants may have toward other inhabitants of the neighborhood, particularly its Hispanic residents. A large number of these latter—who today make up some 11.5 percent of the South End's population—live in the public housing complex in the center of the neighborhood, Villa Victoria. In a monograph produced in the South End, the sociologist Mario Small recounts the misadventure of a tenant who wanted to organize a dinner to announce the launching of a homework assistance program:

At one chic restaurant, she remembered feeling particularly conspicuous, as she and her helper were the two only nonwhite people there. When she approached the manager and politely asked for donations (of food or money), "that lady just started *yelling* at us," she remembers. Gloria recalls with indignation that the manager would not have addressed in the same tone someone whom she did not consider her inferior, someone, Gloria thought, who was white.

The white homeowners exercise their power through the fifteen neighborhood associations in a particularly vigilant manner. Among them, the Union Park Neighborhood Association, where I made my first forays in the neighborhood associations.

The Union Park Neighborhood Association

The Union Park Neighborhood Association brings together the residents of a few residential blocks surrounding a small park decorated with a fountain. It extends as far as the public housing complex Villa Victoria, which marks a break with the brownstone area both architecturally (it comprises one fifteen-story tower) and socially (80 percent of the population live below the national poverty line, and the mean family income stands at $16,286, in contrast to $41,590 for the neighborhood as a whole). These upper-middle-class residents thus directly face the question of encountering other groups—more than in the case of now more homogenous areas of the South End closer to the city center, which have almost no projects, but less than in others further to the southeast where public housing, shelters and charities like the Salvation Army are more numerous.

The association has no membership list, considering every resident to be part of it by definition. That said, the fifteen inhabitants who make up its board drive the organization, while extended meetings bring together a few dozen or sometimes as many as a hundred people. Its social homogeneity is striking. The members of this association are almost all white homeowners: no tenant or nonwhite resident takes part in it, even though there is no explicit exclusion. A remark that one tenant whispered to me after attending one of the meetings was instructive. One of the first questions that he had been asked was, "Do you rent or own?"

The association's budget is as much as $20,000, devoted to the upkeep of the park and employing someone to clean the sidewalks after the garbage trucks have gone. There is a committee overseeing commercial and real estate projects. Association members' presence on the boards of charities allows them to maintain close ties with such groups and keep a close watch over their activity.[56] Lobbying directed at City Hall and/or local businesses is also of considerable importance for development projects as well as street cleaning and garbage collection. Members pay particular attention to the small park, its upkeep and the hours it is open. The replacement of its gates—considered too old, but whose "antique" character nonetheless had to be preserved—gave rise to animated negotiations with the South End Historical Society, to which many Union Park members also belong.

The attention paid to the Union Park garden speaks to the central role that public spaces and the management of them play in local associations. The associations have built up their power of intervention; they also exercise it by means of philanthropic activities that establish their moral authority, devotion to the community and control of "other" populations. Donations; subsidizing the uniforms of a children's sports team from a neighboring project; grants for deserving students from poor backgrounds; or even the meals prepared and served in homeless shelters all mobilize association members. The fifteen neighborhood associations maintain their influence through an extensive social life that generally takes place in the most spacious houses or public gardens like Union Park, which is opened up to the public once a year. Fundraisers, picnics and Christmas parties are well attended. Youth groups are sometimes organized in order to strengthen participation. While some meetings take place in public places such as community or cultural centers, others are organized at a member's own home, while the most informal meetings—for example, those among association presidents— are held in neighborhood restaurants.

The institutionalization of these local groups is nonetheless incomplete. First, City Hall still plays a predominant role in running the neighborhood. A lack of public funding for housing, green spaces and garbage collection certainly does encourage wealthy residents to intervene, since they are able to provide the money necessary for the upkeep or renovation of parks and sometimes even for cleaning the sidewalks. But through its control of

---

56 On links with the civic sector, see Chapter 3.

land-use planning, City Hall remains the central figure of urban affairs. Moreover, the political-financial networks at the heart of Boston politics, and more particularly the Democratic Party, which is all-powerful in the city, structure municipal political life. Thus the owner of a Union Park restaurant—whose father is a real estate developer and friend of the mayor—could turn a deaf ear when the Union Park Neighborhood Association expressed grave reservations over his installation of outdoor seating. And even if the white homeowners are connected to the municipal apparatus, they form a local elite that, contrary to European gentrifiers of similar profile, has largely not translated its influence into election to office, nor claimed a place within the official structure of the Democratic Party.[57] Their grip over space has the peculiarity of having established itself on the margins of the electoral game, political apparatuses and the forms of patronage that have developed within them. The South End's neighborhood associations did become more institutionalized as a result of the urban renewal process; but they achieved this by creating a space where they could intervene in the management of public affairs, and not by the conquest of positions in the political or administrative arena. There are close links between local councillors and neighborhood associations, and each candidate will invariably campaign for their support; and the associations' efforts to encourage voter registration also speak to their involvement in political affairs. Nonetheless, the gentrification of the South End has not resulted in the white middle class, which remains concentrated in the suburbs, taking control of municipal politics as such.[58]

Finally, the neighborhood associations are characterized by a certain unevenness in their functioning. Their fragility is expressed not only in the poor attendance at some of their meetings when there is no important issue to occupy local residents, but also in their recurrent splits and recompositions. For example, in 2007–8 the Union Park Neighborhood Association was

---

57   Here we see how different this case is from the French middle class's residential migrations in the 1970s and 1980s, which involved not only the civic sphere but also the conquest of municipal power. Catherine Bidou-Zachariasen, *Les Aventuriers du quotidien. Essai sur les nouvelles classes moyennes*, Paris: PUF, 1984.

58   According to the Metropolitan Area Planning Council, across the metropolitan Boston area in 2000, 85 percent of the population were white, but this figure falls to 56 percent if we consider the city alone.

torn apart by conflict after it was revealed that the Pine Street Inn charity planned to buy three buildings on one of the streets adjacent to the park. This conflict followed numerous others that had taken place over recent decades, often sparked by charities' presence in a district that since the end of the nineteenth century had been considered "the most 'charitied' region in Christendom."[59]

This was once again the case in 2007, when several members of the Union Park Neighborhood Association started a petition to protest the purchase of three row houses by the Pine Street Inn. These homes, which already housed some eighty former drug users undergoing rehabilitation, were to be transformed into a halfway house for former homeless people. Other residents were angered by the petition, which in their eyes demonstrated an unacceptable level of selfishness and intolerance, and also mobilized. Following two members' semi-clandestine distribution of leaflets, a mass meeting was held for residents hostile to the project. As the voting and membership procedures allowed every resident to participate in the ballot, a statement hostile to the charity's plan was easily voted through. Resignations followed and another body formed whose objective was to support the Pine Street Inn project and defend "diversity" in the South End. This lack of consensus differentiates the fifteen South End associations from those in Beacon Hill and Back Bay, which enjoy their own offices and sometimes even employees, and speak with a strong and united voice. One further characteristic distinguishes the South End associations from the civic scene of traditional upper-class neighborhoods. The South End's associations have built up one particular form of authority: the power to regulate and organize the social mix that prevails within the neighborhood.

CONCLUSION

59   In the words of Robert Woods, a social worker who opened two settlement houses in the 1890s—one in the South End, the other in the West End. Robert Woods (ed.), *The City Wilderness: A Settlement Study by Residents and Associates of the South End House*, Boston: Houghton Mifflin, 1898, p. 245. Apart from these social centers, a multitude of other institutions also offered their social and educational services in the South End from the end of the nineteenth century onward.

The urban struggles of the 1960s encouraged the emergence of participatory planning. The Boston example shows that this could lead to the emergence, in the space of one neighborhood, of a group of white homeowners holding significant power, particularly with regard to real estate developments. As Boston attracted a growing number of high-income professionals, an elite established itself in what had, in the postwar period, been one of the city's poorest working-class neighborhoods.

But it would be mistaken to see the delegation of power to wealthy residents as only a means of clearing the minefield of social rebellion, and the triumph of "local democracy" as the simple instrumentalization of principles that had failed to gain any concrete expression. Acceptance of resident participation led to the construction of public housing projects that give the neighborhood the demographic and architectural face that it has today. Having moved into what may previously have seemed an unlikely location, and encouraged by the public authorities to mobilize and to impose their authority in the management of the local area, these residents have not remained unchanged in their control of space. This elite emerged in the context of urban renewal, the civil rights struggle and the Vietnam War, which deeply shook the middle classes and their faith in the American model. Indeed, this participation is not only a matter of homeowners mobilizing to defend the value of their property, and this elite's control is not limited to its institutional positions. Or rather, while these organizations do greatly rely on municipal backing, they exist only because of resident engagement in them, constructing a particular legitimacy deeply marked by the social movements of the 1960s. This moral authority rests on the value that they accord to diversity, a principle to be defended as well as a reality to be managed. How has this question rallied so many residents over the decades? How has this mobilization contributed to cementing this social group around singular practices and values? To draw out the genesis of this legitimacy, we must look to the type of collective action that developed within the neighborhood associations.

Chapter 3

Philanthropic Adventurers

The civic engagement of the wealthier residents of the South End was not solely a function of the public authorities' desire for interlocutors who would support the renovation of the city center. This mobilization was also part of the history of collective action in the United States; more specifically, it sheds light on what became of privileged groups' social engagement after the upheavals of the 1960s. During this period, as civil rights struggles as well as gay and feminist movements emerged, the traditional civic associations of the well-to-do became the object of virulent criticism. White, largely closed to Jews, blacks and other ethnic minorities, separated by gender and only accepting members of the educated middle or upper classes, pillars of the US elite like the Rotary Club, the Lions, the Kiwanis, the League of Women Voters and even the American Association of University Women were confronted by the radical movements that shook the country. The South End's associations, products of this history, certainly exhibit a particular class profile. The majority of their members nonetheless express a pronounced taste for "diversity." This does not mean that racial prejudices have disappeared, but they are rarely expressed overtly. In this respect, the organizations in this city-center neighborhood project a very different image than do the groups in the residential suburbs, whose mission is to protect real estate value and prevent low-income residents and/or minorities from moving into the

neighborhood.[1] While in the 1960s the South End's neighborhood associations exerted pressure on City Hall to improve urban services, this was
not a matter of stopping the poor, black people and immigrants from
moving in. They were already there, and unlike the traditional attitude of
the upper classes, the neighborhood associations celebrated rather than
repudiated the presence of these populations.

Finally, unlike in the influential clubs of the US elite, men and women
today participate in these associations side by side, and without the most
important roles necessarily being reserved for men. Gays represented a
sizeable minority from the outset, and today their presence in these ranks
is no longer hidden. And while the associations are still entirely white,
today they include a significant number of Jews and Catholics (whether
practicing or not) unlike the traditional elite organizations. Michèle
Lamont has shown that volunteering in civic associations is one of the
practices by which the US upper middle class defines itself.[2] In this sense,
these associations constitute a privileged point of entry for studying the
refashioning of this new elite. This chapter proposes to examine the
concrete forms of relating to the other that these well-off residents' civic
engagement makes visible.

---

1   The neighborhood improvement association movement, which peaked in the postwar period, was born during the expansion of the industrial cities in the 1880s. Since the
upkeep of urban infrastructure relied on municipal funds, departing for the periphery
allowed residents to escape the costly urban tax burden. Moreover, thanks to well-exe-
cuted lobbying efforts, the new suburbanites continue to benefit from many of the city's
public services. Robert Fischer, *Let the People Decide: Neighborhood Organizing in
America*, New York: Twayne Publishers, 1994; Douglas Massey and Nancy Denton,
American Apartheid: Segregation and the Making of the Underclass, Cambridge, MA:
Harvard University Press, 1993, pp. 35–6; Mike Davis, *City of Quartz? Excavating the
Future in Los Angeles*, New York: Verso, 1990.

2   "Participation in voluntary associations is an important source of friendship for
upper-middle-class men with a high degree of geographical mobility. Many companies
make it policy to encourage their workers to get involved in local organizations as a way
for these companies to maintain good relations with the community." Michèle Lamont,
*Money, Morals and Manners: The Culture of the French and American Upper Middle
Class*, Chicago: University of Chicago Press, 1994, pp. 59–60).

At first glance, participation in the South End's neighborhood associations appears to be a surprising mixture, a combination of openness and exclusion, propagating both a "live and let live" philosophy and practice of tight control. The residents who run these associations like to call themselves "pioneers" — experiencing and recounting their arrival as an adventure;[3] this rhetoric extends to those who moved in the 1990s and 2000s, after the most of the neighborhood's renovation had already taken place. At the same time, these "adventurers" engage in their associations in a quasi-professional register. They love the local sociability, which they contrast to the anonymity of the suburbs or the snobbery of Beacon Hill; they get to know their neighbors and greet them in the street. At the same time these residents are also moral entrepreneurs of the ethos of "good neighborliness," enjoying informal encounters with fellow residents — on the condition that these interactions unfold in ways carefully orchestrated in both time and space. Their relation to the mixing of different social groups embodies these ambiguities: "diversity", which is the watchword of their civic engagement and stands at the heart of their discourse on the neighborhood and the manner in which they define themselves, is at once an object of anxiety and also of surveillance. They are diversity's enthusiastic spokespeople but also its watchful wardens. Their legitimacy in representing the community is built on this particular stance, combining an outward bohemianism with a relentless, anxious control.

The defense of diversity has led to the emergence of, to use Pierre Bourdieu's expression, an "interest in disinterestedness," embodied in the neighborhood associations and in specific moments and practices widespread among the upper-middle class. This established a specific relationship to poverty, cementing a group around values and practices that made up a habitus and generated powerful constraints. To be a respected member of the "community" implies investment in the moral sphere, though this is not without concomitant advantages in consolidating a socioeconomic status. The strong intertwining of morality and social status — so characteristic of the United States — today takes specific forms, which this chapter will examine by way of the segment of the upper middle class that moved into working-class neighborhoods. This study seeks not only to describe this moral posture, but

---

3 Catherine Bidou-Zachariasen, *Les Aventuriers du quotidien. Essai sur les nouvelles classes moyennes*, Paris: PUF, 1984.

also to reconstruct its genesis. Where does this form of distinction come from—one where even in a situation of close geographical proximity, an expertly-titrated combination allows for "mixing without merging"?[4]

PRIVATE PROPERTY AND SOCIAL CONSCIENCE

Following the 1960s' profound transformation of race and class relations, the baby-boomer generation frequently showed a desire to break with the traditional environments of the US white middle class. Civic associations in the urban South End offered sites of engagement in which this attitude could be expressed. Nevertheless, homeowners came to participate in these associations in a moment fraught with conflict. When the urban renewal plans proposed by public authorities met with great hostility in the South End, this competing activist force threatened the economic value of the property the new homeowners had purchased, and fundamentally questioned the legitimacy of their presence in the neighborhood. Constructing a bulwark against these threats, a group of "new residents" began to form, on the basis of carefully established alliances.

The birth of the "pioneers"

The recomposition and expansion of the civic sector in the South End began in the early 1960s, when City Hall's decision to pursue collaboration with the community encouraged the restructuring of a local milieu composed of community centers, churches, and the traditional shopkeepers' or property owners' associations. But the most pronounced turning point was 1968. In that year, as it became clear that urban renewal meant the expulsion of the poorest populations, the city's black activists seized on the housing question, engaging in local activism in order to encourage the emergence of "Black Power." It was directly in tandem with this social movement that the white homeowners began to participate in the neighborhood associations. The form that mobilization took in this context provides an important illustration of the gradual split developing in the late 1960s between those who sympathized with the non-violent civil rights activism at work in the southern states, and, on the other hand, the black movement then radicalizing nationally.

---

4   Edmond Goblot, *La Barrière et le niveau. Étude sociologique sur la bourgeoisie française moderne*, Paris: PUF, 1967, p. 41.

The local engagement of white progressives living in an inner-city neighborhood like the South End sheds light on the redefinition of liberalism in the years that followed the great moment of conflict in the 1960s.[5]

Liberal property owners

At the end of the 1960s and the beginning of the 1970s, local battles raged in the South End. These often found the white homeowners in direct conflict with the black and Hispanic radicals. The latter's noisy demonstration outside the 1973 South End Historical Society ball is just one example. They denounced the festivities organized by the society's lovers of historic architecture as an enterprise serving only the interests of real estate agents—and moreover an enterprise conducted with a barely-concealed racism. Activists directly confronted attendees arriving at the ball, expressed overt hostility toward the new white residents within the space of the neighborhood itself. In this activist context marked by growing polarization, the homeowners' associations attracted residents who expressed sensitivity to racial questions, but who recoiled from the social movements' growing radicalism. Beyond the South End, many of these liberals, frightened by what had become of the civil rights struggle in the North in the latter half of the 1960s, gradually distanced themselves from the movement. While the campaigns in the South could win their support, the discourse and demands of Black Power went too far for many of them—and what was later distilled into the word "diversity" had roots in this political reaction.

Indeed, many recent arrivals in the South End in this era showed real social concern while rejecting a confrontational posture, ultimately sharing a common belief in the power of enlightened governance to effect transformation. Many supported Mayor Kevin White or worked for him, like the young Harvard law graduate Colin Diver who turned down positions offered by prestigious law firms in order to provide his services to White in 1968, and was soon faced with with the black community's revolt. He and his wife gave a lengthy interview to the journalist Anthony Lukas, author of the bestseller *Common Ground*, published in 1985, a work in which Colin and Joan Diver incarnated the "urban pioneers" moving into the South End in the second half of the 1960s.

---

5 Carol A. Horton, *Race and the Making of American Liberalism*, Oxford: Oxford University Press, 2005; Kenneth L. Kusmer and Joe W. Trotter, *African American Urban History since World War II*, Chicago: University of Chicago Press, 2009.

The state of mind of a young lawyer from an upper-middle-class family echoed US youth's coming to consciousness, confronted with the spectacle of violent racial segregation in the South as well as the personal risk of being sent to Vietnam. The Kerner Report, published in 1968, predicted an even more dire turn still to come. Commissioned by President Johnson after riots spread to Los Angeles, Detroit and New York in the second half of the 1960s, the report said the country now risked division into two societies—one white, the other black—and reading this account left many consciences shaken. While some responded by engaging in radical movements (even in clandestine activity), many more sought to establish stronger ties within their communities in order to prevent this dystopian future from becoming reality. Colin Diver shared this latter outlook. In his eyes, the legal career he was headed for was far from adequate for the historic situation that now seized his attention, significantly revising his personal and professional horizons. As Anthony Lukas explains, "the new social activism had rendered such conventional careers [in the legal profession] less automatic." Colin Diver and his wife did not buy a house in the suburbs where they had grown up and lived until that point. Joan Diver shared her husband's aspirations. "As long as she could remember [she] had wanted to work for the poor . . . Joan wanted work that would have a direct impact on the lives of ordinary people." Attracted by philanthropy, she worked for a large foundation in the city and supported her husband's plan for them to move into the South End: "Having committed himself to the war on urban poverty and injustice, he felt he should be living closer to the front line."[6]

---

6   J. Anthony Lukas, *Common Ground: A Turbulent Decade in the Lives of Three American Families*, New York: Vintage Books, 1985, pp. 5, 338. This book claims to be a fresco of the struggles provoked by the plan to desegregate Boston's schools in the 1970s, as seen through the lives of three families that really existed, and whose history the author traces across the generations: one family from the Irish working class, a black family living in Roxbury, and a third family, the Divers, who belong to the white upper middle class. The plot, which follows their overlapping involvement in the events of the time, looks beyond simple psychological and/or romanticized portraits, taking the transformations of the city into account as it explains the violence that Boston witnessed in the 1970s. This work, which won the Pulitzer Prize, was written on the basis of thorough research. Incorporating widely documented historical developments into his novelized narrative, the author privileges the role of a few individuals in explaining how these events played out. He was interested in using his characters as ideal-types, a perspective from which I

For them, this was not simply a matter of profiting from the neighborhood's proximity to the city center—with Colin able to ride a bicycle to work—nor of being able to purchase at house at a low cost. The Divers' social convictions drove them toward an engagement irreducible to the simple pursuit of economic interests. For example, they made clear to the real estate agent charged with finding them a home that they did not want to buy a lodging house, even if it offered a better value, as this would mean expelling the existing tenants. Joan further tried to establish a dialogue between white and black mothers at a local school in order to overcome their mutual lack of understanding.

In a tense atmosphere marked by sharp social clashes, many white residents sought a third way. A young homeowner who had recently moved into the area together with his family—and who was also a member of the SEPAC advisory board, the South End Historical Society and his local neighborhood association—created a South End Citizens Association. The group he established brought together "all good-willed inhabitants" and attracted the sympathies of the Divers, who "had hoped that a credible 'middle' might emerge, one with which [the Divers] could ally themselves, for neither extreme offered much hope of the varied, vital, but livable urban community they sought in the South End." Indeed, commenting on the kind of positions that they rejected, Colin Diver exclaimed, "We're being asked to choose between the self-righteous and the self-interested. What kind of choice is that?"[7]

We can see a similar profile and discourse in another Harvard law graduate who became president of one of the main neighborhood associations in 1976. He moved into the South End in 1970 together with his wife, a city planner who had a degree from the prestigious Wellesley College. Like her, he grew up in Newton, a wealthy suburb of the city. The liberal beliefs that he evinced—sending his children to the public schools they were assigned to, as opposed to moving them to private school, serving as a member of the ecumenical Greater Boston Interfaith Organization, himself Jewish—were mixed with hostility toward the black activist Mel King. He stubbornly held to this view even in 2007, calling King a manipulator and accusing him of having stirred up hatred against the white middle classes. It was also in 2007

---

benefited in my own research: the passages devoted to the Divers are a precious resource for drawing out the values and rationales that this type of residents put forward.

   7   Ibid., p. 439.

that this resident and his wife left the South End. Colin and Joan Diver moved out much earlier, at the end of the 1970s, heading to Newton, the suburb where they grew up, as did many other young couples—particularly those with young children. Such mobility shows the extent to which the group here being studied is not reducible to an urban space. Or rather, that the values emerging at the moment when this elite was in formation go beyond the limits of the South End itself, and indeed of Boston. On a much wider scale, the redefinition of liberalism that we see in this period profoundly changed the US upper middle class's relation to other social groups.

The new frontier

The South End's associations allow us to observe up close how values and a particular rhetoric emerge and are then transmitted across the subsequent decades. If the experiences of the neighborhood change as it transforms, a common vocabulary makes it possible to unify these experiences, to give them meaning and elevate their value. Forged in the late 1960s, this vocabulary found a new relevance with each stage of the rehabilitation of the neighborhood, notably the late 1990s development of Washington Street, which became, after Tremont Street, a simultaneously geographic and symbolic new frontier.[8] This participated in the traditional US theme of the constantly-renewed "frontier." In the twentieth century this frontier shifted far from the wilderness of the American West, and applied instead to the "urban jungle,"[9] as well as taken up by President Kennedy in 1960 to describe his program of social reform as "the New Frontier."

The terms "pioneers," "urban pioneers" and "urban renaissance" appeared in the Boston and New York press in the 1960s with the beginning of what was known as the "back to the city movement." An April 9, 1964 *Boston Globe* article entitled "The South End Begins to Stir" described Boston finance commission

---

8   On the significance of Tremont Street, note the episode Lukas recounts in which Colin Diver ran after a thief: "Colin hesitated for a moment. Tremont was a significant boundary to his world, the southern border of the gentrified South End. Beyond it stretched a row of tenements, occupied principally by Puerto Ricans, Dominicans, and Cubans." Lukas, *Common Ground*, p. 628.

9   Neil Smith and Peter Williams, *Gentrification of the City*, Boston: Allen and Unwin, 1986, pp. 15–16.

president moving to Appleton Street as "a great urban adventure." The residents who arrived between the 1960s and the early 1980s describe their move in terms of a "shock": "I was in shock when I saw the house," a resident who came to the neighborhood in 1983 recalled. "The real heroes were the homeowners who took the risk," one Union Park inhabitant told me. Buying a home in a neighborhood with such a negative reputation was perceived to be a risky bet and a critique of a previous way of life, at least as much as a potentially lucrative investment.

The social legitimacy that these new residents drew from their pioneering move to the South End was reinforced by the extent of the work that they carried out on their new neighborhood, often with their own hands. The evenings and weekends spent knocking through walls and renovating buildings, laying carpets and repainting; the memories of sandwiches wolfed down, a life of camping out without a kitchen for months; and the volume of sweat they shed and dust they swallowed: all these were part of the "pioneers" earning their stripes. One resident from a middle-class background who grew up in tony Newton manipulated this persona to perfection during an interview that I mentioned in the first chapter. He bought a house in the South End in 1967 and recounted the shared epic he participated in at the time:

> What used to happen there, on weekends, you would hear people with saws, hammers—they would be fixing their own houses. And in fact, that was what I did. It took me four years to rebuild the house I lived in. But I did it essentially myself. And it was pretty much what the community was like at that time. People bought a house and they renovated it themselves . . . what I would do is I would go to work . . . I'd come home at night. And I would go across the street, Berkeley Street, buy a sandwich, eat the sandwich and work until midnight tearing down walls . . . At the time, no shower, just a tub. Water gray, because of the dust. I went to the local hardware store every weekend, at least once on a Saturday, every week for two years. I essentially worked two jobs . . . very intensely for about two years. For a while there was no kitchen.

This sense of giving oneself over to an adventure is widespread. It takes a collective dimension in the neighborhood associations, which formalize the neighborly and social relations built around the lending of tools and exchange of advice.

This sentiment is deeply anchored among long-standing residents of the South End, and they also transmit it to new homeowners. Indeed, these "new arrivals" and not just the "pioneers" who moved into the South End before them invoke this particular relationship with the neighborhood, combining social convictions and the feeling of living a singular adventure. Far from being a point of division among clearly distinct generations of gentrifiers, the denunciation of "yuppies" indifferent to their "community"—accused of selfishness and ridiculed for their peevish complaints and their inability to accept the nuisances of the urban environment—is very widespread, even if in each era, it designated a different set of individuals.[10] Indeed, it seems as if residents adopt this discourse as they become more integrated—and in doing so mark sharp boundaries between themselves and others they accuse of not sharing the in-group's values.

The strength of the associations and their capacity to serve as the crucible for an enduring identity are based on a specific, shared vocabulary that is nevertheless something different individuals, across diverse migratory and social trajectories, have been able to pick up and deploy. The mix of social fear and moral convictions, summed up in the notion of adventure, persisted across the whole period that this book examines, from the end of the 1960s up until the 2000s, yet these concepts were also regularly reformulated. Certainly, the most recent arrivals have adopted the term "pioneer" and the accompanying rhetoric less often than was previously the case. But a sense of danger has constantly been reactivated in the South End over the decades, even after the collapse of the most activist movements, chief opponents of the white homeowners' dominance in the neighborhood. But until the 1980s, empty plots and building projects were legion, and City Hall supported the construction of mixed project including so-called accessible housing. Later, in the 1990s, the transformation of the industrial wastelands of Washington Street revived the idea of a frontier and of conquest, not "of the West" but of the southeast of the neighborhood. These have continued fuel social fear, even if it is intermittent and has certain spatial limits. The activism of the neighborhood associations varies in accordance with the fluctuating numbers of construction projects, both commercial and housing.

---

10   On the presence of an anti-gentrification discourse among the gentrifiers, see Japonica Brown-Saracino, *A Neighborhood that Never Changes: Gentrification, Social Preservation and the Search for Authenticity*, Chicago: Chicago University Press, 2010.

Above all, the continued weight of the categories used to classify the urban space between the white middle-class suburbs and the inner-city black ghettos always stirs, among the gentrifiers' friends and relatives, an astonishment mixed with disapproval or sometimes even envy. These reactions feed gentrifiers' sense of being a little "insane," living an adventure and transgressing norms with this piece of "madness." "And the fact that we did what most people thought was either foolish or incredibly brave all made it sexier," notes one resident who arrived in 1969. Other accounts concurred. A woman employed to lobby City Hall and who moved into the South End in 1983 after raising her kids in a small town on the outskirts of Boston, explained, "When we moved in, the two houses next door were derelict. They had no doors. It was nothing. My children and my friends thought we were absolutely crazy."

Even with continual departures from among the poorer section of the population, the arrival of ever-wealthier residents did not erase social divisions from the neighborhood. Indeed, far from these divides diminishing, the departure of middle-class households only widened the gap, as the great polarization of incomes in the South End demonstrates.[11] Thus, the theme of urban adventure has also been adopted by retirees and semi-retirees who, after many years in socially and ethnically homogeneous neighborhoods, came to the South End in the 1990s, at a moment when its transformation had already advanced significantly. Among these residents, the appeal of city-center living is mixed with a strong apprehension about the neighborhood's low-income populations, both black and Hispanic. Moreover, the construction of lofts on Washington Street—an artery whose transformation only began in the late 1990s—allowed for the erection of material and symbolic barriers to the street (entrances with entry codes or concierges). Thus the choice to buy a loft now contrasts with what has now become, for these residents, the more "classic" choice of purchase, the brownstone.[12]

In this light, we can understand the strong in-group sociability that persists in the associations even when no immediate danger presents itself. Instead, it is fed by the need that their members feel to rally together in the face of the

---

11   After Jamaica Plain (0.645), the South End is the Boston neighborhood with the highest Gini coefficient (0.634). This coefficient measures the degree of inequality in income distribution.

12   On the taste for lofts as part of gentrifier identity, see Sharon Zukin, *Loft Living: Culture and Capital in Urban Change*, London: Radius, 1988.

risk—both appealing and threatening—that spatial proximity to such different populations represents. One association has organized a reading group;
another, wine tasting evenings. Christmas parties (generally taking place in
the most spacious houses) and annual picnics also have the look of rituals of
initiation into the social group the civic association represents. This can even
take explicit forms: one neighborhood association makes a practice of contacting every homeowner arriving in its territory—their names doubtless passed
on by the estate agents—and organizes a welcome party.

A conquest without the conquered

A further reason why the register of "adventure" became so established—and
has continued to color the neighborhood associations—is that the weakening
of oppositional social movements made it into a hegemonic discourse. The
pioneers experience and present their conquest of the area as a conquest
without a fight, implying that there was no "conquered" group. Residents
who were present in the 1960s and 1970s do speak of the hostility that existed
toward Mel King (even though they insist—particularly so during the George
W. Bush presidency—on everything that makes them sympathize with him
today). Nonetheless, the only battles mentioned are those fought against the
public authorities: to secure the renovation of sidewalks and street lighting, to
rebuff a highway construction project, and, today, for the mayor's office to
guarantee better street cleaning and garbage collection service.

The hegemony that these "pioneers" have conquered is in first part a matter of
socio-demographic developments: demolitions and the concentration of projects
outside the South End to rehome its displaced residents transformed the urban
landscape. We can estimate the number of departures between 1960 and 1980 at
some 25,000 (recall that in 1970 the population stood at 22,775), a large number
of whom were elderly whites, black families and workers from ethnic minorities.[13] Moreover, the mobilization of those who sought to discredit the "pioneers"
suffered the same general decline affecting the radical Left in the US as in other
countries, riven by internal divisions.[14] Demonstrations such as one blocking the

---

13   John H. Mollenkopf, *The Contested City*, Princeton: Princeton University Press,
1983, p. 199.

14   In 1970, Students for a Democratic Society—which at the end of the 1960s represented the largest student activist force in US history—imploded. Across the 1970s the

Historical Society's guided tour in 1970 to shouts of "Pioneers out—take your Victoriana with you," disappeared.[15] In the third issue of the newspaper of the activist group CAUSE we read, "Pioneers refers to the middle and upper-income who keep coming into the community buying up real estate and depriving the poor of adequate housing and self-determination." This paper ceased publication in 1981, when SEPAC, the advisory board controlled by these activists, was dissolved with the end of urban renewal.

In parallel to this, certain community groups became institutionalized as community development corporations (CDCs). The search for funds strengthened their professionalization, and turned community leaders away from more militant, on-the-ground activism. The Emergency Tenants Council, born in 1968, transformed into a construction business and then a social services agency for the massive Puerto Rican complex Villa Victoria. From 1976 to the mid-1980s it was a dynamic association in which many tenants participated. School workshops, community gardens, the transmission of Puerto Rican and Latin American culture, majorettes, and holiday camps were just some of the many activities that expressed an intensive engagement—operating on a professionalized more than political level—before a pronounced loss of interest set in. Mario Small's research emphasizes the absence of any incentive to mobilize. The deterioration of housing conditions in Boston in the 1990s following the removal of rent controls and a price boom largely did not affect these tenants, who benefited from a protected status. Moreover, the youngest, who did not live through the battles of the 1960s, today have a less positive relationship with the neighborhood. For them, it is not the site of important victories, like it was for the older residents who see Villa Victoria as a symbol of their rise from degraded, unsanitary living conditions to modern housing. Rather, given the transformations of the South End, these younger inhabitants experience Villa Victoria as an isolated

---

vitality of the groups that waged civil rights struggles (NAACP, Southern Christian Leadership Conference, the Urban League) declined. After Nixon's 1973 decision to withdraw troops from Vietnam and put an end to conscription, the media took an interest in very few activist groups.

15   On the promotion of taste in "Victorian" culture among the gentrifiers, see Chapter 4.

enclave within a neighborhood now dominated by one group: the white upper middle classes.[16]

Certainly tenant activism has not disappeared. The associations in the large housing projects have representatives at City Hall, ensuring that these residents will not be displaced.[17] But the outlets available have changed for such engagement, shifting activist focus from the neighborhood level to the city or the state. The members of the Villa Victoria management organization and of other CDCs are now busy seeking funding from the public authorities and private foundations. Others have tried to devote their energies elsewhere. The most qualified leaders such as Joyce and Mel King in some sense left the neighborhood behind (although continuing to live there) as they entered into wider political and institutional arenas, from the Massachusetts state legislature to university teaching. Elected a representative to the state legislature in 1973, Mel King brought together a "Rainbow Coalition" around his candidacy in 1983. He like other activists benefited from the relative opening of the political field to minorities who had emerged from the civil rights struggle, as well as from the development of public agencies to deal with the question of discrimination, from the 1980s onward. Thus City Hall appointed a former activist from the South End to address discrimination in the field of housing. MIT, where a movement in favor of a more politically-engaged urban planning had begun in the 1960s, offered an important site of professional "conversion."[18]

Long-standing activists do remain in the neighborhood, but they are in retirement, or have transferred their oppositional stance to forms other than collective engagement—my second ally being a case in point. The vacuum left within the space of the neighborhood is thus all the more easily occupied by the white homeowners.

---

16   Mario Small, *Villa Victoria: The Transformation of Social Capital in a Boston Barrio*, Chicago: University of Chicago Press, 2004.

17   The association at the Cathedral development has thus managed to defeat a proposed demolition/reconstruction project. Marie-Hélène Bacqué (ed.), *Projet urbain en quartier ancien. La Goutte d'Or, South End*, Paris: PUCA, 2005, p. 180.

18   "Another went on to employment at the Boston University Medical Center and the MIT Department of Urban Studies and Planning. Another became a judge, while SETC's founder went on to become part of a black development effort in North Carolina." Mollenkopf, *The Contested City*, p. 196.

Alliances and misalliances

The evolution of the civic scene in the South End during the troubled years of 1965–75 is, nonetheless, a complex question. First, the local battles were far from reducible to a clash between "old" and "new" residents. Up until the end of the 1970s, migratory flows were not limited to the arrival of white homeowners, and only a view distorted by the benefit of hindsight could lead us to imagine that they were then a predominant force, bound to impose their control. It is by digging into the complex relations they engaged in during this period that we can make out the contours of the new group then coming into existence—the group that today "sets the tone" for the neighborhood.[19]

"New" and "old" homeowners

At first, the perception of a shared threat prevailed over both social and racial divisions within the neighborhood associations. White homeowners thus mingled with the traditional lodging house landlords like Louise Fitzpatrick, who ruled the associations' activity.

A Lodging-House Owner
Working-Class Roots and Political Enterprise

Louise Fitzpatrick was born to Québécois immigrant parents in the 1920s. Her father, known as "Dr. Morier," was a psychiatrist whose real level of professional qualification remained a mystery to many at the time, but this did not stop him from enjoying, in the context of their working-class neighborhood, a certain social status. From him Louise, married to a postal employee of Irish origin, inherited a number of lodging houses, which she managed diligently. Indeed, she was able to advance her interests through relentless political and civic engagement. Testament to this is the extent of the archives, collected in over a dozen boxes, that she left behind after moving out of the South End. She kept press cuttings, minutes of the meetings of the many groups to which she belonged, invitations, personal correspondence, a calendar showing the

---

19   J.-C. Chamboredon and M. Lemaire, "Proximité spatiale et distance sociale dans les grands ensembles," *Revue française de sociologie* 11: 1 (1970), pp. 3–33.

constant succession of the meetings she participated in (two or three a week). In this archive we also find a series of BRA technical documents on the renovation of the sewage system and the installation of street lighting, as well as extensive documentation on the regulations for lodging houses. From these papers we get the impression of a circumspect woman who knew how to advance her own business affairs while at the same time treating her tenants with a mix of maternal benevolence, moral vigilance and lastly but certainly not least, financial interest.

Her career developed on the basis of her management of her lodging houses, one of the rare sectors open to women from the upper section of the working class and the middle class. The neighborhood association, of which she became leader in 1967, provided an extension of this economic activity, in turn allowing her to develop her business interests via the network of connections that she established through the political sphere. Each Christmas she organized a tree-lighting ceremony in the public park, which the mayor never missed.[20] A member of the local branch of the Democratic Party, she supported certain municipal councillors, who found valuable support in the neighborhood association.

The Catholic Church was an important element of her enterprise. Her correspondence bears witness to her ties to the Kennedy family—of Irish Catholic origin—and in particular Ted Kennedy, who thanked her personally for the help she had given to his 1964 Senate campaign. The neighborhood association's meetings were held in the rectory of the Church of the Immaculate Conception. A priest's blessing, followed by a speech by a representative or municipal councillor, was a ritual of the Christmas ceremony she organized in the park.

Louise's archives bear the traces of her multiple engagements: negotiation of the renovation of urban infrastructure; interventions in development projects, notably concerning the nearby hospital complex;

---

20   One summer, Mayor Kevin White thanked her for the postcard that she had sent him; she also received an invitation to a ball being given by the mayor and his wife.

publicity for neighborhood watch patrols across the different parts of the South End; but also the struggle—one to which we'll return—against the construction of public housing and against neighborhood bars. But while she shared some of the new homeowners' preoccupations, her engagements sought above all to defend her business interests. Louise participated in a lodging houses' commission, bringing together the different neighborhood associations. In 1970 she campaigned for election to SEPAC as president of her association and "businessman in the field of managing lodging and apartment houses for the past 27 years." At the beginning of the same decade, she threw herself into lobbying, seeking to change the regulations on lodging houses that had, up to that point, forbidden the tenants from cooking in their rooms. In 1971, a municipal councillor wrote to her with news of the final vote on this question: "Enclosed you will find what you have waited so long for. Your 'Lodging House Bill' has finally become a reality."

Many other members of the neighborhood association recall that, in the absence of a higher education degree, Louise Fitzpatrick had a way of speaking and writing that reveal working-class stubbornness and verve rather than an erudite or distinguished style. While she did have cause to visit the homes of Historical Society members, we find no trace of her socializing with the wealthiest South End residents then assembling in the Historical Society. She was not a member of the Historical Society's board, and her name is not mentioned in any of its newsletters. Louise seems to have lacked two major social markers—a taste for high culture and philanthropic activity—and was instead occupied with enriching her economic capital through more classic resources: the patronage of political networks.

But the social capital Louise accumulated in the neighborhood association was soon reappropriated by the more educated homeowners who took the reins in the 1980s and 1990s. In 1977 Louise became "president emeritus," with lifetime voting rights (until she left the neighborhood in 2005), but she saw her position gradually called into question by new homeowners. The statements that association board candidates provided in the early 1980s show that they had arrived in the previous fifteen years: among the eight candidates who mention how long they had been living in the neighborhood, the longest-standing resident had moved to the South End in 1970 and the most recent arrival in 1981. During one meeting in the early 1980s, a resident criticized Louise for her habit of allowing politicians to speak at the traditional Christmas ceremony. And the president who took leadership of the association in 1982—on the one hand a foreigner, but on the other a professional (an engineer from Bolivia)—understood better than Louise had how to integrate himself into the South End's upper middle class. From 1983 to 1985, he served on the board of the Historical Society board as well as on one of its committees.

The gradual transfer of the resources built up by the lodging-house owners not far removed from the working class, in favor of the professionals who moved in beginning in the 1960s in order to access home ownership, marked a crucial stage in the emergence of a mobilized group. And this process was not without its clashes. For these latter, the task at hand was not only to redefine the neighborhood by limiting the visibility of populations considered insufficiently respectable, but also to encourage the arrival of the middle class in a more general sense. In 1963, Peter Whitaker—ancestor of the pioneers—thus tried to mount an offensive against the lodging houses, which, in his view "contribute[d] much to the deterioration of the area." Many lodging-house owners (and we can imagine that Louise was among them) responded vigorously to this, insisting on the respectability of their tenants and redirecting his accusations at the more makeshift lodging houses taking in an itinerant population. "Eventually the resident owners, defending their occupation and their 'good' tenants, overcame urbanite opposition," Langley Keyes recalls.[21]

At the time, these landlords represented a group solidly rooted in the neighborhood. In 1963 the number of lodging houses was counted at 923, taking in between 10,000 and 12,000 tenants (of a total population then

---

21   Langley Keyes, *The Rehabilitation Planning Game: A Study in the Diversity of Neighborhood*, Cambridge, MA: MIT Press, 1969, p. 75.

standing at 35,000), while nonregistered boarding houses comprised between 400 and 900 dwellings, thus adding another 4,000 to 8,000 people. Some 400 landlords lived on-site and — drawing most of their income from the rents — they were highly mobilized.[22] Nonetheless, the conversion of lodging houses into condos from the late 1970s onward considerably reduced their numbers. If the most engaged among them left the neighborhood only regretfully, the estate agents' offers finally won out over the particular interests and connections that had structured this group up until the late 1970s. The lodging-house owners gradually disappeared.

Among the "old" inhabitants present in today's neighborhood associations, there are still a few surviving residents born in the South End — white but generally not Protestant — for whom the gentrification of the neighborhood has offered certain opportunities, notably in real estate. Indeed, during a number of my interviews I was advised that I ought to meet one eccentric South End figure who, through the course of his life, incarnated both the promises of the American Dream as well as the "diversity" of the neighborhood. Despite his economic capital and his keen interest in culture, Richie O'Brien's integration nonetheless came up against certain limits.

The Real Estate Fortune of an "Old Timer"

Richie O'Brien, the model "old timer," was born in the South End in 1949 and grew up in a working-class Irish family. His father, a manual laborer, and his mother, a housewife, brought up eleven children in a two-room apartment, which they eventually succeeded in leaving behind, moving to the city periphery. Richie began working at fifteen years old, delivering papers and shining shoes, before departing for the army. After working as a salesman and playing on his social contacts as well as a certain personal charm, he eventually became a property manager. At the end of the 1960s, he bought several buildings in the South End, which he transformed into condos and then sold at considerable profit.

---

22   Ibid., pp. 41–2.

His engagement in the neighborhood association and many other institutions reflected this improbable career. He was president of the South End Business Association and a board member in one of the neighborhood's most powerful associations. The capital that he acquired through his real estate operations gave him a strong property-owner identity, as well as a deep faith in free enterprise. His belief in the benefits of economic development explains why he often found himself at odds with his new neighbors. When the latter regarded commercial development with suspicion, he was happy to see the neighborhood going up in value.

The differences are expressed in subtle ways. On several occasions I heard him gently mocking his comrades' taste for diversity, noting that they are nevertheless very quick to mobilize against developments liable to attract a less fortunate population. Well-aware of the persistence of class divisions, Richie shared his qualms with me, but immediately emphasized that he had given up on expressing them in meetings. Instead he turned inward, affirming the singularity of his trajectory and of his relationship with the neighborhood (and, at the same time, probably a certain loyalty to his own past) through more personal practices than those practices his group-oriented neighbors emphasized.

In his sixties, divorced and bearing it well, Richie loves flirting and racking up dates, perhaps seeking to compensate for the social barriers he still faces with some highly visible amorous successes. During a partial municipal election in 2007, he supported not the candidate from his own neighborhood association, but a politician close to the mayor coming from "Irish" South Boston. A well-known figure in the South End, he is constantly greeting people in the street, whose diversity he likes to emphasize. Along with these deep local roots—on which doubtless crystallize some of his ambivalence—he speaks keenly of his travels and loves reminiscing about his time in the Navy. Finally, Richie smokes, has little appetite for the food offered in the restaurants of the South End, and doesn't hesitate to express how much he hates dogs—so many ways in which his tastes clash with those of upper-middle-class residents.

Ultimately, the decline of the lodging houses led to the narrowing of the mobilized group, which now almost exclusively involved whites. Puerto Ricans and black residents had very little presence in the neighborhood associations at the moment in the 1960s and 1970s when these associations began to grow in influence. Puerto Rican residents instead mobilized autonomously, demanding the construction of public housing, while black residents organized around their churches and associations. Except for a few leaders also holding positions outside of the neighborhood, like the Kings, few black people engaged in the neighborhood associations, which gradually came to be dominated by whites. White homeowners rapidly took over the few neighborhood associations with a black middle-class majority (often the landlords of lodging-houses): the limited size of the African-American population in Boston probably explains why it was not black gentrifiers who took control.[23] Similarly, the residents of Québécois and Middle Eastern origin who represented their communities in the neighborhood associations soon disappeared. Descendants of European migrant groups—Italians, Portuguese, Irish and Jewish people are today present in the homeowners' associations, but they have not maintained their connections to the old communities long-rooted in the South End. Most importantly, the neighborhood association scene became ever more white as struggles over civil rights pushed racial divisions back into the frame of "whites" versus "blacks." Jewish and Catholic residents, particularly those of European origin who had previously been excluded from the category "white"—which was closely linked to the Protestant faith—were gradually integrated into this category.[24]

---

23   On the migration of the black middle classes and their engagement in the gentrified districts of other cities, see Monique Taylor, *Harlem between Heaven and Hell*, Minneapolis: University of Minnesota Press, 2002; Mary Pattillo, *Black on the Block: The Politics of Race and Class in the City*, Chicago: University of Chicago Press, 2007.

24   Indeed, many historians' works have shown how its definition changed over the decades: "A significant strand of twentieth-century American political life, then, is the story of how 'race politics' ceased to concern the white races of Europe and came to refer exclusively to black–white relations and the struggle over Negro civil rights." Matthew F. Jacobson, *Whiteness of a Different Color: European Immigrants and the Alchemy of Race*, Cambridge, MA: Harvard University Press, 1999, p. 247.

The genesis of gay friendliness

The presence of gays in the South End, which preceded the arrival of the middle class in the 1960s, originated in the interwar development of a gay culture around the bars of the city center.[25] As early as the 1960s, neighborhood associations involved gay and lesbian participation. Although this was not referred to explicitly in the early days, over the years their presence gained more open recognition. At that time in Boston, as across US society as a whole, homosexuality was a profound stigma and gay visibility unthinkable. When the gentrification began in the South End, police raids on bars—and even homes—had only recently come to an end.[26] The question of sexuality does not come up in Lukas's narration of the Divers' story. Nevertheless, it is worth noting that the couple's growing unease did not only result from fear of the physical aggression and burglary to which they fell victim. What they found intolerable, instead, were the prostitutes in the alley behind their house—especially Joan, who otherwise seems to have acclimatized to the neighborhood more easily than did her husband, and particularly through her involvement in the parents' association. The presence of a sexuality considered deviant, so close to her children, drove Joan and several other women to break license plates off the johns' cars and send them to the police.[27]

The early integration of gays was initially facilitated by their not overtly signaling their sexual orientation, as was the general rule in the 1960s. Nevertheless, their behavior could not remain entirely private in a neighborhood where homeowners established close links among one another. Peter Whitaker's taste for younger men was no mystery. Meanwhile, serious suspicions of pedophilia hung over one of the presidents of the Historical Society. Whatever the validity of these accusations—which may simply speak to classic prejudices against homosexuality—we can ask ourselves why they did not lead to a devastating opprobrium being cast over the objects of such

---

25   In the interwar period a scandal sheet called the *MidTown Journal*, run by a heterosexual, offered tales of gay and lesbian Bostonians' lives. It was based in Union Park, in the South End (*Improper Bostonians: Lesbian and Gay History from the Puritans to Playland*, compiled by the History Project, Boston: Beacon Press, 1998).

26   *Improper Bostonians*; George Chauncey, *Gay New York: Gender, Urban Culture, and the Makings of the Gay Male World, 1890–1940*, New York: Basic Books, 1994.

27   Lukas, *Common Ground*, pp. 444–5.

allegations. Peter Whitaker's peccadillos—which people still today talked about today, in front of me—did not prevent him from becoming a very charismatic figure and a recognized spokesman for the new homeowners. The defense of their economic interests had prompted these residents to close ranks. This economic motive encouraged connections not only among new homeowners and gays, but also between gays and the older inhabitants of the South End, like Louise Fitzpatrick, whose sense of morality and religious principles made her hardly receptive to the defense of sexual liberation. As we can see from the story of a white lesbian who moved into the South End near Massachusetts Avenue in 1967, the logics of class prevailed.

The Resources of a Gentrified Neighborhood for a Lesbian Doctor
"Middle Class Is Middle Class!"

Elizabeth Kramer's story is closely connected to her homosexuality. If the South End's status as an unfashionable address in the 1960s sheds some light on the forms of exclusion that gays suffered in their residential paths, Elizabeth's experience also speaks to the resources it was possible to procure in a working-class neighborhood undergoing gentrification. A Harvard graduate, she became a clinical psychologist while her partner was still finishing her dissertation. The two women rented an apartment between the downtown area and the South End, near two bars that they frequented. However, urban renewal led to the destruction of the building they lived in, and it was not without great stubbornness (the BRA official rejected their application the first time around by insisting that the offer was open to "families" only) that they succeeded in securing the available financial assistance—for "relocation"—to buy property in the South End in 1967.

Elizabeth then got involved in the life of the neighborhood, particularly in the community gardens, while also taking an active role in the Democratic Party's gay and lesbian caucus. For her, the South End was a site of potential integration—not that she was transparent about her sexual orientation ("I wasn't out, because the term 'out' hadn't been invented! Everybody was in the closet."), but due to the tolerance made possible by the accumulated array of deviancies that characterized this working-class neighborhood, as well as by the homeowners' common interests. When I asked what kind of welcome she received upon her arrival, she recalled, "The reaction of the neighbors: 'You're fixing up the property. Middle class is middle class!' They didn't care that we were a lesbian couple, we were fixing up the property. Which as I said was a wreck, and they were delighted."

Since the interwar period, there had been numerous gay bars in the inner city, but they were almost nonexistent in the South End. Cruising sites were, moreover, scattered across the city: public toilets, bathhouses and Boston's city library were the best known.[28] Urban renewal, which led to the demolition of a large part of the inner city, as well as the influx of middle-class residents into the South End, explains the emergence of a gay scene in the 1970s and 1980s. Nonetheless, with some establishments exclusively catering to gays and others reserved for them on certain nights of the week, there was a strong "porousness in the boundaries between gay/gay friendly/non-gay locales."[29] Many accounts of this period tell us that the parks and even the alleyways of the South End were places where men met up and could have sexual relations, even if Fenway Park—not far from the neighborhood—was better known for this. This relative margin with which to maneuver can be explained by porous boundaries between public and private that still characterize working-class districts like those that George Chauncey describes in his work on New York. While that historian's analysis concerns the first third of the twentieth century, we can imagine that the presence of deviant populations in the South End's then-overcrowded streets did create spaces where gays could live their homosexuality as a semi-secret.[30] In addition to these

---

28   *Improper Bostonians.*

29   Colin Giraud, "Les gays et la renaissance urbaine du Marais au Village," *Études canadiennes* 64 (2008), pp. 63–78.

30   "Although gay street culture was in certain respects an unusual and distinctive phenomenon, it was also part of and shaped by a larger street culture that was primarily working-class in character and origin. Given the crowded conditions in which most working people lived, much of their social life took place in streets and parks. The gay presence

were more unexpected meeting places, beyond the bars and parks (and, quite simply, the streets). One building on Tremont Street transformed into an arts center in 1970—which regularly hosted a flea market—occupies an important place in gays' memories of this period. "The periodic flea markets in the Cyclorama building, somewhat resemble a gay bar with bric-a-brac."[31] The bars opened at a moment when relations were changing in the neighborhood, even if it would be mistaken to imagine a sudden visibility of the gay population in contrast to an earlier period of total invisibility.

Indeed, when looking at the sociability of gay South End homeowners engaged in the renewal of the neighborhood, their presence is best understood not in terms of invisibility, but rather of them not making their sexuality explicit, or of them maintaining a silence accompanied by forms of tacit recognition. For example, one of the presidents of the Historical Society, a banker active in SEPAC and in his neighborhood association, never made public his homosexuality (either verbally or through a specific way of dressing or speaking). As my second ally told me, he was often accompanied by a man of very effeminate appearance, whom he introduced to others as a "friend" but never hid. However, on official social occasions like the ball, the obligation for men to attend accompanied by a woman—often a lesbian—allowed and still allows no exceptions. The degree of transparency changed in the 1980s, with the arrival of inhabitants whose residential moves coincided with a very strong assertion of their identity, as part of a coming out process that was sometimes combined with both political and civic activity. One former South End inhabitant commented in a book published in 1976, "Nowadays, [the South End] is recognized as an extension of the great central Boston gay ghetto."[32] And we can read in a 1983 article published in a Boston gay newspaper, Bay Window (whose offices were located in the South End): "The South End has come to be known as Boston's gayest area—clone territory. 'Everybody' in that neighborhood is ultra-gay: Levi 501s, pierced ears, cock rings, military haircuts, little black moustaches, body-builder muscles,

---

in the streets was thus masked, in part, by the bustle of street life in working-class neighborhoods." Chauncey, Gay New York, p. 228.

31   A. Nolder Gay, The View From the Closet: Essays on Gay Life and Liberation, 1973–1977, Boston: Union Park Press, 1978, p. 73.

32   Gay, The View from the Closet, p. 69.

poppers, joints, colored hankies."[33] Thus in contrast with the earlier experience of Peter Whitaker and many members of the Historical Society, a gay man openly living with his partner could succeed Louise Fitzpatrick as the head of the neighborhood association in the late 1970s.

Beyond these explicit signals marking the gay presence in the public space, the article's author also refers to two bars opening in the 1970s. However, the affirmation of the South End as a "gay neighborhood," the mixed character of the neighborhood associations, and the absence of overt reprobation, went hand in hand with a gradually increasing control of gay visibility from the 1980s onward. The influx of openly gay residents asserting their interests in a more favorable political context did not lead to a proliferation of establishments reflecting their identity. The AIDS epidemic in the 1980s and the development of online hookup sites in the 1990s clearly played an important role in the collapse of the "gay bar system."[34] Another consideration in explaining this is the South End's lack of a local gay rights movement, unlike neighborhoods like San Francisco's, marked by the struggles in which Harvey Milk played a central role.[35] The Boston political apparatus took on a different composition in the 1970s and 1980s as new alliances formed, with gays becoming a component of Kevin White's constituency. The attitudes of local political figures also changed, through the efforts of the gay and lesbian caucus of the Democratic Party in Massachusetts, established in 1973, which fought for the adoption of gay rights legislation (a *Gay and Lesbian Civil Rights Bill* was passed in 1989). Some politicians did gradually begin to speak openly of their homosexuality in the 1990s, but the scandal that plagued the first "out" politician destroyed all hope of political careers or lobbying based on the "gay district" of the South End.

Lastly, the lack of community mobilization can be explained by the en masse departure of low-income gays as the neighborhood became more and

---

33   Jack Stone, "Gay living in Boston's South End," *Bay Window*, March 1983.

34   Gayle Rubin, "Studying Sexual Subcultures: Excavating the Ethnography of Gay Communities in Urban North America," in *Out in Theory: The Emergence of Lesbian and Gay Anthropology*, ed. Ellen Lewin and William Leap, Urbana, IL: University of Illinois Press, 2002, pp. 17–68.

35   Randy Shilts, *The Mayor of Castro Street: The Life and Times of Harvey Milk*, New York: St. Martin's Griffin, 1982.

more expensive. But the gentrifiers' engagement in neighborhood associations also played a role in the South End's diversion from its apparent trajectory into a "gay district." Precisely when the gay friendly attitude was coming into formation, the neighborhood associations seem to have sharply curbed the emergence of exclusively gay spaces. The author of the article cited above, appearing in *Bay Window* in 1983, thus mentions the hostility of the main neighborhood association to a gay bar located in its area: "There are still some problems, though. When I talked to Larry Basile the other night he was a little annoyed by the behavior of some of the local residents—to be specific, the E Neighborhood Association (yes, them again) who have now been joined by another group."

Louise Fitzpatrick's archives bear the trace of the same reluctance, which mixed various preoccupations. The announcement of a bar "for women" opening in 1982 provoked immediate opposition. Among the many sets of minutes that the neighborhood association president collected, in the July 21 1982 meeting records we find an account of an interview with the bar's owner, who already had another establishment in the city center. The first negative reaction came from a gay real estate developer, who referred to "incidents" that had taken place in this other bar, and emphasized the exclusionary nature of gay-only sites. But he, like the other meeting participants, mainly revisited the themes that the campaign waged against bars since the mid-1970s established as part of the official rhetoric of the white homeowners. One raised the specter of alcoholism: "G. says it could turn in to another big bar with '200 drunks,'" while another went further: "L. speaks up for parents on Mass Ave. The children 'don't need another bad example.' Don't need 'any more drunks' on Mass Ave." Yet another explained that she didn't "want to 'set a precedent' for what would happen on Mass Ave. We have 'set a tone' there. Doesn't think the club would be 'beneficial to the neighborhood.'" Not only had years of mobilization preceded this episode, but it came only a few months after the association's intense campaign against a neighboring bar, Smith & Sheehan. Louise Fitzpatrick's archives contained a hefty sheaf of documents produced by the working group that the neighborhood association set up in order to close down this bar. For example, among these papers are the very precise instructions given to the volunteers charged with calling their neighbors to get them to attend the meetings. The lesbian bar episode quite likely reactivated the already-established perception of equivalence between the presence of bars and damage to the neighborhood's reputation, playing on the allergic reaction immediately triggered by any mention of "alcoholics."[36]

More broadly, the bar's opening was connected to the conversion of buildings previously dedicated to residential use into commercial premises. This was perceived as running counter to the desired evolution of the neighborhood, and not at all the kind of change that those working in real estate wanted, as in the case of the developer G., even though he was gay—namely, the arrival of new homeowners. The conflict over the lesbian bar crystallized a mix of preoccupations regarding anything that might curb the rising property values in the South End, together with a reluctance about any locales seen as being too visibly exclusionary. A more detailed historical study would be necessary to evaluate exactly what degree of homophobia—or in this case, lesbophobia—may have been at work here. A gender division, reinforced by the minimal presence of lesbians in the South End, may have also played a role here.[37] Indeed, it seems that while the South End's heterosexual residents may well have been homophobic, they could not express this openly, given the balance of forces in place since the 1960s. At a minimum, their homophobia was restricted to expression only in terms of resistance to homosexuality being too visible. The weight of the interests at play here led, in practice, to simply accepting (or making do with) mixed sites like neighborhood associations, where gays participated in the common mobilization of homeowners. The overt hostility that some people did express toward homosexuality targeted exclusive establishments alone.

From the outset, white South End homeowners' engagement was thus marked by a certain openness. But the forms that this openness took resulted not only from the baby-boomers' participation in '60s protest movements, but also to the sharp backlash against that activism. Moving into a working-class

---

36   On the creation of a task force to close down the bars considered the most infamous in the district, see Chapter 5.

37   The South End along with Jamaica Plain was then classed among the Boston neighborhoods with a "heavy concentration" of gay populations. It still is, if only male population is taken into account; conversely, it is not among the areas with the highest lesbian population. Gary J. Gates and Jason Ost, *The Gay and Lesbian Atlas*, Washington, DC: Urban Institute Press, 2004.

neighborhood like the South End and establishing selective alliances in their new neighborhood was indeed a response to the shaking up of the social structure in the 1960s. But if the social structure required rebuilding on a new basis, the manner in which class boundaries were reconstituted showed that this process was also an urgent effort to maintain its solidity. Allying with the lodging-house owners to put up a common front against the radicalism of social protests; breaking open the isolationism of the Protestant middle class but keeping blacks and Hispanics at a distance; including gays in civic associations while preventing the formation of a "gay district." Such were the underlying premises from which the definition of diversity would emerge. What remains to be understood is what practices brought that definition into being.

LOVE AND CONTROL OF DIVERSITY

The upper-middle class's characteristic discretion does not make them any less active in their efforts to protect its spaces. Never reluctant to appeal to the public interest, the wealthy upper middle class knows how to defend its own interests. French and US works have shown that philanthropy is one of the many strategies that prominent family lines have used to maintain their social rank over the generations.[38] Undoubtedly, we can find financial interests and class logics at play within Bostonians' local engagement: the following chapter, devoted to the South End Historical Society and realtors, brings these to light. The cause of diversity, nonetheless, shows us another dimension of this engagement, which does not solely function according to logics of exclusion that ensure the reproduction of social status. Or rather, it seems as if exclusion and the reproduction of status go hand in hand with forms of inclusion, signaling a notable change in the nature of social boundaries. Here, I argue that the watchword "diversity" expresses a singular relationship with poverty, established in the last decades of the twentieth century. This term, which emerged from the movement critical of modern city planning and from internal transformations of the Left, offered a common reference point to a segment of the privileged class that had been shaken by the social upheaval of the 1960s and 1970s, and

---

38   Susan A. Ostrander, *Women of the Upper Class*, Philadelphia: Temple University Press, 1984; Diana Kendall, *The Power of Good Deeds: Privileged Women and the Social Reproduction of the Upper Class*, Lanham, MD: Rowman and Littlefield, 2002.

then faced with the rise of neo-conservatism in the 1980s: diversity became part of the formation of a new liberalism. Our task now is to examine the term's meaning, and to analyze the practices that defined a new relationship with poverty, distinct from the traditional forms of spatial exclusion. Firstly, we should note that the management of diversity cannot be reduced to control over "undesirable" inhabitants; it is also a matter of making new arrivals accept the presence of "others." Some members of the neighborhood associations thus exercise an intermediary role, taking it upon themselves to manage the coexistence of different groups in the South End. Ultimately, a whole system of social legitimacy was erected around the new value of diversity, and the expression of that value became the object of management and control.

Diversity

The gentifiers' credo

The practices of wealthy South End residents stand at odds with the outlook generally associated with the privileged groups' efforts to distinguish themselves. Far from rejecting the working-class signifiers as vulgar and uncouth, as Pierre Bourdieu has analyzed, these residents have ascribed them a certain dignity, to the point of establishing them as one criterion for appreciating spaces, practices and tastes. Among the segments of the upper middle classes that are invested in diversity, the public expression of racial prejudice elicits sharp reproach, while signs of openness to others (nonwhites, the poor, gays) enhance rather than diminish reputations. Rather than the total abolition of distinction, what we are analyzing here is distinction in a new and singular form, a combination of inclusion and exclusion in which a certain kind of openness plays a role in the consolidation of social status.

Diversity was the most recurrent slogan throughout my interviewees' discourse, particularly in their answers to the first question that I put to each of them: "When and why did you move to the South End?" Apart from the term's characteristic vagueness, this notion is very closely associated with two themes, which arose in two different moments: on the one hand, the critique of urban planning in the early 1960s, which the gentrifiers then integrated into their own rhetoric; and on the other, the reformulation of progressive or liberal doctrines in the early 1990s, which also concerned a much wider group of people.

The first of these moments attributed value to diversity, conceived as a force that would generate local conviviality. As such, in the interviewees' comments, we find references to a diversity that seems to give the inner city its character. Jane Jacobs presented this idea in her 1961 essay, and it subsequently spread throughout the popular media; and as many works show, it became a social marker for people living in gentrified urban areas.[39] Jacobs's *The Death and Life of Great American Cities*, whose polemical target was the urban renewal policies, denounced the development of artificial and isolated spaces, the suburbs, accompanying the disappearance of urban communities. Her argument is bolstered by a description of Greenwich Village in Manhattan, a lively community bringing together different populations in its streets and businesses, constantly encountering one other and interacting. The vision of urban space that Jacob's pamphlet encouraged—among the general public as well as among professionals working in urban policy—rested on a strong dichotomy between the old city centers, seen as spaces of conviviality and exchange, particularly on account of the mixing of populations and their animated streets; and, on the other hand, the uniformity and ennui of the suburbs in terms of both their planning and their social composition. In my interviewees' rhetoric, we can hear an echo of this argument, which was spread first via counterculture and then through the mainstream press. They also express this perspective through their practices, since—following the gentrifiers' devotion to the idea of the street—many members of the neighborhood associations are also active in 'Walk Boston,' an organization founded in 1990 that promotes pedestrian use of the city.

The rhetoric of a mixed society establishes the South End's great distinctiveness as compared to the other central neighborhoods of Boston like Beacon Hill, as well as the suburbs. It contrasts the "vibrancy" of the South End—a word the interviewees used over and over—to suburban ennui, just as it contrasts the neighborhood's heterogeneity and conviviality to the suburbs' homogeneity and anonymity.[40]

---

39   Jon Caulfield, *City Form and Everyday Life: Toronto's Gentrification and Critical Social Practice*, Toronto: University of Toronto Press, 1994; David Ley, *The New Middle Class and the Remaking of the Central City*, Oxford: Oxford University Press, 1996.

40   Gabriella Modan brings to light the oppositional pairs structuring the discourse of the white residents of a gentrified district of Washington: city versus suburb, heterogeneity versus homogeneity, ideology versus reality, order versus disorder, public versus private, interaction versus individualism. Gabriella Gahlia Modan, *Turf Wars: Discourse, Diversity and the Politics of Place*, Malden, MA: Blackwell, 2007.

So after taking me on a long historical tour of the neighborhood, emphasizing on the interior architecture of the brownstones ("there is beautiful molding, and the ceilings and chandeliers"), one resident, a member of a neighborhood association and Walk Boston, explained, "I like [the South End], it's terrific. I like it because people say good morning to each other." And when I asked her if this was not also the case in the suburbs, she said, "No, and not the case in Beacon Hill [where she lived before buying a house in the South End] and not the case in Back Bay . . . I like it here much better because you can get to know people. It is friendlier." The evocation of neighbors who greet each other in the street and trust each other with their keys is a recurrent theme, constantly contrasted with Beacon Hill, which these residents deem too snobbish or anonymous. The term "live and let live" has become a "credo," as in the neighborhood that Elijah Anderson studied.[41] One inhabitant, again a member of a neighborhood association, explains: "I like the mix of people. I like the energy that is there, all the age groups, all the different ethnic backgrounds, all different people of sexual orientation. To me that makes it very energizing. I like that about it. Beacon Hill, it was more the one type of person. And I didn't find it so friendly as a group. Living in the South End, I got to know my neighbors."

Residents also particularly strongly assert this taste for diversity because it offers—as in the case of many other renovated districts—a form of rationalizing objective constraints. Migration into the South End was, indeed, one among various possible courses of action in the face of a boom in real estate prices that began in Boston in the mid-1990s. Valorizing diversity boosts the neighborhood's symbolic value—though the South End still lags behind Beacon Hill and Back Bay economically. It also has the power to make migration into the neighborhood appear to be the result of the new arrival's singular personality and tastes, and thus as an informed and conscious decision. Nonetheless, we find this theme of diversity cropping up in a wider segment of the upper middle class—even among those who live in the very residential neighborhoods that South End inhabitants criticize, but who share in a similar way of life in other respects, as well as common political positions. Indeed, diversity is characteristic of a wider relation to the other that signals a major recasting of American liberalism.

---

41   Elijah Anderson, *Streetwise: Race, Class and Change in an Urban Community*, Chicago: University of Chicago Press, 1990, p. 12.

Diversity, racism and euphemizing exclusion

The civil rights struggle led to an important schism in the history of US liberalism. The radicalization that Black Power and the New Left expressed, as well as the riots in the second half of the 1960s, drove a wedge between the radical movements and a growing segment of the Left whose priorities were passed over in favor of new demands that now targeted not only discriminatory laws but also the structural roots of poverty and segregation. Well outside of the Left's internal divisions, the term "white backlash," which appeared in 1973, designates whites' reaction to this powerful questioning of the foundations of American society and the democratic system itself, whose links to the country's racial structure had also become the object of condemnation. During the 1970s and even more so in the 1980s under the Reagan presidency, the Left also suffered an attack from a quite different direction: no longer from radicals denouncing its hypocrisy and collusion with the system, but from a Right that adopted the language of liberalism itself to attack the tactics used in the struggle against segregation; they claimed they threatened equality through "reverse racism." Repudiating white supremacy and explicitly condemning racial discrimination, the neo-conservative movement of the 1980s turned its fire on affirmative action policies in the name of equal opportunity. Diversity now became increasingly important as a rallying point for a Left facing concerted attacks. In this context, living in a state with a progressive reputation, Bostonians appeared to be the embodiment of now sharply-criticized East Coast "liberals," supposedly as arrogant as they were quick to make a hypocritical show of their liberalism. Moving into a mixed neighborhood was one way of expressing concrete resistance to this stigmatization as the US Left reorganized itself during the 1960s. Appreciation of diversity was a common trait among these new arrivals, as well as among wealthy households in more peripheral neighborhoods who otherwise occupied a similar political position.

What exactly is the meaning of "diversity?" From the 1970s, this paradigm came to replace the notion of compensating for historic discrimination in judicial rationales for upholding affirmative action.[42] Now, universities could take applicants' racial characteristics into account in the selection process if these

---

42   Daniel Sabbagh, *L'Égalité par le droit: les paradoxes de la discrimination positive aux États-Unis*, Paris: Economica, 2003

would contribute to "cultural diversity." Subsequently, the business world picked up on this notion, presenting diversity as a source of greater productivity. The categories in question widened, and affirmative action debates' initial focus on racial discrimination gave way to a proliferation of different minorities taken into account, the sheer number of which itself became one dimension in assessing the success of diversity.[43] President Clinton, elected in 1992, not only pushed black and ethnic minority appointees to the forefront of his administration, but also women and gays. At the same time, the civil rights question tended to fade from the political class's attentions in favor of a more consensus-based, elite vision of minority questions.

> Clinton adopted the safe strategy of appointing minorities and women to his administration and eventually to federal judgeships, while remaining low-key on civil rights . . . During the 1990 diversity was the winner. Democrats understood that, as a political tactic, supporting diversity was less risky than endorsing affirmative action—it redefined the issue not as a preference for minorities or women but as a public good that supposedly utilized the potential of all citizens.[44]

Today, the comments my South End interviewees offered on the question of diversity invariably unfolded in a series of different social categories they named as present in the neighborhood; their strong valuing of the sheer numbers of these different groups drowned out any consideration of whether social relations might put at odds the interests of the rich and the poor, blacks and whites, heterosexuals and homosexuals. In the 1990s this diversity, conceived as a common good favorable to all and not implying any redistribution of status or power relations—in the South End at least—became an established means of legitimation and marker of identity. In the statements that candidates for the board of Louise Fitzpatrick's association provided in the early 1980s, the word "diversity" did not appear once, while today it is present on almost every association's website. One of these tells us that "The

---

43   Peter H. Schuck, *Diversity in America: Keeping Government at a Safe Distance*, Cambridge, MA: The Belknap Press of Harvard University Press, 2003.

44   Terry H. Anderson, *The Pursuit of Fairness. A History of Affirmative Action*, Oxford: Oxford University Press, 2004, pp. 223–224

Ellis Neighborhood is a corner of Boston that is rich in history, art, architecture, and cultural diversity." A consultant we will meet again later on explains:

> We wanted to live in the part of the city which could offer what we consider the best of the city, which was diversity. In all its flavor, diversity in terms of age of people who live there, ethnic mix, the vibrancy of the South End art, the homosexuals, the low-income housings, the empty-nesters.

This rhetoric allows liberals to profess a distinct attitude of progressivism, while at the same time diluting the racial question among the multitude of categories that make up diversity. It has the virtue of combining what Steven Brint called an "egalitarian culture"—which had to be reaffirmed in the face of the neocon offensive—with a "white ethnic culture . . . which is largely Democratic, but worried about crime and resistant to perceived preferential treatment of the poor and minorities."[45] In the South End, this position translates into a robust condemnation of race hatred—though it can go hand in hand with prejudices that are expressed in euphemistic fashion. Tellingly, I heard overtly pejorative comments about black people only once in my study, and they were made by a couple who were particularly active in their neighborhood association. Having mobilized against the Pine Street Inn homeless shelter buying three row houses on their street, they became one of the targets of the countermobilization to uphold "diversity."

During a meeting organized at this couple's home, to which I managed to get myself invited, a discussion developed around children's educational attainment levels and how this related to their parents' race. Black parents were described as irresponsible, with Chinese and Hispanic parents considered to be more serious-minded. The discussion shifted onto the effects of history and of racism on today's persistent inequalities, with our hosts ultimately judging historical discrimination as "25 percent" to blame (they considered black parents' disinterest in education responsible for the other 75 percent). "You have to stop at racism, because that's what they want to hear," the lawyer husband argued. Doubtless hoping to help a foreigner understand

---

45   Steven Brint, "Upper Professionals. A High Command of Commerce, Culture and Civic Regulation," in *Dual City: Restructuring New York*, ed. John Mollenkopf and Manuel Castells, New York: Russell Sage Foundation, 1991, pp. 155–76.

the extent of social problems in the United States, the couple continued this argument by turning to Boston's black neighborhoods, in their eyes peopled by a fundamentally hostile population. Seeking to bolster her point, the wife—an accountant—told me this anecdote: returning from vacation, their trip passed through Boston's Mattapan neighborhood. Having made what they considered the "error" of driving through a black area at night, she said to her husband, "You can run as many red lights as you want, but get me home right now!" and told him to lock the doors, fearful of faces on which she told me she detected a menacing desire to "smash in your car windows."

By contrast, the interview I had conducted with her the previous year had begun in a fashion much more typical to the neighborhood. Responding to a question on the South End, she vaunted her "multiculturalism." But at the end of our interview, when I asked whether the neighborhood had any negative aspects, she spoke at length on the concerns about safety and black and Hispanic people's presence in the streets. An anecdote about the particularly noisy youth she had seen in the subway opened into a long discussion on black parents' level of responsibility, remarking that "It's always blacks. But they call you a racist if you say that," concluding by saying that she does have black friends. At no other point in my study did I ever hear such explicitly racist comments as the ones this couple made. As I will discuss in the final chapter, racial divisions were expressed more subtly, through the condemnation of certain behaviors around alcohol, smoking, and relations between the sexes.

The couple I just mentioned were unstinting in the hostility they voiced toward the Pine Street Inn's plans for three row houses across the street from them. Among the PSI's other opponents, some spoke in euphemistic terms and even denied the existence of social divisions. Take the case of the resident who, worried about the just-announced arrival of thirty new tenants, said, "It's tough for everyone, whether you've got money or not." For their part, this couple, initiating the first petition against the PSI's project, did not hesitate in asserting the homeowners' superiority over the tenants and expressing their concern over "population density," using the vocabulary of the most conservative suburban neighborhood associations. This was the main argument that they put forward in opposition to the PSI's purchase of the three row houses, demanding that the association only be allowed to buy one of the houses.[46]

---

46 As one of these residents explained, "The neighbors have a preference for

However, others soon organized a response to this mobilization. The champions of diversity circulated another petition affirming everyone's right to live in the South End, be they tenants or homeowners:

> We believe it is imperative to maintain and increase well-managed, low-income housing in Boston and to stem any further net loss of this housing. We support a South End which has long been an economically diverse community. We welcome residents of all economic, ethnic and social backgrounds to share in the vitality and neighborliness of the South End.

The years 2007 and 2008 were punctuated by a series of community meetings. Dozens of residents, municipal councillors, a state legislator and even a real estate developer attended, coming together in shared condemnation of "selfishness." Thus we see a certain rejection of the explicit stigmatization of the poorest; yet as we shall see, this stance was not incompatible with the exertion of tight control over demographic diversity.

Diversity and social status

The changes in the field of city planning, as well as the wider transformations of the political terrain, shed light on the carefully-titrated degree of openness represented in the taste for mixed neighborhoods among these upper-middle-class homeowners. But in order to understand their definition of diversity, we must also bring into consideration a whole tradition of civic engagement in the United States, which is not always thought as standing in contradiction with economic and business interests. The valorization of community, far from being the same as the general interest, in fact implies the affirmation of, and respect for, each of its components. "Helping others is also a matter of emphasizing one's privileged position

---

ownership. It's really ownership and investment in a neighborhood that makes the neighborhood better and stronger. When you have ownership the people who own those apartments care about crime and they care about trash and they care about the schools. When you have a neighborhood filled with renters, particularly absentee landlords, the neighborhoods tend to deteriorate fairly quickly." Rachel Kossman, "Pine Street Inn Acquires Upton Street Property," *South End News*, October 22, 2008.

within the community."[47] Devotion to the community strengthens one's social status both symbolically and materially. As Michèle Lamont notes, the boards of cultural bodies, charities or neighborhood associations are sites of meeting and exchange that can often prove profitable in the professional sphere as well.[48]

Nevertheless, if civic engagement in a mixed neighborhood like the South End does not harm social status, there are limits to what benefits it can offer. Local associations certainly are places for accumulating capital that can potentially be reconverted within the context of increased upward mobility and strategies for engaging emerging professional niches. The markets opened up by gentrification—property, businesses linked to renovation or to dogs—demand the creation of local networks, and neighborhood associations are a useful tool for this. They became even more so during the 1990s, when access to email lists became a resource unto itself. An email about a restaurant—for example, if it sponsored an association's event—had the merit not only of being distributed among a large number of wealthy inhabitants, but also of appearing as a piece of news linked to the life of the community rather than as a mere advertisement. Participation in neighborhood associations offers access to a social capital unrelated to what was procured through the traditional Bostonian elite's institutions. Contrary to participation on the boards of the Boston Symphony Orchestra or the Museum of Fine Arts, it offers no immediate benefits. But for the upwardly mobile middle class, it can compensate for a lack of inherited social capital, marking one's enrollment in an upper-middle-class sociability. Thus one black lawyer who arrived

---

47   Agnès Camus-Vigné, "Community and Civic Culture: The Rotary Club in France and the United States," in *Rethinking Comparative Cultural Sociology: Repertoires of Evaluation in France and the United States*, ed. Michèle Lamont and Laurent Thévenot, Cambridge: Cambridge University Press, 2000, pp. 213–28. See also Robert N. Bellah, *Habits of the Heart: Individualism and Commitment in American Life*, Berkeley: University of California Press, 1985.

48   "Participation in voluntary associations is an important source of friendship for upper-middle-class men with a high degree of geographical mobility. Many companies make it policy to encourage their workers to get involved in local organizations as a way for these companies to maintain good relations with the community." Lamont, *Money, Morals and Manners*, pp. 59–60.

in the neighborhood in 1971 could, through his local engagement in the South End and its advisory and charity organizations, achieve the status of a Boston elite.

The Role of Local Resources in the Construction of an Improbable Elite

Today enjoying an income of more than $300,000 a year, Bill Simmons grew up in a middle-class household in a working-class district of New York. His father, a doctor who had migrated from the Caribbean, kept a close eye on his son's education, which took the most prestigious channels from elementary school through university. As a new arrival in Boston and a black man, even one with very light skin, he had to penetrate a milieu still relatively closed off to ethnic minorities. He initially did so on the basis of his status as a prominent local figure—a member of his neighborhood association. From his arrival in 1971 he became involved in planting trees, which he organized and financed. As a member of the Kevin White campaign committee set up in the South End in 1975, he also became a candidate for the SEPAC advisory board's elections, and from 1985 was a member of the neighborhood community center's board. In this he followed the example of his suburbanite professional colleagues—though certainly on a less prestigious terrain than theirs—who were municipal councillors or members of city infrastructure boards.

His involvement in the life of his local associations allowed him to enter the municipal scene of upper-middle-class sociability. Indeed, today his ties to the civic sector involved a range of engagements—making him, as they say, one of this milieu's "usual suspects." To emphasize the extent of the obligations that this represents—and thus insisting on the moral dimension of his public persona—Bill offers this quip: "I told these people, well, there are three meetings in the same day, so I have an excuse, I'll only go to one. Or maybe do a drive-by—you pop your head in and say 'hi . . . hello'—and you realize that there are a bunch of the same people doing the same thing, with their black neckties." In fact, his position in the world of civic associations now stretches far beyond the South End, as he has become a member of many professional associations and cultural institutions as well, sanctioning the status of a prominent Bostonian more definitively than engagement in a local association ever would.

The boards of neighborhood associations—especially those situated in prestigious parts of the South End—can bring more direct benefits, but this has only come to be the case in more recent years. Above all, they cannot be understood solely on the basis of the too-narrow interpretative framework of economic interests. Rather, the careers being constructed here are not only professional, but also moral. Joining the neighborhood association and abiding by its rules (attending its meetings more or less frequently, and in any case its fundraisers) contributes to the construction of a moral figure, providing evidence of one's "good neighbor" credentials. This interweaving of financial motives and disinterest can be seen clearly in the case of the vice president of one neighborhood association. At 48 years of age, Amy Barber decided to set up her own property consultancy agency, and her local engagement proved a trump card for meeting clients. That said, money was not her only motivation, as she explained to me during our two interviews. The first of these took place in her kitchen, with its "Provençal" decor, in a house whose five or six floors I climbed, from the ground-floor gym to its roof terrace. After I had asked for a second interview, Amy very sweetly emailed to propose a further meeting. "If it's a nice day, we could go out on the terrace at 28 Degrees, where they do my favorite oysters—$1 each during happy hour."

The Engagement, Interests and Disinterest of a Consultant

Amy Barber arrived in the South End in 1994, and two years later she and her husband—who do not have children—bought a house on a street near the city center. Born in 1958 to a father who was a doctor and a mother who was a nurse, she holds an economics PhD from a prestigious West Coast university and is a management and investment consultant. Her husband is a businessman, and together their incomes add up to $500,000 a year. Her desire for diversity is part of a relatively cohesive set of values. She calls herself a Democrat, meaning that she supports the idea of some limited social redistribution. "I believe that government should provide a safety net for the poor. I believe that people need help. I believe in a lot of things that we don't have, like health care and decent public schools, [but I'm] not a communist. Not to the extent in Europe. In some part of Europe, it's gone too far. People just live on unemployment forever."

Her notion of diversity translates to her strong roots in the neighborhood, centered on frequenting local restaurants and manicurists' salons, as well as engagement in her neighborhood association. Her interests extend beyond the South End, and she emphasizes that she has many friends and is not limited to a small local circle. Her use of the local residential space is paired with mobilities and sociabilities across different levels. Originally from California, to which she still has strong attachments, she is married to an Englishman and goes to Europe four times a year. The first of our interviews took place the day after she returned from a ski trip to France, and her remarks on Boston were punctuated by comparisons to Paris and London. She also mentioned her frequent visits to New York and Washington, DC. These points of reference allowed her to distance herself from Boston, which in this educated white elite still has a reputation as a provincial city of isolated neighborhoods. She thus compared the South End to a village or a neighborhood in Paris, while at the same time invoking its diversity to contrast its multiculturalism with the overly traditional character of this New England city.

Her access to positions of authority in her neighborhood association speaks to professional competencies easily redeployed to the purposes of fundraising. Amy was asked to organize a charity auction: "I am highly organized. I know they tapped me for that, for my skills. I know how to run teams of people that are meant to do a lot of things. I had fifteen people and I organized them into subcommittees." She had no difficulty contacting South End business owners and realtors, and, aware of the reciprocal interests that united her with them, asked for their support in exchange for cross-promotion of their business through her fundraiser. In her description, we can see the implicit assumption that it is possible to combine the best interests of all concerned in harmonious fashion. She emphasizes the moral but also the technical dimension of her engagement in the community. What she is putting to work here is a true competence, of a quasi-professional character.

The links between her professional activity and her civic engagement are expressed also at another level, which demonstrates a subtle economy of financial interests and symbolic goods. As she explains, her engagement in the neighborhood association corresponds to a willingness to engage in unpaid work at a time of her life when she and her husband enjoy a very comfortable financial situation: "We have enough money and I want to spend more time working . . . but not for money!" This is no longer just a matter of donating 2 percent of their income to charities, but also of developing a more targeted engagement, finding a cause with which she can identify.

So we can see that this quest for meaning is closely related to her professional trajectory and her social position. At the same time that she joined the neighborhood association, she also decided to join a development NGO working in Latin America. Like her practices in the city, her engagement is spread across multiple levels. As a student she had participated in a development project in Latin America; twenty-five years later, she wrote to the NGO putting herself forward as a candidate for its board, offering her social and financial capital. (She was not accepted, however. Though disappointed by this, she was considering applying again the following year.)

In the same way, and tracking both with changes to her own status as well as the structure of the civic sector more generally, her engagement as a feminist also transformed significantly over the course of her life (even if, responding to my question, she hesitated in adopting the label "feminist," no doubt because it sounded too "militant"). During her youth, she participated in anti-blockade actions protecting abortion clinics. Today she makes substantial financial contributions to Planned Parenthood and the National Abortion Rights Action League.

Entrepreneurs of diversity

The defense of the social mix implies an appreciation of minorities, living side by side with other groups as a part of the whole. It is also expressed in a number of commitments as well as practices and sociabilities that do not function solely on the basis of exclusion. The type of collective engagement that the South End's associations exhibit has its roots in the management of urban renewal, and rather than a total rupture with the three classic figures of engagement in the United States as described by Robert Wuthnow—the organization man, the club woman and the good neighbor—it represents a reworking of these categories. It does so both through a certain dismantling of gender boundaries and above all through the objective of the engagement—namely, the local organization of social coexistence. It thus establishes a highly regulated means of managing conflict, as well as forms of negotiating with the public authorities and an ethos of goodwill and peaceful discussion. What results is a form of control exerted over all those it seeks to transform into "good neighbors."

Fighting for diversity

The defense of the social mix is indissolubly both a battle to promote diversity and a fight for the power to organize it. This was evident in the way of the struggle over housing for formerly homeless people played out, pitting the residents who opposed this development on their street against those who defended it in the name of diversity. In spite of the petition circulated by the former group, the Pine Street Inn (PSI) did ultimately succeed in buying the three adjacent row houses. Still, it ended up negotiating and selling one of the houses at market value, but this outcome nevertheless reaffirmed the charity's right to buy property and house low-income populations there. A significant group of South End residents engaged in a tireless struggle to achieve this victory on behalf of the PSI: creating petitions, writing columns, setting up meetings and email lists and making buttons that were sold in the streets and offered to the mayor, representatives and various personalities. They spared no time or energy in rebuffing the residents opposed to the project, who were seen as selfish. At the same time, paradoxically, this engagement offered the white homeowners the opportunity to reassert their power over the organization of this diversity, as the negotiations between the various stakeholders would demonstrate.

Negotiations across 2007 and 2008 altered the parameters of the PSI project, and the residents standing up for diversity participated actively in these discussions. Considering other residents' concerns legitimate, they first sought to placate opponents by insisting on setting the selection criteria that PSI would apply to future tenants. They insisted that PSI carefully examine applicants' criminal records, and that they would exclude those who had committed sexual crimes. They constantly reiterated the need to supervise these populations, even though they were adults, some of whom had jobs. One eleven-page document drawn up by PSI and distributed at a public meeting addressed the size of the buildings, the selection of the residents and the supervision to which they would be subject. The association detailed a list of employees who would be responsible for this supervision—counselors and superintendents—and announced that visits would be strictly controlled.

> All guests and visitors must sign in and out with the date and time in the guest book. There are no exceptions to this rule. Overnight guests and visitors are allowed, provided that adequate advance notice is given to the House Manager. No guest or visitors permitted to stay more than three nights in any given week.

It thus offered reassurances to residents concerned about the tenants' visibility in public space, like the South End inhabitant profiled earlier who made disparaging comments about black people, and who in an interview with a journalist expressed fear that these three row houses would "really define the street."[49] As we can read in the document that sought to reassure homeowners, "Residents are allowed to sit on the front steps but will not be allowed to congregate in front of neighbors' residences on Upton Street. No smoking is allowed on the steps or around the front entrance." Rather than ordinary tenants subject to the same laws as the rest of the neighborhood, the future inhabitants of the three row houses were considered people in need of special surveillance.

Above all—and most importantly—the negotiations led to a notable decrease in the number of occupants housed by the PSI project, in order to address the "population density" objection that its opponents had previously advanced. Invoking the need to improve sanitary conditions and thus to

---

49   Reported by Linda Rodriguez in "Nightmare on Upton Street," *South End News*, March 20, 2008.

increase the size of each dwelling, the number of tenants allowed fell from forty-five to thirty-seven, and then to thirty. Even though this decision provoked protest among the residents who advocated for the shelter, they eventually rallied to the idea that it was necessary and desirable for there to be some mix among the buildings' future inhabitants. So 25 percent of the residents of the three row houses were to be above 60 percent of the median income level—that is, earning around $36,000 a year. As we read in the circular of June 28, 2008, these were people who could bring "another level of economic integration into the neighborhood. It also gives balance to the house by adding a group that may be more outgoing, more apt to participate in neighborhood projects, and able to serve as a bridge between the poorer residents who from PSI's experience tend to stay to themselves and the neighborhood at large."

Thus we understand the extent of support mobilized for the cause of diversity. The most eminent members of the residents' associations and other local groups signed the petition. Brian Hanson, for example, a respected figure we have already mentioned who was ill in this period, nevertheless made an appearance at a meeting along with his wife. Inhabitants who had been hostile to the construction of social housing in the 1970s and 1980s also supported Pine Street Inn. For her part, a resident from the Villa Victoria development participated in the mobilization, while activist leader Mel King and the black state representative Byron Rushing were also present at the first meeting. But almost all of the supporters of this cause were white homeowners, who thought of diversity as a value that "we" show in relation to "them." Indeed, from the conflict that divided all these players nevertheless emerged an assumption common to both camps: namely, the need for a balanced distribution of the population across space, as well as the legitimacy of "the community" (which boiled down to the white homeowner group) to decide the demographic diversity in its territory, even if setting the terms for that diversity was a fiercely contested process. The term "density," mixing an environmental claim with "sociological" considerations, indeed signals a clear principle: the necessity of balancing of populations across space, in function of their social status and "ethnic" origin. We see, further, how this fight for diversity brought "other" populations onto center stage, as it became a matter of organizing the just distribution and control of these residents. Certainly, these "others" were not the threatening tenants whom the first set of petitioners described. But it also established a dichotomy between the idle, dangerous poor and the deserving poor. The concern motivating this sharply-drawn line between these two groups, outlining the boundaries of the population designated as the legitimate recipients of aide, shines through in a discussion on campaign buttons that took place in one meeting. A slogan was proposed for these badges, "All are welcome," but many of the meeting attendees objected: they ought not let anyone imagine that they were defending delinquents and rapists, they explained.

More broadly, one argument was constantly invoked in support of diversity, namely that the three row houses' existing tenants—men undergoing drug and alcohol rehabilitation—were pleasant and obliging, so why wouldn't their successors be so as well? They participated in the annual neighborhood cleanup and cooked hamburgers for the neighborhood association picnic. It was common for people to speak of how "they blend in," and this was combined with the idea that passing these houses you would not even notice that they were "different." The necessity, in the eyes of many South End homeowners, of maintaining a certain percentage of low-income populations in the neighborhood was accompanied by constant efforts to limit their visibility. As we will see, this logic is comparable to the approach to the gay population, even if it operated through different modes and different interactions.

Socializing residents to diversity

One episode demonstrates particularly well how, following in the footsteps of urban renewal, a small group succeeded in establishing institutionalized forms of negotiation for neighborhood affairs. These mobilized residents invested the figure of the "pioneer" with the priority of rational engagement in public affairs, producing a very particular activist identity—namely, that of "responsible" residents, those who collectively take charge of the development of the neighborhood in the name of "diversity", a process which (thanks to the ambiguity of this term) necessarily also includes the legitimate apprehensions some feel about diversity. Acknowledgement of these perspectives implies controlling—and if need be, combating—those populations who might threaten property interests, but it also means reconfiguring particularly the new residents' fear of the other as, instead, pride in adventure and an altruistic engagement. There is a whole learning process devoted to educating them to a particular habitus: the responsible resident is subject to certain rules of cohabitation and tolerance, open to discussion, and recognizes everyone's right to participate—whatever their race, sex, social class or sexual orientation—so long as they respect the formal frameworks of a carefully policed discussion.

These "moral entrepreneurs" particularly distinguish themselves through the register in which they engage others—one that emphasizes the happy medium, goodwill and conciliation, all typical of the inhabitants who took sides with the homeless shelter. These shelter advocates devoted themselves to organizing a series of meetings whose objective was to reach a compromise over a negotiated social mix, underpinned by confidence in technocratic means of managing conflicts. During the dispute sparked by the PSI project, they hired a professional facilitator to put together a public meeting and promote dialogue. The long-standing community leader Mel King did get a hearing in one discussion, but none of his suggestions were accepted. Despite his radical past, he has become respected as a "historic" figure who had played an important role in Boston life. In 2007, one neighborhood association even awarded him a prize, and given that for many of its members—not least the oldest—King embodied the political enemy par excellence, this ceremony marked the brutal depoliticization to which he was subjected, now deprived of the activist base that existed up until the 1980s. His call for protests in front of City Hall, or even his appeal simply to ignore the residents who were hostile to the homeless were not heeded. But he had expressed the deepest disdain for these residents, whereas the new partisans of diversity gave a frosty reception to any rhetoric that too abruptly disregarded the other side's position: for instance, there was sharp condemnation of a blog, produced by one gay former resident of the South End, when he denounced yuppies and gentrification, declaring *The South End is Over*. Messages sent over the list-serv for the mobilization to support the PSI commented in rather hostile terms on his impassioned article on the PSI affair. That is not to say that they were above using epithets to describe the project's opponents in private conversation. But publically there was a strong tone of compromise, which meant considering all inhabitants' views as legitimate concerns. This stance was all the more important for the contrast it offered with the two polarized positions, such that, with a certain margin for maneuver, these residents could situate themselves in position of the "reasonable" happy medium.

This task of seeking to "mend fences" is part of the conflict avoidance characteristic of upper-middle-class culture, as Michèle Lamont has studied.

This attitude allows for a particular means of managing the social and racial cleavages that still deeply affect US society. More than simply a matter of political correctness, this "social correctness" promoted by certain linguistic and behavioral norms seeks to regulate social relations. This proceeds by way of an effort to "master the form of exchange among individuals and groups, all the while protecting the identities of all."[50] In fact, here we have not just euphemism based on a rhetoric occluding all the relations of domination and unequal social relations. Instead, this rhetoric implies recognition of the other, while also inviting the other to do likewise, and adopt this pacified exchange framework as her own. The white South End homeowners' slogan championing consensus, "give back to the community," is a telling expression of this commitment to a regulated and reciprocal exchange. Sites external to the South End allow for further expression and development of this "social correctness." Many of my interviewees participate in interracial dialogue forums. Others, Protestants and Jews, are members of the Greater Boston Interfaith Organization, a liberal association that seeks to promote ecumenical links among the city's religious and ethnic communities, while also fighting for a certain measure of social progress.

Indeed, the wealthy residents attracted to the cause of diversity express their ethos by way of their commitment to managing tensions, clearing any "minefields" and wiping away any dimensions seen as too overtly conflictual. They thus present diversity, defined—as we have seen—as the harmonious and mutually beneficial cohabitation of different groups, as an extraordinary and desirable objective whose achievement is dependent on everyone's goodwill. As Elijah Anderson tells us, they thus constitute and transmit "a peculiar combination of neighborliness and self-defense." This "good neighbor" ethos implies, as the sociologist writes, a real opening up to the other: a "community's ethos and social script [that] call for decency and tolerance toward others."[51] Nonetheless, the underlying assumption is that for all the new homeowners, this social mix is a difficult reality that they need to be initiated into: "Certainly some of the neighbors don't like the Salvation Army and the halfway house. But they usually come out for cleanups and stuff like

---

50   Éric Fassin, "La chaire et le canon: les intellectuels, la politique et l'Université aux États-Unis," *Annales ESC* 2 (March–April 1993), pp. 265–301.

51   Anderson, *Streetwise*, p. 253.

that . . . That's part of the South End. A mission of the neighborhood associations is to bridge that gap, have people to talk to people they wouldn't talk to," explains one South End resident who is very active in her neighborhood association and in organizing various charity fundraisers. Their objective is to convince the new arrivals of the advantages of such openness in terms of regulating and collectively defending their interests.

This intermediary role, promoting the happy medium, implies a certain savoir-faire. The new residents have to be helped in their initiation to diversity, all the while remaining "good neighbors, [these] affable members of the community who respected boundaries, kept their home in respectable condition, and did not pry into the intimate details of neighbors' lives, [who] abided by well-established norms of civil behavior that included routine acts of kindness and hospitality."[52] The installation of a roof terrace, or the renovation of a building's facade—but also infractions against the rules (trash not left in the right place or at the right time, or not picking up dog litter)—residents mount a rigorous surveillance of all this. A small group, conscious of its mission, takes on these tasks, reinforcing its identification with a "pioneer" spirit. Indeed, there are always a few members, between five and twenty according to the size of the association, who take on a far from negligible burden of responsibility: preparing and running meetings; attending city-level meetings, notably the public hearings organized by City Hall; responding to residents' countless emails, and so on. The source of this legitimacy is located in a managerial and almost professional register that many association presidents exhibit, often retired people or women who work part-time or at home, or even those not engaged in professional life but who have impressive credentials. Just as in the neighborhood associations of affluents suburbs, lawyers, lobbyists and real estate developers work side by side, all the while accumulating economic resources and social capital. A former president of the Union Park association has an office in his house in which he has a meticulously ordered archive of files concerning the neighborhood. His office, in which he has hung a photo of himself with Bill and Hillary Clinton, provides further evidence of his intensive activity. Meanwhile the president of the largest South End

---

52   Robert Wuthnow, *Loose Connections: Joining Together in America's Fragmented Communities*, Cambridge, MA: Harvard University Press, 1998, p. 37.

neighborhood association plans to hire a secretary, following the examples
of associations in Back Bay and Beacon Hill.

But the reference to community is closely intertwined with a technocratic
register. The diminishing of small town life as the framework for American
existence, as urban populations have grown, has not put an end to the figure of
the citizen invested in his immediate environment.[53] Many residents inherited
such dispositions—given updated expression in the South End today—from
their parents, who were active in their parish, in parent-teacher associations or
in Scouts groups. Thus a tradition of local engagement has been able to persist
across the generations, sometimes even despite strong ideological and genera-
tional splits. Such is the case of one South End resident born in 1959, an urban
planning consultant whose father was a manual worker; the resident now lives
with his same-sex partner, a realtor. He joined the neighborhood association
upon his 1977 arrival and is also a member of the board of a homeless shelter.
He explains, "My parents are civic-minded people. Although I think I am very
different from my parents [he laughs] ideologically . . . They are one way, I am
another! They've always been . . . it's almost hereditary now, it's in our DNA
that we need to be involved in the community."

Feminine engagement?

This singular management of social diversity is matched with a gendered
form of organizing that marks a break from the traditional figure of the woman
active in her community but restricted to the church and the parents' association at local schools. The South End's neighborhood associations organize
traditional philanthropic activities that consist of donations to charities and
goodwill visits, predominantly undertaken by women. Many of them regularly go to serve meals to homeless people, often preparing the food
themselves. Nonetheless, these commitments reproduce gender divides only
imperfectly. Certainly men are more involved in negotiations with the
mayor's office and the management of development projects. And the distribution of tasks according to gender is often accompanied by difference in the

---

53   While its source is in the figure of the citizen designated the town father, this
reference point has repeatedly been re-appropriated and reformulated over the centuries,
and it is still very much present today, even if it is very much combined with pronounced
forms of individualism. Bellah, *Habits of the Heart.*

intensity of local involvement, as one couple make clear. He is an architect, member of an association board and in charge of a committee. She is a music teacher. Without children, they left their previous house in a rural area outside Boston in order to move into the city center in 1998. Not knowing anyone in the neighborhood, they regularly attended the meetings that their association organized, as well as the Historical Society ball. The husband's trenchant positions contrast with his wife's indecision, timidity and conflict avoidance: "I can give my opinion, and if you want it, that's fine. It you don't, that's OK." The prominent role her husband played in the neighborhood also contrasted with her engagement in less visible and less valorized tasks. She generally participated in the organizing the fundraising soirée: "I'm always involved with decorations or putting ads in the newspapers." During a mobilization against a construction project, she collected signatures on the street and distributed leaflets through mailboxes. The power of gender divisions struck me also on other occasions, particularly when I heard a former neighborhood association president explain why she had given up her position: "I don't like politics." I could not help but compare her retreat—in the face of the dynamics of power—to the assured, cynical, even manipulative attitude of two other residents who spoke with me. The pleasure that both of these men took in explaining to me—as well as playing at—the intersection of personal interests and power relations struck me as particularly gendered.

But this classic division of tasks and attitudes also seems simultaneously to have been subverted. Many women forcefully asserted themselves—some of them very far from the image of the housewife—redeploying their professional competencies in their civic engagements. Some of them had moved to the South End after break-ups, divorces or separations, and they were often driven by the desire to rebuild a private life and social ties outside of conjugal, family and heteronormative frameworks. Across recent decades— and strikingly so in the second half of the 1960s—the US divorce rate has risen considerably.[54] For the increasing numbers of women living alone, the gentrified neighborhood offered an opportunity to break with an atmosphere they

---

54   Going from 2.5 per 1,000 marriages in 1965 to 5 per 1,000 in 1976. The number of marriages ending in divorce has increased from 1 in 4 to 1 in 2. James Patterson, *Restless Giant: The United States from Watergate to Bush v. Gore*, Oxford: Oxford University Press, 2005.

were often out of step with in many residential suburbs.[55] The percentage of people living alone in the South End by the year 2000 was thus particularly high: 49.2 percent, compared to 37.1 percent for Boston as a whole, and on the rise (the 1990 figure for the neighborhood had been 44.3 percent). The inner-city neighborhoods and the civic life that takes place there offer material resources—as literature on gentrification has underscored—but also social and affective resources.[56] Single women between fifty and sixty years of age, who are not necessarily ready to play a secondary role nor one limited to the "social" domain, are thus an important force among South End homeowners. Their mobilization rests on forms of commitment whose intensity seems in some cases proportional to the degree of personal affirmation they gain from the break with oppressive conjugal links and the burden of domestic work.

One woman actively engaged in the fight for diversity in the South End is an example of this. Born in 1946, the granddaughter of Russian Jewish émigrés and daughter of a lawyer and a primary school teacher, she grew up in New York, earned two master's degrees and made her career in public relations and then in tax administration. Separated from her lawyer husband and living out a semiretirement, she bought an apartment in the South End in 1998. Her activist inclinations (in part inherited from her parents, who were very involved in Jewish community associations) were updated some thirty years after her activities on Manhattan campuses then at boiling point during the Vietnam War. At the end of the 1990s she sought something different from her previous existence in a Boston suburb focused on the domestic space and married life. A lover of jazz and folk art (a movement of autodidacts, as opposed to the fine arts), she has a pronounced appreciation for difference and the cultural

55   M.P. Baumgartner, *The Moral Order of a Suburb*, Oxford: Oxford University Press, 1988; Laura Miller, "Family Togetherness and the Suburban Ideal," *Sociological Forum* 10: 3 (1995), pp. 393–418.

56   Damaris Rose, "Economic restructuring and the diversification of gentrification in the 1980s: a view from a marginal metropolis," in John Caulfield and L. Peake (eds.), *City Lives and City Forms: Critical Research and Canadian Urbanism*, Toronto: University of Toronto Press, 1996, pp. 131–72; Liz Bondi, "Gender, Class and Gentrification," *Environment and Planning D* 17 (1999) pp. 261–82; Neil Smith, *The New Urban Frontier: Gentrification and the Revanchist City*, London: Routledge, 1996, pp. 98–101.

melting pot. She actively supported Barack Obama in the 2008 presidential elections and does not hesitate to call herself a liberal or even a bit of a radical. A member of a liberal Jewish congregation with a gay rabbi, and a fierce advocate for diversity, she tries to translate this watchword into action: through a sociability open to different cultural horizons, through travel and through her participation in Boston's organized interracial dialogue.

Maintaining a social life, friendship network and love life freed from the family setting, she is always looking to meet people. Omnipresent (along with her dog) on the streets of the neighborhood, she is a loyal customer of the restaurants constantly opening up in the South End, where she spends considerable sums. This expresses not only her social status but also her break with the domestic tasks that used to be incumbent on her. She is resolutely involved in "on-the-ground" engagement, collecting signatures for petitions and soliciting passersby to participate in charity fundraisers. When a gay pride parade passed through the South End, she set up a table in front of her house to greet the marchers. Deeply shocked by the campaign against the Pine Street Inn project—and living a few yards from the buildings under dispute—she led the group advocating for PSI, and had a falling out with one of her closest friends over the matter.

Practicing diversity

Over the course of decades of gentrification, the valorization of diversity has been accompanied by a strengthening of control over populations designated as "the other," and a scarcity of encounters between white owners and other residents on terms other than those of sharp inequality. In the same period, however, a gay-friendly sociability has extended across the neighborhood.

Proximity and inequality

The intertwining of social commitments and class status—which these residents do not experience as incompatible—accounts for the presence of sometimes contrasting figures in the neighborhood associations. Businessmen and women earning $200,000 a year or more here meet with certain residents of more modest means, notably former activists, no longer engaged in political struggles, for whom the neighborhood association offers a sort of refuge. Indeed, one very religious man, a nurse married to a school headmistress, told me that he moved into the South End in 1983 following several years in Africa in order to "live among the poor." He did not hesitate to express radical positions and even evoked the word "communist" in more favorable terms than did Amy Barber, profiled above. "I believe it is very important to support social programs . . . it almost led me toward communism." After a vicious tirade against the wages of corporate CEOs, he followed up with a statement that left the final thought hanging: "That's why I am working hard so that Bradford Street is a good environment because I can affect the small changes in the local, but I can't affect . . ." Come what may, he continues to organize weekly barbecues in the small park on his street every summer.

But the less well-off owners like him are generally white. While some residents engaged in common struggles alongside tenants and poor and nonwhite populations in the 1960s and 1970s (like the fight against a planned highway that would have sliced through the South End), their relations with these latter are increasingly a matter of philanthropic activity. The nonprofit associations that have traditionally played a crucial role in the mechanisms of wealth redistribution in the United States saw their dependence on private donors increase as a result of heavy cuts in federal aid across the 1980s and 1990s. Tax-deductible donations from members of neighborhood associations—and even from these associations themselves—are much sought after. The demands of rationalization and cost effectiveness incumbent on these associations translate into the exertion of increased pressure. And if these associations are to tap into the generosity of foundations and large companies, they have to show signs of good management, thus opening up a margin for intervention from the South End homeowners who sit on their boards. The presence of management professionals in these bodies is a serious guarantee of their good standing, in turn affording a measure of control to the individuals who bear these credentials.

The former president of one neighborhood association is now on the board of not only an association for the rehabilitation of drug users but also an educational center for formerly homeless people, both located in the South End. The son of a New York commercial lawyer, he was a top manager in a major Boston bank before retiring early. In 1999 his children finished their studies and got married; he and his wife decided to sell their suburban house in order to buy a place in the South End with the desirable Union Park address. Like many residents who are active locally, his engagement became more intense during the first years of his retirement. Through his participation in numerous boards—whether of profit-seeking companies or of charities—he pursues a semiprofessional activity that is lucrative in terms of accruing symbolic capital, rather than financial gain. Thus he became a consultant for United Way, a national organization that facilitates smaller local charitable groups, including by bringing them to the attention of donors, particularly major enterprises. And when he visited a South End charitable association as a consultant, he was solicited to join its board.

The political, financial and symbolic support won by this wealthy resident brought in return—both for himself and for the homeowners who live near him—a certain right of inspections in their area. This has translated into their encouragement of a particularly coercive program implemented by the drug rehabilitation organization where he is a board member. For a six-month period, former drug users in the program are subjected to strict boundaries and rigorous rules concerning their comings and goings. The early retiree vaunts the merits of this program: "It's their last chance. If they don't pass, they go back to jail." This pressure is a gauge of the pliability that allows them to fit into the neighborhood's life—albeit in a subordinate position—while participating in a diversity that others appreciate: "We like them being there, because it is a very safe neighborhood, and they volunteer for a lot of things. They volunteer for two cleanups that we have every year. If people need a handy man, we frequently hire somebody from over there. So it works quite well. And plus, our neighborhood is quite diverse."

The spatial proximity among the neighborhood's wealthy inhabitants and residents of more modest means gives rise only rarely to collaboration. In 2005 a body was set up at the community center seeking to bring together all South End groups, not limiting itself to homeowners' associations. The first meeting rallied thirty-five groups, and subsequently twenty-five people regularly attended its gatherings, whose objective was to promote social mixing through concrete actions oriented toward exchanges between representatives of different cultures and social milieus. This promotion of diversity led to workshops in which the presidents of neighborhood associations and tenants' associations met. Nonetheless, this process quickly collided with white residents' demand for results. "The only people I had heard say, 'Can we start working on something?' were the white folks who said, 'This is great but what are we going to work on?'" explained the social worker at the head of this initiative, which was not pursued any further.

Rather, spatial proximity is accompanied by strongly unequal relations, which philanthropic practices serve more to illustrate than to attenuate. Without doubt, this is best demonstrated by the term that a retired banker used to refer to a resident of a shelter he visited, and whom he helped and advised: he "adopted" him, just as his wife "adopted" a former prostitute. Relations with other local groups, notably tenants' associations, are, moreover, nonexistent. An account that Mario Small reproduced in his monograph on the Puerto Rican enclave of the South End is enlightening in this regard. A Villa Victoria tenant who planned to organize guided tours of the neighborhood and wanted to involve other residents in this was met with flat refusals:

> Daniela, a light-skinned woman whose English betrays a heavy Spanish accent, was trying to organize a tour of the South End and the Villa that would involve both residents and voluntary organizations from the greater South End. Trying to put into words the covert prejudice she sensed, she explains: "You know how many doors I knocked on? I'm talking about the South End. I went to the neighborhood associations, the neighborhood right down there [she points]—let me not mention any names . . . Do you know how many doors I knocked on to get help, to have people even just sit with me? . . . We had some contribution but no one wanted to get involved . . . When I went to knock on the doors of these [neighborhood] associations, I swear to you it was like a slap in the face."[57]

When questioned on the lack of tenant involvement in their associations, the owners advance a different rhetoric, based on tenants' responsibilities and the lack of interest that they demonstrate in South End affairs—though of course the question of what the issues of the neighborhood really are depends on widely differing preoccupations. The former president of one association thus recounted her frustration after numerous fruitless attempts to get tenants from the Tent City development to come to a meeting. She wanted to bring residents together in order to exert pressure on a noisy bar situated nearby. No one from this development showed up, and she concluded, "There is a big gulf between people like me and people there." In order to illustrate this

57   Small, *Villa Victoria*, p. 116.

divide, she emphasized their incapacity to bring pressure to bear on City Hall, insinuating that an association with illegal activities also tended to keep them away.

The contrast among such different inhabitants' interests and relations with the neighborhood comes through clearly in an interview I conducted with one of the few black residents that I encountered at an association meeting. As it happened, he was the superintendent of a building belonging to the PSI, the association that had wanted to buy the three infamous row houses. The building he worked in already housed formerly homeless people. He had to attend these meetings because of his job, though he did so without ever intervening or showing any of the homeowners' energy or enthusiasm. During a later interview, he commented on his move to the South End and his relationship with the neighborhood only in terms of restraint, quite unlike my usual interviewees. Before passing an essentially negative judgment, he only gave a hint of an answer to my question "Do you like the South End?"—a subject on which my typical interviewee would enjoy expanding at great length. From his perspective, the place where he lives is very much linked to his work and the housing market, over which he has very little control. Born in Louisiana in 1953 and brought up in a family of eight children—his father a manual worker—he traveled to the North in search of better working conditions and to flee the racial segregation of the South. He did not associate the South End with any sort of diversity, a word that he never used.[58] He spoke of slurs directed at him, including the "N-word." At the same time, he did not appreciate gays kissing in the street. Above all, the restaurants are far too expensive for him to afford. When he can, he escapes to a more working-class bar in Roxbury in order to play pool with his brother—the pool halls of old having completely disappeared from the South End.

The sociability of fundraisers only rarely punctures neighborhood associations' in-group mentality. All those I participated in, generally having been invited by an interviewee who paid the required contribution on my behalf, were organized around a buffet or a sit-down dinner, or sometimes a jazz

---

58   On the different uses of the term "diversity" and the other watchwords that black tenants' movements privilege, such as "rights," see Ellen C. Berry, "Divided over Diversity: Political Discourse in a Chicago Neighborhood," *City and Community* 4: 2 (2005), pp. 143–70.

concert. Some of their rituals allow donors to reaffirm their social status: for instance auctions and in particular silent auctions consisted of items for sale are presented on tables around the room, with participants invited to write the price they are willing to pay on a piece of paper, visible to all. The final, highest bidder takes the item. Auctions organized by more influential associations — one of which regularly involves a television host — have more attractive prizes. Nevertheless, the different South End associations' fundraisers demonstrate how diverse they are, both in terms of how these evenings play out and who attends. The less wealthy or those dealing with more controversial issues like youth offenders function more in a mode of activism, with the support of the most progressive white homeowners. Indeed, the fundraiser that one youth organization held gave me the opportunity to hear a speech praising the youth of the neighborhood's black and Hispanic communities. The event revolved around the artworks produced by children and adolescents together with artists from the neighborhood, which were auctioned off. Half of those in attendance, children and their parents, were black, and there was also a large number of Hispanic people present. Many neighborhood association members were there. In the entirety of my research, I saw almost no other occasions when white residents and residents of color mingled like they did at that event.

A conditioned gay friendliness

What does sexual orientation have to do with diversity today? The presence of gays is part of the social mix that the homeowners vaunt, and we see them within the neighborhood associations as well.[59] However, this integration, symbolized by the rainbow flag at the entrance of certain restaurants, concerns only a specific portion of the gay population — namely the affluent white segment. Nonetheless for this segment, integration does give rise to exchange and a common sociability, in public and private spaces, that does not apply (or only in very limited numbers) to upper-middle-class black residents, for example. A certain visibility is also accepted, since gays are overtly present as such. Nonetheless, they engage in this sociability within mixed spaces that mark a break with gay-only locales like the

---

59   The South End is one of the two Boston neighborhoods characterized by a "very strong concentration" of gays (Gates and Ost, *The Gay and Lesbian Atlas*). The percentage of households that are not families is, moreover, much higher than in the city as a whole: 67.6 percent in the South End as against 51.9 percent for Boston as a whole.

bars, businesses and civic association sites that played a major role in twenti-eth-century urban homosexual life, and that still endure in other gentrified districts across Europe and North America. Their integration into a gay friendli-ness that excludes any assertion of gay community as such is clearly demonstrated by the case of one South End resident and the professional, residential and biographical possibilities that have presented themselves to him across his life.

Steve Sandford, a white man born in 1960 to a small business owner and a housewife, grew up in a small Massachusetts town. He left to study in Boston and moved to the South End in 1982. "It was a gay-identified neighborhood. It was the obvious place that a gay kid moving to Boston would live. And it was afforda-ble," he recalls. His move to the South End coincided with political engagement dating back to his high school years, and which led him to support the career of the first openly gay politician in Massachusetts. When the politician was ruined by scandal, he fell back on his real estate activity before working for mayor Ray Flynn, and then converting his social capital in the more lucrative field of consulting. Today, as the head of a flourishing think tank, he earns $400,000 a year and has renounced any idea of a career in politics. Married to a househus-band and father to two adopted children of Asian descent, he maintains a sociability that is almost exclusively based on his family life; indeed, more often than not he spends his time with heterosexual families. When I interviewed him one Sunday morning, his husband was making pancakes for their children while the two of us sat in the lounge. It is far from coincidence that the person who put me in contact with this man was one of the leaders of the dog park campaign, and more recently engaged in the parents' association set up at one local public school. This association's effective lobbying expressed South End parents' increasing engagement, in tandem with the apparent transformation of the neighborhood into one more adapted to family life. The increasing number of strollers in use and shops for children add to young parents' visibility. These trans-formations, which are an irritant to many gays, also contribute to the subtle condition sets for their presence in the neighborhood.

Ultimately gays—who might instead have mounted collective mobiliza-tions and lobbying efforts rooted in the South End—did not become potential competitors to the heterosexual gentrifiers in seeking to appropriate the neighborhood. This made it easier for the heterosexuals to develop sociability and common engagements with those gays who shared their high socioeco-nomic standing. All the same, this integration was accompanied by subtle forms of exclusion, or at least an injunction to discretion, the requirement to abstain from behavior considered too identity-bound or having excessive sexual connotation. The latter was relegated to occasional and less visible spaces and moments, though as we shall see in the final chapter, the dog park, which became a site for encounters, authorized forms of flirting analogous to those of heterosexual residents. The greater presence of families in the South End from the 1990s onward encouraged the integration of gays, at a time when the improvement in the neighborhood's reputation as well as white parents taking control of a public school convinced a growing number of families to raise their children there rather than in the suburbs. The increasing similarities between certain gays and heterosexuals in their private lives also played an important role in this regard. This was a result of the growing number of heterosexual divorcees, and of the increased involvement of gays in legitimized forms of conjugal relations (gay marriage was legalized in Massachusetts in 2003) and family life (adopting children).[60] Their shared lifestyles based on strong consumer patterns and a common interest in keeping certain undesirable populations at bay contributed to a redefinition of sexual deviance. This now became less linked to sexual orientation as such—homosexuality not being a stigma in any discourse, whether formal or informal, explicit or implicit—but instead to the ways of expressing that orientation, as well as socioeconomic and ethnic divisions that excluded nonwhite and poor gays. Today, heterosexual gentrifiers exhibit a benevolent but always vigilant attitude, as became clear in one meeting that I attended.

The Control of Gay Visibility
The Negotiation Over Gay Pride

A group working on preparations for Gay Pride went to a neighborhood association to propose its plans for the march to head through the South End that year. The group included a French man living in Boston, and

---

60   It is also possible that communitarian bonds proved less necessary for gays of higher socio-economic standing than for those of modest means. Philippe Adam, "Bonheur dans le ghetto ou bonheur domestique? Enquête sur l'évolution des expériences homosexuelles," *Actes de la recherche en sciences sociales* 128 (1999), pp. 56–72.

in a later conversation, he told me, "These guys are the biggest pain in the ass." During the meeting, though, the tone was respectful, indeed, policed. After the presentation by two Gay Pride representatives, many detailed and rather fussy questions were posed in a serious, severe tone. One resident emphasized that in recent years the street sweepers only came by the following day. Another announced, "I've three questions and a comment I'd like to make." The fact that this was the South End's most powerful neighborhood association doubtless explains the scrutiny to which the proposal was subjected.

While the plan had to be considered in a professional manner, an agreement was quickly reached in favor of the parade going through the South End, and permission was granted without even the need for a vote. In addition to the gay friendliness that makes up part of the South End gentrifiers' identity, and aside from the control that they were able to assert during this meeting, it seems that many of the association members were alert to the commercial benefits of Gay Pride passing through the neighborhood. And ultimately many heterosexuals joined the march, holding the association's banner, and publicizing their participation online.

The life that has developed around a block of lofts in Washington Street bears witness to the recomposition of these social boundaries. Since 1999, the block's ninety-eight units have welcomed many dozens of inhabitants arriving simultaneously to the recently renovated area. The space's quickly growing reputation has encouraged encounters among homeowners and mobilization in the neighborhood association. Parties are periodically organized on the rooftop in summertime, with barbecues where the inhabitants and their friends come together. Above all, the park facing the building, and within it, the dog park, are important sites of sociability. It is here that informal invitations to nights out are made. Meanwhile the diners bustle with young couples, gays and retirees, with the latter coming from the residential suburbs and often mingling for the first time in a private sphere that includes homosexuals as well as heterosexuals. Twenty percent of the loft units were sold at below market price. Artists who were able to buy property through the terms of this mixed program also contribute to the invigoration of the area, even if the least wealthy among them sometimes experience the symbolic violence of the staggering economic divides generated by the arrival of ever-richer homeowners.

The violence these "others" are subject to—these artists and gays, who are relatively well accepted or even valorized for the diversity that they represent—comes through clearly in the account given by a man who owns his own apartment but faces a precarious employment situation. His regret for the lost South End of the 1980s is doubtless an expression of nostalgia for his youthful insouciance and partying, as well as of his current economic difficulties, which are evidently more difficult to bear given that he lives in an increasingly wealthy area. But these sentiments also have to do with the disappearance of a certain gay visibility and the weakening of the role of sexuality in gay identity. Complaining of the ostracism that the (hardly respectable) drag queens today suffer at Gay Pride, he notes that he was once even advised that he needed to get married and have kids. "A single man is scary," he concluded. As this account emphasizes, not everyone in the gay community welcomed the gay friendly integration. However, some have rallied to the idea of "mixing in" and refusing the "gay ghetto." One gay resident, a consultant who has lived in the South End since 1977 and is a member of his neighborhood association, told me, "I wouldn't want it to be a gay ghetto because that isn't normal. It doesn't reflect society as it is. Of course I want to be in an accepting community—a community where a lesbian couple, where two gay men can walk the street and hold hands if they want . . . We certainly see more families with children here. I think it's just wonderful."

But other voices make themselves heard as well, speaking to the fact that gays nostalgic for a more communitarian South End can also be the defenders of a kind of neighborhood where low-income residents are better accepted. Thus Steve, the gay consultant and now a father, opposed the South End inhabitants who were hostile to the Pine Street Inn project and stood up for the presence of formerly homeless people in the neighborhood. He spoke of how he always liked to see people in social reintegration programs (former addicts, former prisoners) walking the streets or the stairs of his block. Winking as he spoke, he made it quite clear that despite his integration into the neighborhood's heterosexual sociability, he regretted the disappearance of a way of life made up of cruising and ephemeral encounters, even if it is his own biographical journey and his current family life that have distanced him from this other lifestyle more than anything.

The most visible gay opposition to this upper-middle-class gay friendliness came from a blog called *The South End Is Over*. Its anonymous author published a series of essays mocking the yuppies, their luxury condos, their Ugg boots and their granite and steel kitchens. It should be noted that this incarnation of the reviled yuppie is highly gendered: the yuppies in question are mostly women, and more specifically, mothers.

Soy Lattes And Deluxe Strollers
The South End Is Over!

The blogger's critique mainly targets consumption: sophisticated coffees like soy lattes, heirloom tomatoes at more than $5 a pound, fifty-dollar foie gras omelets, the rise of valet stations on neighborhood streets—but also SoWa, an arty area of the South End so labeled in imitation of New York's SoHo.[61] His criticism very often targets families—but mothers much more than fathers—with reference to what he sees as the imposing, noisy presence of babies and (deluxe) strollers in cafés. These women symbolize the offhand and brazen attitude that he denounces in the yuppies who have just arrived from their suburbs. Moreover, the articles that he has published on the site are punctuated by remarks on what he sees as heterosexual couples imposing their behavioral norms: "I was out to dinner with five other gay men the other night . . . We said our gay goodbyes, and like all homos everywhere, each of us gave each a hug and a kiss goodnight. We were appalled by the shocked expressions from the Ugg-wearing 'trendsetters' staring at us through the windows of the Butcher Shop. You would think we had given each other a big juicy group blowjob by the looks on their suburban/Back Bay/Beacon Hill faces . . . I remember a day not long ago when a kiss goodnight between two homos in the South End

---

61   "I think it is about time to tell the people what SOWA really stands for: Severely Overprivileged White Assholes," notes an entry from October 16, 2006. On SoWa, see Chapter 4.

was *de rigueur* and shocking to no one. In fact, prior to the Butcher Shop, a great gay little restaurant named 'Rave' occupied that spot, and before that, a gay coffee shop called 'Mildred's'."

This site had such a reach that—despite its author's anonymity—the *South End News* devoted an article to it in 2009. Nevertheless, that same year the blog ceased publication.

CONCLUSION

The upper middle class's engagement in favor of diversity exhibits a subtle interplay of proximity and distance. Spatial proximity is a fact, and neighborhood associations take the responsibility for socializing residents to accept this—even if, as we will see in Chapter 5, exclusive locations have been established within the neighborhood. Social distance, expressed in the highly unequal or nonexistent relations among different status groups, leads to the assignment of subordinate places—and even subjection to surveillance—to some groups, while simultaneously affirming their right to some space in the neighborhood. This mix also functions on the basis of a recomposition of social divisions, explained by the elite group's own formation process: openness to the affluent portion of the gay population, associated with the efforts made to renovate the neighborhood; the maintenance of class boundaries after its brief alliance with the lodging-house owners who disappeared from the South End with the explosion of the condo market; and the recomposition of racial divides around the same opposition between whites on the one hand and blacks and Hispanics on the other, but with some populations formerly considered "nonwhite," like those Irish, Italian, Québécois or even Lebanese origin now being deemed white or else leaving the neighborhood entirely.

This chapter has demonstrated how transformations of the family sphere and sexual questions have contributed to the transformation of class stratification, and more specifically to the recomposition of upper-middle-class values. An analysis of the engagement that a group of well-off homeowners carried out in a mixed neighborhood sheds light on a major episode of US gay history. One of the most interesting aspects of George Chauncey's book on New York is its refutation of any linear conception of this history: he shows that the gay milieu in the second third of the twentieth century was much less tolerated and visible, and more segregated than it had been from the end of the nineteenth century up to the 1940s, and moreover that gay culture was born not among the white middle class, but existed in the working class—notably in black, Irish and Italian neighborhoods. The works on "gay neighborhoods" that began appearing from the 1980s onward—concerned with giving their object scientific legitimacy, but also expressing a political desire for visibility—tended to emphasize the autonomy of gay cultural spaces, which were sometimes described as "quasi-ethnic communities" emerging after decades of invisibility.[62] As a counterpoint to this sometimes homogenizing depiction, this study of the South End sheds light on the relations between homosexuals and heterosexuals post-Stonewall—characterized by greater tolerance, certainly, but nonetheless based on a strong element of control.

However, the "diversity" which low-income populations, ethnic minorities and gays participate in to different degrees did not become a central point of reference and a consensus marker of identity until the 1990s. It cemented the dominant upper-middle-class group, following the struggles that marginalized those most overtly opposed to minorities' rights, such as particularly conservative members of the South End Historical Society. These individuals did nevertheless play a considerable role in the history of neighborhood's transformation, notably through their deployment of "high culture" for the purposes of restoring the South End's symbolic stature.

---

62   Lewin and Leap, *Out in Theory*; Stephen Murray, "The Institutional Elaboration of a quasi Ethnic Community," *International Review of Modern Sociology*, 9: 2 (1979), pp. 155–75.

Chapter 4

Creating Historical Heritage

"Omnivorous" has become the descriptor that best captures the upper middle class's relationship to culture. This term, advanced in particular by US sociologist Richard Peterson, has come to summarize the thesis of a profound transformation of cultural tastes.[1] The lifestyle of Americans of high social standing is no longer limited to canonical, distinguished tastes. On the contrary, its tendency is now to expand to take in aspects of popular culture and practices as well. Many scholars have used the results of studies of musical tastes to support the hypothesis that there was a historical turning point after World War II, with a decline in attitudes of "snobbery" defined by exclusion. Omnivores, then, are those who, beyond their cultivated tastes, also engage in practices that are considered low- or middle-brow; and as a population, omnivores' numbers are on the rise. Their behaviors express a new attitude toward popular culture: no longer rejecting or stigmatizing it, but rather recuperating certain elements—even "gentrifying" them, as Richard

---

1 Richard A. Peterson and Roger M. Kern, "Changing Highbrow Taste: From Snob to Omnivore," *American Sociological Review* 61 (1996), pp. 900–7; Richard A. Peterson and Albert Simkus, "How Musical Tastes Mark Occupational Status Groups," in *Cultivating Differences*, ed. Michèle Lamont and Marcel Fournier, Chicago: Chicago University Press, 1992, pp. 152–68.

Peterson puts it—and incorporating them into the dominant culture.[2] With this "gentrification" we see an integration of cultural products, especially musical ones, now consumed by a variety of different social groups. This chapter proposes to revisit this analysis in light of the particularly exclusionary deployment of "high culture" in order to transform a working-class neighborhood. Focused on the South End Historical Society, this chapter also sheds new light on the "bohemian" spirit of the gentrifiers.

The Historical Society, founded in 1966 and comprised, from the beginning, almost exclusively of upper-middle and upper-class white homeowners, is among the local groups active in the South End. Unlike the neighborhood associations, though, each of which represents a few city blocks, the Historical Society claims to represent this area as a whole. After many years of lobbying City Hall, in 1983 the Society succeeded in obtaining the designation of "historic landmark" for the South End, thus protecting its Victorian architecture from any demolition or exterior modifications. Not only did the neighborhood thus acquire distinct cultural prestige, but its economic value also increased. This lobbying effort was the local expression of a more general movement beginning in the 1960s, which rediscovered inner-city architecture at a time when residential suburbs—and, more broadly, modernist town planning—were the object of increasingly forceful critiques. Moreover, the link between the rise of historic preservation and the rising status of older, run-down neighborhoods is not unique to Boston. We see the same movement, accompanied by the stigmatization of the architecture of large housing projects, in other cities in New England and in Europe.[3] The significant housing stock in brownstones and the similarity of the South End's architecture to the wealthiest neighborhoods, Beacon Hill and Back Bay, in a city that already had a well-established tradition of historic conservation, made this preservation project that much easier. But unlike other historic preservation

2   Peterson and Kern, "Changing Highbrow Taste," p. 906.

3   Max Page and Randall Mason, *Giving Preservation a History: Histories of Historic Preservation in the United States*, London: Routledge, 2004; Brett G. Williams, *Upscaling Downtown: Stalled Gentrification in Washington DC*, Ithaca, NY: Cornell University Press, 1998; Gordana Rabrenovic, *Community Builders: A Tale of Neighborhood Mobilization in two Cities*, Philadelphia: Temple University Press, 1996; Jean-Yves Authier, *La Vie des lieux. Un quartier du Vieux-Lyon au fil du temps*, Lyon: PUL, 1993.

efforts, often based on a valorization of alternative milieus and the working class,[4] the first gentrifiers in the South End emphasized a heritage resting distinctly on the values of high culture associated with the wealthiest classes. The connection between this architecture and a cultivated elite (those who lived in the neighborhood when the Victorian houses were first built) merits underscoring for this discussion, and close examination. Through the promotion of the Victorian architecture as reason to move into the neighborhood, and of the figure of the "pioneer" recovering the treasures of the past, these gentrifiers established sharp lines of demarcation between themselves and the people they suggested had let these riches go to seed—namely, the immigrants arriving from the 1880s onward.

Continuing our reflection on the interplay of inclusion and exclusion at work among the wealthy, this chapter seeks to understand the conditions under which cultural distinction continues to be activated, including among the segment of the upper middle class that has come to live in working-class neighborhoods. This is all the more surprising since the cultural tastes that South End residents foreground today lean toward "exotic" restaurants, loft apartments and "Open Studios" days of visits to artists' workshops. In order to understand why the more conventional signifiers of high culture, in contrast to these symbols of bohemian preferences, have nevertheless constituted such an important resource, we must look back to the particularly intense struggles, both political and symbolic, that once raged in the South End. Seen in the light of these conflicts, it would be reductive to interpret the gentrifiers' invocation of Victorian high culture as simply the transmission of an immutable heritage, in a city comprised of similarly prestigious institutions. The stakes that the history of the neighborhood represents speak to something quite different from an "objective" definition of its heritage. Rather, it ought to be understood in terms of the battles that polarized the field of civic engagement from the late 1960s to the late 1970s—struggles to determine how land would be used within the framework of the urban renewal project, including the possibility that some would be allocated to the construction of public housing. As with historical

---

4   Patrick Simon, "La société partagée. Relations interethniques et interclasses dans un quartier en rénovation. Belleville, Paris XXe," *Cahiers internationaux de sociologie* 98 (1995), pp. 161–90.

preservation movements during urban reform at the turn of the twentieth century, the defense of architectural heritage was inextricably linked to a project to transform space. The epigraph of the 1969 South End Society newsletter—"Using the Past to Serve the Future"—gives a clear signal of this relationship in the period we are studying. The key terms and representations that the Society promoted, based on a three-period narrative—Victorian glory, decline, and reconquest—provided the basis for the battle, waged together with other groups, to put an end to public housing construction. The "future" that this cultural institution worked toward contributed in a powerful way to revising urban policies in favor of market forces and to the legitimacy of white homeowners to live in and transform the South End. The most conservative members of this group and their cultural vision were ultimately sidelined; but their activities and advocacy, which decisively reoriented the gentrification movement, nevertheless shed light on the complicated genesis of a "liberal" elite.

CONNOISSEURS, CONSERVATIVES

The Historical Society is a society of "amateurs" who have gradually succeeded in becoming recognized as authentic "connoisseurs" of South End history. Studying this institution, whose role I had initially underestimated, allowed me to discover a crucial dimension in the formation of the group in question. The recurrent references to diversity, the assertion of openness and tolerance, and the virulence of anti-Bush sentiments had all given me the impression that this milieu was cemented by relatively similar political orientations, as their consistent vote for Democratic candidates and invocations of their liberal faith seemed to demonstrate. But as well as constructing itself on the basis of some unexpected alliances,[5] one of the characteristics of this group is that it has built its social and local base through ideologically contrasting initiatives. More than its founding members' responses to my questions on their political outlook, it was an evening at a ball that made me aware of the particularly conservative foundations of the Historical Society's cultural enterprise.

---

5   See the analysis of "Alliances and Misalliances" in the previous chapter.

A "Sensitive" Terrain
The Limits of Ethnographic Immersion in an Upper-Class, Conservative Milieu

I was enthusiastic about having the opportunity to attend the Historical Society ball, one of the organization's main events. Thanks to its secretary—a man who was rather critical of the association's direction, and who resigned not long afterward—I managed to get invited to this fundraiser, whose tickets usually cost $95 (or $120 for those also present for cocktails at the start). Thinking that in borrowing a pair of black high heels—absent from my own wardrobe—I had made sufficient concessions to the dress code, I naively turned up by myself, thus breaking the binding rule of such society events: the obligation to attend with a member of the opposite sex.

The call to order came immediately; it did not help that I found myself seated next to an architect apparently known to everyone but me as an exceedingly unpleasant character. He proceeded to alternate between remarks on the laziness of the French, who "take six weeks' holiday a year" while Americans "work and don't complain about it;" derisive references to Harvard elitism and academics' privileges; and finally his less-than-friendly opinions on French women, apparently provoked by my dress, which he deemed too short. During the ball I got to experience directly the weight of conjugal norms in this milieu, the hatred for the welfare state and the obsession with "government handouts"—but also the power of racial divisions. The decision to use the Hispanic cultural center next to Villa Victoria, with its majority population of Puerto Ricans and their descendants, clearly put people off: attendance was disastrously low that year. The contrast with the very warm reception that I, this white, Harvard-affiliated Parisian academic, had received up to that point contributed to my tolerance reaching its limit that evening, as I was faced with the spectacle of wealth and the subtle but nonetheless powerful forms of keeping the poor controlled and at a distance in this gentrified neighborhood. Despite his wife's attempts to keep up the appearance of social decorum, the architect's verbal assault continued. After a few more or less choice words on the virtues of the welfare state and on my interlocutor's sexism, I headed for the exit.

A social-historical look at the 1960s and 1970s reveals a mobilized group noticeably different from the lovers of diversity portrayed in the literature devoted to gentrification. Equally surprising were the close links between professional trajectories and sexual identities on the one hand, and on the other, the association members' capacity to impose themselves as the legitimate if not monopoly authority in cultural matters. Indeed, since its creation the Historical Society has brought together upper-class and upper-middle-class homeowners, real estate agents, gays and conservatives.

A distinguished cultural engagement

The Boston upper classes, the Brahmins, built their power on close ties to culture, and this connection was strengthened with the 1636 foundation of Harvard College, which the sons of the leading families attended. The elite's systematic engagement in music and the fine arts in particular dates from the beginning of the nineteenth century, making Boston the "Athens of the United States."[6] Yet as Paul DiMaggio has shown, the construction of a high culture closely linked to the Boston elite dates from the second half of that century, with rapid industrialization and the *en masse* arrival of immigrants taking away the white Protestant elite's control of municipal affairs and awakening panic among their ranks.[7] The erection of a solid boundary between "high culture"

---

6   In 1826, the prestigious Athenaeum cultural center opened the city's first art gallery. A few years later the Boston Academy of Music was established. Frederic C. Jaher, *The Urban Establishment: Upper Strata in Boston*, Urbana: University of Illinois Press, 1982, p. 34.

7   Paul DiMaggio, "Cultural Entrepreneurship in Nineteenth-Century Boston: The Creation of an Organizational Base for High Culture in America," *Media, Culture and Society* 4 (1982), pp. 33–50.

and "popular culture"—enforced by nonprofits managed by trustees—was a response to this threat. The Museum of Fine Arts or even the Boston Symphony Orchestra—together with other institutions linked to the historical preservation movement—thus formed a particularly developed cultural milieu.

The founders of the South End Historical Society and its most active members in its early years worked in professions requiring high levels of qualification, with high incomes and managerial roles: lawyers, bankers, doctors, architects and planners. The listings for these professions in a municipal directory allow us to count more than half—or even two-thirds—of the active members of the Historical Society as belonging to the upper middle classes (60 percent in 1966, 57.5 percent in 1976, 68.7 percent in 1978, 63 percent in 1979).[8] However, they did not belong to the Boston elite. And the society's board did not include any "professional" historian whose knowledge is certified by the academic world.

The South End Historical Society at first only had weak links with Boston's most exclusive high culture milieu. These ties initially depended on a couple who moved to the South End in 1967. The husband, a banker from a wealthy New York family, came to work in Boston and became a member of the Historical Society's board in 1973; his wife headed the Society from 1978 to 1985 and still maintains a high-ranking position even today. Both of them are also active in their neighborhood association, pointing to the close connections among the different local groups. In the mid-1970s, moreover, he participated in the campaign seeking to shut down bars, while she is today part of the association that manages the small park near her home.[9] An engineer's daughter born in 1939, she was a member of the Junior League and the Daughters of the American Revolution, very selective institutions of the wealthy upper middle and upper classes that combine social, philanthropic and cultural functions.

---

8   The *City Directory* is an annual directory published by City Hall, featuring the name, address and profession of Boston residents; however, it is put together in a nonstandardized and not always reliable manner. Details were missing for 15 names out of the 106 board members for the years 1966, 1973–4, 1975, 1976, 1978, and 1979. The interviews I carried out with the founders of the Historical Society nonetheless allow us to check this skew in some measure, and to specify the person's socioeconomic status when only their professional sector was mentioned.

9   On the role of these associations in transforming public spaces, see Chapter 5.

Particularly active in the historical preservation scene, in 1983 she assumed leadership of an organization that had since 1978 brought together some twenty-five associations resisting the demolition of old buildings in Boston.

Another banker—a member of the South End Historical Society board and was one of its fourteen founders—also belonged to the Boston Historical Society, whose charter served as a model for the South End's.

Investment in "high culture" can be explained first by the symbolic devalorization that buying property in the then-stimatized South End represented. Owners were all the more driven to take an interest in decor and interior design—and to thus emphasize surviving antique elements—because this valorization could compensate for (and over time, increase) the low economic value of the property they owned. Up until the 1970s, it was possible to buy entire four- or five-story houses for a few tens of thousands of dollars. The desire to bridge the gap between social position and geographic location was a powerful force driving engagement in the Historical Society. Its first president, a middle manager at the First National Bank who has built up an impressive collection of documents and photos from the Victorian period since moving into the neighborhood in 1964, explains: "One of the reasons we started the Historical Society . . . [was that] we were tired of the reaction of our suburban friends to the South End. I remember a taxi driver, [as I was] getting a ride home—'Do you really want to go to the South End?' I was outraged!"

Beyond this symbolic revalorization, a distinguished sociability was organized within the Historical Society. Renowned historians gave talks. The news bulletin periodically mentioned classical music concerts. As for the annual ball, this spoke to the desire to import the social codes of the wealthy classes—even doing so in over-the-top fashion—in order to compensate for the area's "ghetto" stigma. In conformity with these social rituals, from 1971 onward the Society organized a costume ball, providing the papers the opportunity to talk about this new gentry. That year, a *Boston Globe* article devoted to the people it presented as the South End's "new" residents—at a time when black and Puerto Rican immigration was still sharply rising—focused most of its attentions on the Historical Society. Following the model of "society" reporting, it listed the personalities in attendance, who were thus symbolically integrated into a local elite marked by this seal of cultural distinction. And it was this taste for the architecture of yesteryear that defined this list of wealthy residents, among whom we find Colin Diver, mentioned in the previous chapter.

University of Massachusetts Chancellor Francis Broderick and his wife, architect Basil Alferieff, Colin Diver of the Mayor's office, Polaroid vice-president Mark Sewall, the Junior League's Show House lamplighter Mrs. Joseph Park Jr and her husband; Dr. Richard Gott, Kahlil Gibran and his Jean, and hundreds more are among the South Enders who love their 13-foot ceilings and 25- by 50-foot living rooms.[10]

The first articles on inner-city "pioneers," appearing in the mid-1960s, were already describing them as architecture lovers: "If the South End is a slum," explained Peter Whitaker, whom we met in the previous chapter, "it's one with some grand parks, with houses having 14-foot ceilings and 15-foot drawing rooms."[11]

The fourteen people who founded this Historical Society on February 24, 1966, were soon joined by many hundreds of members—386 in 1977 and 489 by 1981. While I could not identify the social characteristics of all of its members, the profile of the board members suggests a strong homogeneity in both social and ethnic terms. It remained almost entirely composed of white residents—from 1966 to 1979 two black women did participate, one of them being the wife of a consultant. When I attended the ball in 2007, I did come across one black man at the cocktail reception beforehand, but the few dozen residents who began dancing at 10 p.m. were all white.

Culture and business

That said, we should not see the Historical Society simply as an organization of wealthy residents seeking added value for their homes and distinguished cultural engagement that does not require "scholarly qualifications."[12]

---

10   Marjorie Sherman, "South End Glows as Suburbanites Move In," *Boston Sunday Globe*, October 17, 1971.

11   Anthony J. Yudis, "Discriminating People Moving In," *Boston Globe*, April 10, 1964.

12   Unlike in France, where the historical preservation movement is linked to the central state and an already-established professional body, in the US preservationist movement, urban elites and their economic interests play a highly significant role. From this point of view, the South End's Historical Society is very much part of the "pro-market preservation" whose emergence in Providence, Rhode Island, Briann Greenfield portrays

Professionals whose jobs relate to urban policy are heavily represented on its board—from architects and decorators to city planners and real estate agents. From 1966 to 1979, they made up between 15.7 percent and 25 percent of its members. Their influence is not only a matter of numbers; they also have close connections to the mayor's office.[13] Out of all these professionals, those working in the housing sector play a particularly prominent role, including the three people who founded the real estate agencies that dominated the South End property market up until the 1980s. One of them has organized tours of the neighborhood since 1967, consisting of visits to around a dozen homes to examine their interiors. This tour, together with the ball, has become one of the main dates on the Society's calendar. These realtors' involvement in the Historical Society is explained by their relatively atypical position, not belonging to any real estate firm. This little-regulated sector did not yet have the degree of concentration that it reached in the 1980s, and entering this profession only required passing a relatively easy exam. Two of the three South End residents setting up their own agencies in the 1960s were women. For women with university degrees and a certain amount of economic capital, real estate was one of the few professional outlets in which they were permitted to apply their resources, along with teaching and lower-ranking medical professions. One of these two women headed for Boston after receiving a physical education diploma from a Massachusetts college and then marrying an engineer who had graduated from MIT. The couple first lived in Beacon Hill and in Cambridge. They moved to the South End in 1965, when she was pregnant, and they bought a house there for $7,500. Their move to the South End was facilitated by their contacts and intermediaries. Peter Whitaker—who, as we saw in Chapter 2, was actively engaged in revalorizing the neighborhood with the BRA—played an

---

in her work ("Marketing the Past: Historic Preservation in Providence, Rhode Island," in *Giving Preservation a History: Histories of Historic Preservation in the United States*, ed. Max Page and Randall Mason, New York: Routledge, 2004, pp. 163–84).

13   One founding member living in the South End since 1964—when he was recruited by the Boston Redevelopment Authority as an urbanist—was married to the 1973–77 vice president of the Historical Society. She was appointed a member of the commission established by City Hall in 1977 that was responsible for the awarding of the label "historic neighborhood."

important role in this regard: indeed, he told the young couple about the South End. Whitaker was also the first to publish an advertisement for the other real estate agent, Betty Gibson, in his paper, *New South End*. Gibson's own trajectory was similarly atypical. Having secured her college degree, she became one of the first women naval officers, then opened up a fashion boutique, and finally worked for a real estate firm in Beacon Hill before opening her own agency.

From this period onward there were a number of real estate agents in the neighborhood, though they were not all professionalized to the same degree. The success of the tour's founder can be explained by her ability to mobilize contacts that she made locally in order to make herself known, and recognized, among potential homeowners. This allowed her to gain exclusive sales rights. Her husband's engagement in the web of neighborhood associations and the municipal advisory board consolidated the couple's positions. But as my second ally put it one day, being a good real estate agent also involves remembering to read the obituaries, in order to make quick contact with those inheriting a property that might now go on the market. She also specialized in lodging houses; her first sales were on behalf of a woman who owned twelve such establishments. She quickly picked up the nickname "kitchen broker," because she initially ran her business from her kitchen, and her activity in the Historical Society allowed her to organize informal meetings that soon resulted in deals. Another advantage of running the annual tour, a major source of funds for the Society, is that it also visits houses that are on the market.

> In 1967, the First Annual South End House Tour was organized by the Society with twelve houses on display . . . Realtors were excited with the prospect of showing potential customers the possibilities behind the staid Victorian facades.

As the real estate agent who initiated the tour explains, "The Historical Society, they would help us. If I have a house on the market, it would be on the tour. So we got good publicity that way." For suburbanites the tour is an opportunity to come under the cover of cultural activity to the South End, which they see as a neighborhood with a poor reputation. Beyond this trip's focus on architecture, the cocktail reception adds to its distinguished tone; for example, in 1975 they "sipped champagne with strawberries and hors d'œuvres . . . while piano music was provided." But its objective is above all to make a South End address seem a less improbable option for outside visitors, providing them with arguments they could use to justify—to themselves and those around them—abandoning their more valorized habitats in the suburbs.

One of the Historical Society's first committees—formed in September 1966, five months after its founding—was devoted to organizing the tour, proving its importance. First used were the houses of the residents most engaged in the South End: Peter Whitaker's for the inaugural tour, the second year the home of the real estate agent who organized it, and many others in the decades that followed. We see on the map of the 1977 tour (p. 33) that the houses visited were limited to a certain part of the neighborhood. This corresponded both to the limits of the historic district and to the more sought-after streets like West Brooklyn, West Newton and West Canton—and it was here, moreover, that many board members lived. The map of the tour also clearly shows the overlap among the spaces of mobilization, the conceptual categories that it promoted, and the new geographic frontiers defining

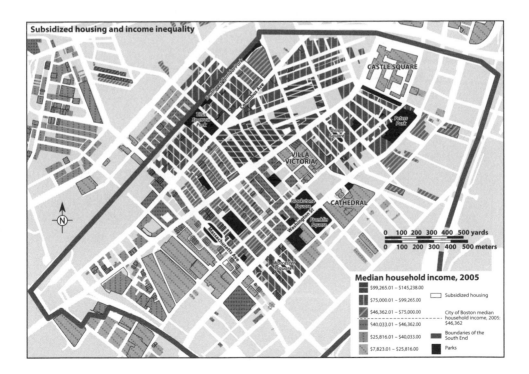

the neighborhood that was now being redesignated. In other words, the three dimensions of gentrification that we are here investigating—the social, symbolic and spatial—are clearly in evidence here. Parcel 706 and those surrounding it thus saw the most rapid gentrification. It was here that the most intensive collective action took place: indeed, the boundaries of the most powerful neighborhood association corresponded to this area. Many members of the Historical Society lived here, and it was here that Brian Hanson set up the first anti-crime patrol.

The Geographical Center of Gentrification

Why did these few parcels see the most rapid transformation? Proximity to the city center surely played some role, as did the lack of vacant and abandoned plots of land or the remains of buildings destroyed by fire. But this part of the neighborhood also differed on account of its relatively small black population. In 1950, black residents made up less than 10 percent of the parcel 706 population, while elsewhere they were above 50 percent or even 75 percent. In the following decades we can observe growth in white-inhabited areas, extending outward from these blocks. In 1980, parcel 706 was 74 percent white. In that same year, management professions made up half of the population. The city parcels surrounding Union Park were also sites of intensive mobilization: Peter Whitaker was a member of his neighborhood association, and other leaders of the movement against bars also lived there. Their project to revalorize their area was stymied, however, by the presence of the Castle Square development to the north, Villa Victoria to the south and the Cathedral project to the east. As such, until the renovation of Washington Street, Tremont Street remained a powerful mental boundary separating the "good" South End from the "bad." In 1980, the parcel where Castle Square was situated was 60.1 percent Asian, while Cathedral's was 35 percent black and 34 percent Hispanic. The parcels beyond Massachusetts Avenue were more than 90 percent black in 1980.

Some parts of the neighborhood showed a striking change in the mismatch of the South End's mean income and that of Boston as a whole. The mean income in parcel 706 was 56 percent of Boston-wide levels in 1960, but 180 percent in 1980. The income level here was now higher than that for the city as a whole, and similar to that of Boston's most chic districts like Back Bay and Beacon Hill; meanwhile, the percentage of the population that was white (83.2 percent) was similar to that of suburbs like Brookline or Newton.

The real estate agents gradually built up a reserved market, and they did so all the more easily because the big real estate firms were at that time focused on the profits they could draw from major inner-city renovation efforts and the extension of the residential suburbs. From the 1960s to the beginning of the 1990s, real estate activity did develop in the South End, but within the limits of the existing housing stock. The neighborhood's reputation remained quite negative until the 1970s. Very closely associating economic poverty with moral degradation, this reputation encouraged a number of young homeowners, notably parents whose children were reaching school age, to sell a few years after moving into the area. We thus understand why a parents' association intervening in the management of a neighborhood public school formed only much later.

This turnover of residents generated profits for real estate agents, as the owners would often turn to the agent they had gone to when they initially bought the property. Nevertheless, these profits did not reach the same level as could be made on construction projects on vacant lots. The abandoned industrial sites that these operations could build on were situated on the margins of the South End, around Washington Street, in the eastern part considered the most disreputable. South End real estate agents, opposed to the destruction of old buildings that would bring developers far more power-ful than themselves onto the market, could not increase supply, so instead they had to work on encouraging demand. The path they chose in order to drive migration to the inner city was not to wait for building renovations, the improvement of urban infrastructure and the transformation of social compo-sition to increase the neighborhood's value. It was additionally a matter of "contribut[ing] to the changing of the image of the South End among those outsiders who still think of it as a colossal skid row," as one of the first Historical Society reports explained in April 1967.

Though not the sole origin of the reorganization of the Boston housing market, the real estate agents' efforts to construct new residential tastes did make a real contribution to it. The kitchen brokers' initiative was crowned with success, to the extent that they established themselves also on the city-wide scene. After having been president of the South End commercial association, Betty Gibson became secretary of the Greater Boston Real Estate Board, one of the city's most powerful economic and political institutions, and home to Boston's developers.

A respectable homosexual sociability

The involvement of a number of gay people in the Historical Society also helps explain the reason for its success. Gays' role in the architectural renovation of gentrified neighborhoods, and also in historical preservation movements, has already been emphasized, and many accounts of the South End speak to this.[14] Out of the eight presidents from 1966 to 1995, five were gay, including one woman. Social traits similar to those of their heterosexual comrades-in-arms helped lead gay residents toward the Historical Society. First, for the real estate agents, financial interests were at stake. Two out of the three main agents were gay, namely Betty Gibson and a man specializing in a gay male clientele. Moreover, a significant number of gay members of the Historical Society shared the group's conservative political leanings. Two of them, very active until the 1980s, today express support for Republicans and a strong hostility toward civil rights movements and their legacy. One of them has been a registered Republican voter since the 1970s.

At the same time, these gay men's involvement in the Historical Society must be understood in relation to their working lives, and, moreover, their sexual and family trajectories. The gay members of the Society—at least those active during the period concluding with its achievement of the label "historic

---

14   "When the South End Historical Society was established in 1966, several of the founders were gay, says Amy McCollum, the Society's current executive director." Scott Kearnan, "Proud History," *South End News*, June 5, 2008. On this subject, read Manuel Castells, "Cultural Identity, Sexual Liberation and Urban Structure: The Gay Community in San Francisco," in *The City and the Grassroots: A Cross-Cultural Theory of Urban Social Movements*, London: Edward Arnold, 1993, pp. 138–70; Will Fellows, *A Passion to Preserve: Gay Men as Keepers of Culture*, Madison: University of Wisconsin Press, 2004.

district" in 1983—were all born before 1940 and discovered their homosexuality in the morally conservative climate of the 1950s, before the Stonewall revolt
in New York in 1969 unleashed the demand for rights based on the assertion of
a gay identity. Joining the Historical Society reflected their ambivalent relationship with the neighborhood. Living in the South End allowed for a homosexual
life because it meant establishing geographical distance from their family and/
or professional milieu, and it also helped allow for encounters with other gay
people; but they could not live this life in the open, homosexuality still being
considered outside the limits of respectability. Indeed, the Historical Society
organized its activities on the basis of explicitly heterosexual norms. Within it,
we find housewives whose husbands occupied comfortable professional positions: indeed, the wives' presence—directed toward social relations and the
cultural and philanthropic spheres—was apiece with the upper class's traditional gender division of social tasks. Moreover, even though eminent members
of the Historical Society did elsewhere participate in a homosexual sociability,
a gay man would normally go to the annual ball accompanied by a lesbian
friend. While this gay socializing took place in homes more than in bars and
clubs, it seems—if we believe certain accounts from the time—that the prohi-
bitions related to sexuality and drug use could here be temporarily lifted in
private spaces.

The Historical Society crystallized these ambiguities. In a sense, the
gays who participated in it re-appropriated (or re-signified) heterosexual
forms. For example, they adopted the costume ball, an emblem of upper-
class distinction, as part of a kitsch taste representing a degree of subversion
of heteronormativity—and in so doing, they were following in gay cultural
tradition. Collecting antique objects, photos and documents is based
more broadly on the valorization of a past in which they have found
models other than those of the family environment or the dominant society. One former Historical Society member's home interior bears witness
to this. In his multi-story home, amidst the dust, there is an accumulation
of antique objects and countless reports. Not an inch of furniture, shelv-
ing or wall space is left unoccupied. On the ceiling, above the Victorian
wallpaper of somber gray and green hue, there is an immense painting
where nude ephebes and angels mix, a vividly colored imitation of
Renaissance style, which we also find in the homes of other gay upper-
middle-class South End residents. The fresco that decorates the walls of

the office where I carried out my interview with him features the names of twenty-odd famous homosexuals, from Michelangelo to Proust via Leonardo da Vinci and that of the owner himself, thus propelling him into the lineage of these great men.

BRICK AND WROUGHT IRON

In 1966, at the time that the Historical Society was founded, the arrival of young white households in the South End had not yet fundamentally transformed its social composition, nor its image. The US perception of space remained strongly structured by the opposition between residential suburbs and run-down inner cities, and Boston neighborhoods—including the prestigious Beacon Hill and Back Bay—were also affected by residents departing for the periphery. Moreover, until the early 1960s the South End's brownstones interested architects no more than they did the public authorities, who in a Boston Redevelopment Authority report from 1962 referred to these houses only in terms of "dilapidated buildings."[15] How, in these conditions, was it possible to bring the architectural offerings of the South End to the forefront, and thus to enhance the neighborhood's reputation? Its ennoblement relied on the production and promotion of new categories of perception, summarized in the adjective "Victorian."

Why these categories, and not a historical narrative privileging the culture of other groups and other eras? Was the reaction against urban renewal, crystallized in Jane Jacobs's 1961 essay, not also accompanied by a symbolic rehabilitation of what had until then been considered mere slums? Given their sociological and ideological profile, the members of the Historical Society were little inclined to promote the South End as a working-class district rich in its diversity, as the oppositional city-planning milieu in contact with black and Hispanic activists in the South End was doing. The Society's

---

15   A guide to Boston architecture published by two architects' associations in 1954 recommended passing only briefly through the South End by car in order to tour its few buildings worthy of interest. Just two pages are devoted to this neighborhood. In 1970, a guide published by the Boston Society of Architects and the MIT Press gave it equal space to other neighborhoods. Donald Freeman, *Boston Architecture: The Boston Society of Architects*, Cambridge, MA: MIT Press, 1970.

investment in "high culture" was the fruit of a certain acculturation, explained by the spread of elite tastes among the Boston middle classes, who ever since the end of the nineteenth century had also wanted to distinguish themselves from the proletariat. Above all, its focus on "Victorian glory" proved a particularly effective strategy, owing to the Boston cultural and preservationist scene and the gradual integration of its preoccupations into the urban policies of the 1970s.

Obtaining a label

The specific type of historical heritage ultimately established can be explained by the allies that contributed to advancing such an enterprise, who were mostly situated outside of the neighborhood. Initially, though, the means used were homemade and led to local alliances.

Support From a Black Elite

Before the Society acquired its own offices, its meetings were hosted by a women's group, the League of Women for Community Service, founded in 1918, which was one of the numerous associations of the black middle class. At the end of the eighteenth century, some of these women had even managed to penetrate the world of the Brahmins.[16] An elite gradually developed around associations and churches seeking to promote respectability and cultural "elevation" as a means of combating racial prejudices. And this was not without a certain disdain for black migrants from the South, seen as a threat to their hard-won place in polite society.

Links with cultural institutions materialized the "privileged relationship" with whites that this black middle class had developed, and contributed to determining the boundaries between respectable black South Enders and the rest of the black population. Despite the very

---

16   Robert C. Hayden, *African-Americans in Boston: More than 350 Years*, Boston: Trustees of the Public Library of the City of Boston, 1991; Adelaide M. Cromwell, *The Other Brahmins: Boston's Black Upper Class, 1750–1950*, Fayetteville, AR: University of Arkansas Press, 1994.

weak representation of African Americans on the Society's board, its bulletin demonstrated the connections between this black elite and the Historical Society, which indeed was part of the Museum of African-American History founded in 1963.

Above all, the success of this enterprise can be understood against the backdrop of the nationwide preservationist movement's advances in the interwar years, though in Boston it had its roots in an older history (the Massachusetts Historical Society was created at the end of the eighteenth century). The taste for history was not only one of the particular dimensions of the Brahmins' relationship to culture; it was at the heart of an identity construction that drew on English culture as well as glorification of American independence. In the nineteenth century, the countless sites of the 1776 revolution located in Massachusetts became the object of careful maintenance. Boston was also the city where Nathan Appleton founded the highly regarded Society for the Preservation of New England Antiquities in 1910.[17]

Among the cultural heritage that now came to be valorized, architecture, particularly that of Beacon Hill, was of particular significance. Charles Bulfinch (1763–1844) established himself as one of the first American architects, with Europeans long having been called on to build the great US cities. He is nationally recognized for works like the Massachusetts State House, the renovation of Faneuil Hall, the Boston General Hospital and even the city park, the Boston Common. The architecture at the heart of this heritage is situated in inner-city districts like Beacon Hill, constructed at the beginning of the nineteenth century. We also find it in two neighborhoods erected a few decades later: the South End, which Bulfinch planned, and Back Bay. Preservationist and author of works on Boston history, Walter Muir Whitehill

---

17   Institutions like the Athenaeum, a prestigious public library and cultural center, also made up part of this movement. The Boston Historic Conservation Committee was created on the initiative of Walter Muir Whitehall, president of the Athenaeum from 1946 to 1973, and Harriet Ropes Cabot, of the Boston Society, in order to protect the houses of Beacon Hill, which became a historic district at the end of the 1960s. The Cabots were a famous Brahmin family. Mark Abrahamson, *Urban Enclaves: Identity and Place in America*, New York: St. Martin's Press, 1996.

belonged to numerous historical societies and was an authoritative figure in the field of local history. The mayor's office solicited his help for the bicentennial celebrations, and indeed during the celebrations in July 1976 he delivered an address at the State House in the presence of Queen Elizabeth II, the mayor and the governor of Massachusetts. It is telling that one of the South End Historical Society's first initiatives was to invite him to speak. The renowned historian gave a talk there in 1966, becoming its first honorary member. Nevertheless it was not until 1983 (when the South End was officially awarded the label "historic") that the Society and its efforts acquired genuine legitimacy. In this, the Society benefited from a movement promoting the brownstones—indeed, the term "brownstoning" was used even before the word "gentrification" made its appearance—that had begun in New York in the late 1960s. The movement's roots lay in that city's Park Slope neighborhood, undergoing significant appreciation in this period.[18]

Above all, the expansion of federal legislation encouraged the South End historic preservation movement, with the creation of the National Trust for Historic Preservation in 1949, the approval of the Historic Preservation Act in 1966 and the National Environmental Protection Act in 1969. This legislation expressed the gradual rejection of demolition as a means of urban regeneration, under the impact of the growing criticisms of urban renewal. In Boston this turn resulted in the 1977 creation of the Landmarks Commission, charged with granting "historic" labels; and in response the Historical Society created a committee to propose the neighborhood's own candidacy. Beyond the rhetorical effort providing the essential justifications for this application, the association threw itself into an enterprise of publications, photography and memorabilia collection. This was all centered on a particular period, with the October 1973 Historical Society bulletin calling on residents to gather "other material pertaining to the South End, or general historic matter from the end of the nineteenth century." In 1971, the Society had photos taken of all the houses in the neighborhood—3,200 in total.

---

18   In 1968, one inhabitant of Brooklyn's Park Slope created a group called the Brownstoner Revival Committee, as well as a magazine, the *Brownstoner*, which much like the South End Historical Society offered advice on renovation. Loretta Lees, Tom Slater and Elvin Wyly, *Gentrification*, New York: Routledge, 2008, pp. 6–7.

In this period, the preservation scene in the USA was largely not central-ized and standardized.[19] The Society thus faced no competition to its legitimacy in constructing and writing the history of the South End. In the absence of any body of specialists, the Landmarks Commission was comprised—as the city website specifies—of nine members, "all residents of the City of Boston, who represent the architectural, preservation and business communities as well as the community at-large." This "communi-ty-at-large" included a number of members of the Historical Society itself, who thus directly participated in judging the South End's candidacy. There were serious clashes between certain members of the Historical Society—particularly the most conservative and most hostile to public housing—and City Hall, whose BRA agency was engaged in the construc-tion of homes for low-income households. Nonetheless, the Society's primary objective accorded with what would become the public authori-ties' own preoccupations as they abandoned demolition as a means of inner-city renovation: the appreciation of the neighborhood through the arrival of new populations.

Under Victoria's patronage

From its creation, the Historical Society organized workshops in which a process of socialization took place, on the model of the tours. One of the Society's first decisions, as noted in its first newsletter appearing in September 1966, was to produce "a pamphlet which is aimed at the education of the public on the do's and don'ts of house renovations, with especial emphasis on preserving architectural details." These workshops were also a form of social-izing people in the taste that it sought to promote, its aim being not only to "help new owners with the unfamiliar tasks of stripping paint, repairing plas-ter, cleaning medallions, repairing windows, [but also] learning something about the wonders of Victoriana."

----

19   The preservation scene was made up of local societies, national-scale founda-tions and a federal structure created in 1949, the National Trust for Historic Preservation, although this last institution played only a restricted role, contenting itself with estab-lishing a list of historic sites—a label bringing only limited assistance to local organizations. Diane L. Barthel, *Historic Preservation: Collective Memory and Historical Identity*, New Brunswick, NJ: Rutgers University Press, 1996.

It constructed this narrative of the South End's history on the basis of perspectives similar to those then informing historians' output with regard to Boston as a whole—foremost the works of Walter Muir Whitehill. Whitehill, who was a fervent admirer of Bulfinch, focused his attentions on the development of an architectural legacy as the Brahmins made their mark on the city. The documents that the Historical Society prepared allow us to see the hierarchies to which such an interpretative approach could give rise, when applied to the particular history of the South End. The bulletin was almost wholly devoted to architecture and decoration, and in 1973 it adopted as its logo the wrought iron that framed the brownstones' external staircases. Above all, the valorization of these material elements rested on the close connection between space and a social elite, glorifying the latter. Not only did it explicitly associate "Victorian splendor" with the upper class of the second half of the nineteenth century, but it implicitly attributed the neighborhood's decline to the poor populations that followed. Its description of home interiors, emphasizing the separation between the masters' and servants' spaces, and of a family life divided among different rooms, also implied what populations it left out of its definition of the "real" South End. It excluded immigrants and the working classes, but also prostitutes, beggars and barflies, who occupied public space while flouting familial norms.

The interest in an "objectively" valuable heritage thus allowed for a series of higly effective operations of distinction. The adjectives the Society used to describe houses, particularly elements of interior or exterior decor, were based on pairs of opposites evoking the refined and the crude, elegance and bad taste. It vaunted "graceful rows of red brick" (tour booklet, 1968) and "charming Victorian rowhouses and residential squares" (tour booklet, 1977). It emphasized "elaborate parquet floors of the Edwardian period" (tour booklet, 1977). A series of singular nouns—"splendor," "beauty" and "glory"—to which it attached various adjectives, like "nineteenth-century" and of course "Victorian"—portrayed objects, buildings and populations as belonging to one same "spirit" or "character." The real estate agent Betty Gibson's recurrent use of this vocabulary, along with her large hats and flash lifestyle, contributed to making her the "grande dame" of the South End, such as was her intention. The adjective "Victorian" invokes not only moralizing prudishness; since the interwar period it has been one of the official categories of architectural and literary history, even if only after 1959 was it defined as "a house built during the reign of Queen Victoria" in the United States.[20] Some of the descriptions in the tour booklets make recurrent use of this shibboleth. In 1997 the Historical Society tour planned to visit eleven houses, and the term crops up in the booklet no fewer than six times. In 1978, the Society organized a visit to "Victorian Connecticut." Ten years before the label "historic" was granted to the South End, on the occasion of the neighborhood's first enrolment in the national register in 1973, it was described as "the largest Victorian brick rowhouse district in the United States." The adjective speaks to a continent, the "Old Continent"; a royalty and economic power combined with an Empire at the height of its expansion; and a queen whose first name and the length of whose reign (1837–1901) seem to represent the invincibility of aristocratic power. Thus we see the erasure of the transformations that shook the United States in that period—namely the formation of the urban proletariat and its rising power, signified by the development of labor unions and, from the 1870s, the first labor strikes, as well as the arrival of immigrants, which marked the history of the South End from the 1880s onward.[21]

Despite the scholarly inspiration of these tour booklets, under the influence of the real estate agents they were written in a style different to classic historical output. They express a preservationist impulse, though without implying that the neighborhood ought to remain exactly as it was in the past. The Society's semi-erudite references to architectural and decoration styles— Italianate, Greek, Revival—and the formulae of the guided tour (the tour often passing by way of a church) are mixed into a more succinct and pragmatic language: the language of advertising. Indeed, from the interwar period onward the real estate agents had promoted development operations that

---

20   *Oxford English Dictionary*, 1993–7.

21   Paradoxically, this historical return to the Victorian period and its town houses leads to another phenomenon taking place from the same epoch being passed over in silence: the first middle-class migration to the suburbs and the craze for quite different architecture in the United States: that is, detached houses. Indeed, it was at the end of the nineteenth century that the semi-rural areas of Boston like Dorchester and Roxbury became "streetcar suburbs," sought after by a white population that wanted to flee the inner-city racial mix.

catered to US middle-class comforts, all the while respecting the architectural past.[22] So they raised no objections over houses being split into
apartments of one or more levels (as condos) or the installation of modern
kitchens and multiple bathrooms;[23] rather, they criticized the transformation
of original houses into tenements or lodging houses. Meanwhile, churches
were protected by the label "historic"—which forbade any modification of
their facades—but no regulation prevented them being bought and sold such
that they could be turned into luxury apartments. Indeed, at the beginning of
the 1980s, the Baptist church on Clarendon Street, in the center of the neighborhood, was converted into several dozen apartments.

The role of economic interests—whose impact is felt more indirectly in
traditional cultural institutions that are run by administrators and professionals—thus distinguishes the Historical Society from its more prestigious
counterparts. This did not prevent the Society from achieving authority
locally at least, if not completely being integrated into the Boston scene. In
1973 Mark Goldweitz—one of the neighborhood's most powerful landlords,
whose wife was a member of the Historical Society's board—rented offices to
the association, and it ultimately bought a property of its own by way of realtor Betty Gibson. Meetings now took place at the association's
headquarters—with their period decor—as did classical music concerts. In
1975, the format and the paper stock of the Society newsletter became more
sophisticated, and the masthead now regularly bore a wrought iron motif. In
1978, the Society offered trips around New England, and the April 1978
newsletter mentioned its having taken on an employee. Above all, the efforts
it made to valorize architecture in the South End by resuscitating the historical role of a prior elite earned the Society a certain recognition. Not only had
the Historical Society joined other prestigious institutions like the Bay State
Historical League and the Bostonian Society, but this latter in turn joined its
South End counterpart in 1977. It seems that even Walter Muir Whitehill
changed his opinion. The chapter entitled "The Flight from the South End"

---

22   On the Australian context, see Gary Bridge, "Estate Agents as Interpreters of
Economic and Cultural Capital. The Gentrification Premium in the Sydney Housing
Market," *International Journal of Urban and Regional Research*, 25: 1 (2001), pp. 87–101.

23   Indeed, on one occasion I came across a classified ad describing a house composed
of "4 bedrooms and 3.5 bathrooms."

in his first book on Boston centered on a narrative of this neighborhood's decline.[24] But as the first Historical Society president told me, "He spoke at one of the very early South End Historical Society meetings, back when I was president, and I had dinner with him and his wife at Betty Gibson's house. He no longer looked down at the South End the way he had when first writing *Boston: A Topographical History.*"

CULTURAL DISTINCTION VERSUS PUBLIC HOUSING

The room to maneuver that the Historical Society enjoyed would also have allowed it to mobilize other reference points; for instance, it could have constructed a history that did not exclusively revolve around the Victorian past and the social elite associated with that era. The resources that Bostonian heritage provides do not alone explain the Society's focus on a high culture. The Historical Society's strategy ought to be understood in the light of the local struggles in which it engaged, for high culture also offered a weapon against the perceived imminent threat of minorities—particularly blacks— and their virulent anti-elite discourse. If the protest movements in Boston were radical, the reaction they provoked was itself particularly violent. It especially took the form of a revolt arising from the white Irish districts, opposing the school desegregation measures implemented from 1974 onward. The South End Historical Society's actions, the plans that it promoted and the activity it pursued in opposition to public housing are a less well-known aspect of the history of this white backlash. This group expressed a more subtle form of resistance, but it was no less tenacious. And we must also take this into account in order to understand mobilized homeowners' lack of interest in valorizing "diversity" prior to the 1990s, as well as the limitations of the valorization that did emerge subsequently.

At the heart of the struggles

The Historical Society occupied a privileged place within the world of civic associations emerging from the late 1960s onward. It was one of the new groups that appeared in this epoch, like the City Hall's advisory board,

---

24   Walter Muir Whitehill, *Boston: A Topographical History*, Cambridge, MA: Harvard University Press, 1959.

SEPAC, or more ephemeral and informal groups like the neighborhood watch groups and the forces seeking to close down bars. Much like the neighborhood associations, it assumed greater importance in the 1990s once SEPAC had disappeared and activist movements had declined. In this period, following the creation of the Landmarks Commission, the Historical society fought actively for the South End to be recognized as a historic district However, while it was one among the groups that claimed to represent the whole South End from the early 1970s on, this concealed the weight of commercial interests that lay behind the universalism of its "cultural" banner.

The Historical Society brought together South End inhabitants of mainly conservative outlook. This did not stop it from enjoying widespread recognition, translating into many hundreds of residents taking out memberships. Its endeavors had a positive echo among a wide range of homeowners who sought a symbolic revalorization of their addresses, but also simply a sense of local belonging, to which knowledge of the neighborhood's history would contribute. Another index of the Society's base was the fact that it enjoyed significant representation within the most powerful of the neighborhood associations. The inhabitants belonging to both the Society and to neighborhood associations were particularly active in negotiating urban renewal with the BRA in the 1970s. Many among them were elected to SEPAC and made financial contributions to the planting of trees or even the installation of lamps in previously barely lit streets. Likewise, the South End's sidewalks were considered of low quality—often cement, sometimes simply covered in asphalt. The Historical Society and the neighborhood associations mobilized around the replacement of the sidewalks with brick in the mid-1970s, and they succeeded in negotiating the laying of "period" bricks.[25]

In the 1970s and especially in the 1980s, the Historical Society was supported by the economic interests of the realtors and developers engaged in the highly lucrative operation of turning lodging houses into condos. The Society also entertained close relations with City Hall—with some among its members who worked there acting as conduits—and through the Landmarks Commission. Yet it also did so in a more unofficial way, through

---

25   The South End had never actually had brick pavements. The "historic" dimension often referred more to the urban forms of the Back Bay and Beacon Hill—reproduced on postcards for tourists—than to the real past.

the developers' campaign financing for mayoral candidates.[26] While its own political views were marginal, the Historical Society thus came to occupy a central position in the South End, as demonstrated by the fact that it was at the heart of the struggles raging in the 1960s and early 1970s. Indeed, in 1969, the South End Tenants' Council, which initially mobilized against the Mindick brothers, pursued its campaign by targeting developers, some of whom were part of the Historical Society. But soon the tenants' movements were not only agitating around the poorest residents' housing conditions, but also explicitly denouncing the arrival of gentrifiers. They invoked the "real" South End — made up of poor inhabitants and minorities, and not real estate agents and the incoming rich residents. As such, the third issue of the activist group CAUSE's paper, the *People's South End News*, described the South End's property owners as "Criminals of the South End. These are landlords who rob the people of decent, low-cost housing. They do not belong in our community."

As we saw in Chapter 2, another South End landlord, Mark Goldweitz, was targeted by squatters. Having first been a tenant before buying a house in 1971, he acquired forty-five buildings and renovated 279 apartments, which he then turned into condos. In accordance with the tastes promoted by the Historical Society, he devoted himself to minute restorations valorizing houses' "historical" elements, as combined with the comfort and modernity that the new arrivals sought. He was the first landlord to do this, additionally restoring woodwork, plastered ceilings and marble fireplaces. But he did not limit himself to "preservation" only. His luxury cars and suits were at odds with the traditional South End property owners' style, and he also invented "modern" means of conserving buildings, such as sanding down the wall plaster to show off the bare brickwork, installing skylights and arranging roof terraces.

The Historical Society faced direct challenges, notably from the radical group, South End for South Enders. One of the Society's earliest tours, in 1971, was blocked by a demonstration led by Mel King declaring, "The Historical Society is a Lackey of the Real Estate Agents." A couple of years later, in 1973, Society members attending the annual ball were greeted by

---

26   Susan S. Fainstein, *The City Builders: Property Development in New York and London, 1980–2001*, Lawrence, KS: University Press of Kansas, 2001.

250 activists shouting, "Stop the Victorian criminals," and "South End Historical Society is an upper-class KKK." These activists gave a quite different meaning to the word "Victorian," as their leaflets distributed at this event explained: "The luxury housing developers and others at this ball can be considered as nothing less than true enemies of the poor, the real South Enders . . . So here this obscene 'Victorian ball' goes on and those who love our townhouses but don't want us to live in them sip their champagne and dance gaily."[27]

During these struggles that were waged in the name of the "true" South End, poor populations' right to remain in a neighborhood whose prices were about to mushroom clashed with respect for private property and financial investments. The Historical Society played a key role in these struggles, and for activist groups it came to symbolize wealthy and racist elitism disguised as a matter of cultural taste. The Society was concerned not just by the direct attacks that it was subject to, but also by the dangers that it foresaw in this period—which were not limited to the threat the activists posed. The Society's members were troubled by the BRA's plans, whose direction—a matter of uncertainty after 1968—fluctuated in tandem with the political and social balance of forces, and which, given the significant means committed to urban renewal, could be of considerable impact. The proposed large-scale public housing projects posed an immediate threat to remake the neighborhood's architecture into the image of the brownstones.

In fact, at the end of the 1960s there was a sharp contrast in the South End between the rows of often run-down brownstones—sometimes divided by empty or abandoned lots, or what remained of buildings demolished after fires—and the large plots assigned to public housing. For the Historical Society, the task at hand was to stop these construction projects going ahead, since taking in the worst-housed residents—often black people—threatened the revalorization of the neighborhood. The economic interests at play here were further sharpened by the profits already realized in what was a very lucrative neighborhood, thanks to its very low purchase prices. Mark Goldweitz, who renovated fifty-six buildings between 1971 and 1973, took in $156,520 a year, on the basis of an investment of $399,380 in thirty-two buildings—that is, an

---

27   J. Anthony Lukas, *Common Ground: A Turbulent Decade in the Lives of Three American Families*, New York: Vintage Books, 1985, pp. 264, 434–5.

annual return equivalent to 39 percent of his investment.[28] So we can understand what drove the Historical Society to elaborate a certain history of the South End. Property interests and the Society's members' hostility toward radical movements encouraged the relegation of immigrant and poor populations to a symbolic invisibility, in favor of a new, reforming figure: the "pioneer."

Indeed, the Society's efforts to valorize Victorian splendor always went hand in hand with the promotion of a minority who would be sensitive to this view. This thus allowed it to add a new phase, reconquest, onto the end of the somber narrative of decline presented in Walter Muir Whitehill's works. It presented this sensibility, a mix of cultural taste and knowledge of the "real" South End, as the basis for an engagement bringing a new neighborhood into existence. One anecdote recurred in several of the accounts that I collected: the spectacle one winter day, when the South End was covered in snow and free of garbage and other traces of its decline, of the neighborhood appearing as it did in its glory years. And this was a look to which some hoped it would return permanently.[29] The spring 1991 Historical Society newsletter, in an article on its own history, explained:

> Some people were beginning to realize the neglected beauty of the buildings and the richness of the community, but the word had not yet spread to the world. After decades of decline and abandonment, the South End still bore the stigma of a slum. Newspaper articles graphically described its skid row, its prostitution, its unsavory barrooms, its despairing elderly in dingy rooming houses, and its trash-filled alleys. Only a small minority bothered to savor its architectural gems.

The legitimacy of this reforming "pioneer" figure was strengthened by the lionization of the neighborhood's first realtor.

---

28   1972 Harvard Business School report, cited by John H. Mollenkopf, *The Contested City*, Princeton: Princeton University Press, 1983, p. 183, n. 3.

29   We find an interviewee of Herman Rappaport's recounting this story: "Producing a mystical effect, the snow covered the dirt and grime which had become characteristic of the neighborhood. The swell-front row houses regained their long lost elegance. Snow-covered Union Park assumed a nineteenth-century appearance." Alan Herman Rappaport, "From Skid Row to Brownstone Chic: Neighborhood Revitalization in the South End of Boston, a Case," thesis, Harvard University, 1975.

A Heroic Figure
Betty Gibson

My interviewees' recurring references to Betty Gibson, in an admiring and sometimes nostalgic tone, told me of her role in South End history long before I understood the significance of her position in the real estate sector. Her significance was not limited to her professional activity during her lifetime, but extended to what was made of her after her death in 2001 — the legacy of a woman among the pioneers who saw the neighborhood's "potential" before everyone else, amidst the dust and the rubble, and "opening the eyes" of the unaware.

On the website of her agency—which was bought up by an international realty firm—we read, "In 1962, Betty Gibson, a woman with a pioneering spirit and great vision, founded our company in Boston's South End. With its bow front Victorian row houses on picturesque, if neglected, side streets, Betty knew the South End was a neighborhood destined for rebirth . . . The South End has surpassed the expectations of even the most visionary people like Betty Gibson."

This figure appears as a heroine in numerous accounts, as a woman who was able to change the course of history. It's relatively unsurprising that the "John Wayne of gentrification"[30] was a lesbian—it speaks to the recomposition of the frontiers of gender and sexuality within the elite studied here. In any case, her canonization in neighborhood history allows for an emphasis on financially disinterested activity rather than commercial interests, and also—on account of the demiurgic character attributed to her activity—in turn reduces the previous state of the South End to a void. One resident offered this recollection: "One of our neighbors was the woman who created the South End. Her name is Betty Gibson. She was a real estate agent. She lived on this street on my block. She was one of the first to see the potential of these houses."

---

30   Neil Smith and Peter Williams, *Gentrification of the City*, Boston: Allen and Unwin, 1986, p. 17.

A relatively critical article in the Boston paper *The Phoenix* in May 8, 1979 described her as "the first lady of 'gentrification.'" And under a photo of a Victorian interior (probably Betty's own home), the article carries a quotation from an activist SEPAC member, stating that "she doesn't care about the history of people, only buildings"—her motives being essentially financial. Yet by the mid-2000s Betty Gibson had become almost above criticism. The memory of the opposition that she sparked has disappeared together with the decline of activism. Today all that is left is the image that she herself patiently constructed—the aristocratic, visionary posture that she assumed, along with the manner of speaking and clothing that went with it.

The Committee for a Balanced South End

The Historical Society's rhetoric and the very stark divisions it established between the pioneers of urban renaissance and the populations who had been part of the city's decline is thus also explained by the struggles in which it was engaged. Indeed, in the mid-1970s the Society waged a counteroffensive, also expressed in its increasingly open resistance to the construction of public housing. A group closely connected to the Society led this struggle, namely the Committee for a Balanced South End. The husband of the realtor who organized the tour was at the origin of this committee, together with two other residents: a property manager who was the founder of a neighborhood association exclusively for homeowners, and an architect who was a member of the Historical Society board. Within the initial circle we also find five other Society board members. And as a sign of the initiative's first adherents' extended networks, a neighborhood association decided to give official backing to the committee.

This body was less long-standing and organized than the Historical Society, but it is no less important. Firstly, its effort to block public housing was at least partly successful. Secondly, it provides a terrain for observing an essential process of group formation: the definition of the group's limits. The relative sidelining of some of its members, considered too extremist by the Historical Society's leaders, traced the boundary of what was and was not respectable, and clearly pointed out what were unacceptable discourse and practices.

The birth of the Committee for a Balanced South End came in response to radical activists taking over the advisory board SEPAC. This initially prompted fourteen residents to submit a 600-signature petition to the mayor's office, before they established the committee in December 1973. More generally, the creation of the Committee for a Balanced South End took place within the context of a rising reaction against the civil rights movement, both in the North and the South. Not only did the radicalism of Black Power alienate liberals, it also made the white conservatives' opposition more visible and audible. The 1968 election of Richard Nixon, who claimed to represent the silent majority, marked an important moment of this white backlash. Moreover, the president supported the opponents of the Boston school desegregation plan—a plan that had elicited particularly virulent reactions in this city. The situation took a turn in 1974 when, after years of unsuccessful struggle by organizations like the NAACP, a Supreme Court judge forced the city's school board to desegregate the education system. It thus implemented a plan to redistribute pupils across the different parts of the city—except for the residential suburbs. Moving children from Irish areas to the schools of Roxbury, and black children to South Boston, East Boston and Charlestown, sparked anger in these Irish bastions. There were violent protests, backed by municipal councillors like Louise Hicks. The backlash included demonstrations against the arrival of buses transporting black children, which was greeted with hails of stones. There were attacks and murders.[31] In this context, a more open opposition to the public housing struggle led by black leader Mel King came to be expressed in the South End. He had a certain base of support at this time, having been elected a member of the state legislature. The Committee for a Balanced South End's activity even more explicitly posed the stakes that had been in play ever since the beginning of the mobilization and the creation of SEPAC—namely, the use of the local authorities' land reserves during the urban renewal period. It demanded a moratorium on public housing construction and for the plots controlled by City Hall to be made available for homes that would be sold at market value.

From 1974 to 1976, the Committee for a Balanced South End initiated court proceedings six times. In 1974, its objective was to stop the renovation of

31   Ronald P. Formisano, *Boston Against Busing: Race, Class and Ethnicity in the 1960s and 1970s,* Chapel Hill: University of Carolina Press, 1991.

185 public housing units by a community corporation that had formerly been a tenants' association. The mobilization was not limited to the new white homeowners only—one of the members of the Committee was the energetic lodging-house owner Louise Fitzpatrick. The Historical Society did not officially support this initiative, but that did not keep its most active members—who were linked to City Hall—from fighting the construction of public housing, as they today acknowledged in my interviews with them. While the Historical Society did not officially support the Committee's efforts, it did bring its resources to the fight. The court proceedings were based on laws protecting the "environment," but the question of historic preservation was ever present. The records of the proceedings launched in 1978 summarize the plaintiff's arguments, demanding on the basis of the 1966 National Historic Preservation Act that the BRA not make any decision potentially "causing or allowing the demolition of the buildings presently standing on the site of the proposed project, many of which are historically and architecturally significant."[32]

The majority of the Committee's suits ended in failure.[33] Nonetheless, after the Committee's participation in a hearing in Washington, the Secretary of State for Housing and Urban Development imposed a moratorium on the construction of subsidized housing in the South End, halting a project that the BRA had earlier approved—providing 145 units for low- and middle-income households. Of course, this decision was bound up with the restrictions

---

32   The "historic" argument was all the more effective (even when the neighborhood did not yet have this label) because the other side put forward no alternative historical narrative. Certainly, some issues of the SEPAC newsletter from the late 1970s retraced the history of "old inhabitants"—from a black NAACP member to a Russian Jewish immigrant who was a prominent figure in the labor movement. But the absence of any written transmission of working-class history made it difficult to mobilize figures and reference points that could have challenged the exclusive focus on architecture. Richard Hoggart, *The Uses of Literacy*, New Brunswick, NJ: Transaction Publishers, 1998.

33   One case was brought in 1974 in opposition to the construction of 181 dwellings in the Villa Victoria development, and another against Pine Street Inn's renovation of four buildings in 1976 to house formerly homeless people. The proceedings that sought to stop the construction of 181 public housing units on Tremont Street were not successful either; though the judge forced the builders to keep 25 percent of the dwellings at market price, there was a lack of takers and thus they returned to the subsidized sector.

on federal funding under the Nixon presidency. But the Boston mayor's office's policy turn in these years also owed a great deal to local mobilizations. The BRA report on public housing, produced in 1978 after the battles that raged through the South End, explained that "past experience clearly demonstrates that most fully subsidized developments have had considerable difficulty maintaining long-term social and financial stability." And it concluded, "As part of a concerted effort to avoid these persistent problems in the future, the BRA will support those proposed housing developments, beyond those currently designed, that include a substantial number of market rate units, in order to guarantee a feasible and realistic income mix over an extended period of time." Long before the construction plan launched in 1988, here was a first recognition of the principle of mixed units. At the same time, the majority of the projects constructed in Roxbury and Dorchester as part of urban renewal had now finally been completed. As such, while the urban renewal carried out in the South End gave birth to a local elite attached to diversity, it is worth remembering that in Boston like elsewhere, urban renewal had clearly increased the social-spatial segregation of the city: "An important secondary effect of urban renewal was to accelerate racial turnover, expand the ghetto, and shift the threat of ghetto expansion from elite white districts to working-class white neighborhoods."[34]

A fragile respectability

The Committee for a Balanced South End showed that the definition of the class and racial boundaries at play in the construction of the South End gentrifiers' identity was not without its tensions. The mid-1970s saw a conflict break out, crystallizing around the publication of a booklet devoted to the neighborhood's history. This was commissioned on the occasion of the bicentennial celebrations, which were of particular significance in Boston, a key site in the 1776 War of Independence. This event strengthened the historic preservation movement, with the South End Historical Society benefiting directly from the public authorities' forays into a glorious past. Indeed, the American Revolution had played a central role in the emergence of the first patriotic and historical societies in the late nineteenth century, a number of

---

34   Douglas Massey and Nancy Denton, *American Apartheid: Segregation and the Making of the Underclass*, Cambridge, MA: Harvard University Press, 1993, p. 56.

them formed around the sites where the heroes of US history like George Washington had distinguished themselves. And the preservationists had little difficulty mobilizing this Revolution again two centuries after the fact, in order to strengthen their positions.

All this activity encouraged the South End Historical Society's growing integration into the Boston cultural scene, which also partly explains the sidelining of the Society's members who were engaged in the Committee for a Balanced South End. The most extreme among them was commissioned to draw up a history of the South End, to be included in a collection covering every Boston neighborhood. The June 1975 Society newsletter announced that this volume would be coming out shortly. However, the Historical Society never came to an agreement over the text, and it was not published. Reading the eighty-page manuscript—which is still today kept in the Society's archives—it is easy to see the close connections between its author and the Committee for a Balanced South End, of which he was a member. Among the Historical Society activities emphasized in this text, the author referred to the court cases seeking "to halt the destruction of the architectural fabric of this historic and architecturally important neighborhood." The manuscript is essentially composed of a series of pieces detailing the history and architecture of the South End, and it also includes a section devoted to "famous and colorful South Enders." The passage on Malcolm X—crossed out by the manuscript's reviewer—clearly shows the writer's ambivalent attitude toward the black leader.

The conflicts here were partly ideological. The racism of certain Committee members goes some way to explaining the discredit into which they fell, with the author threatened with a defamation suit. He spent part of his time writing violently indignant letters that caused a certain annoyance among the authorities, as the exchange of correspondence my second ally archived demonstrates. The public housing body wrote to him on January 23, 1974, reproducing a passage from the historian's earlier missive:

> Is the lifestyle of the poor (garbage thrown out of the windows, drunkenness, panhandling, radio speakers in windows, total disregard of private property, blowing horns in the street rather than ringing doorbells, drugs, prostitution, urinating in alleys on private property and even out windows, noisily living all night on the street in the summer, and complete lack of discipline over children) compatible with a decent urban environment?

The public housing body responded,

> We feel that many of the "issues" you have raised—such as . . . the claim of
> past crime problems because "teenagers from these large families invaded
> homes, stole property, mugged residents, terrorized the elderly, and regu-
> larly rolled customers as they left the whore houses"—are unworthy of a
> response and we will not dignify them with one.

The Committee for a Balanced South End's president's similar positions and
strong-arm methods (going as far as arson, according to some accounts) also
began to become common knowledge. Moreover, the group was openly
backed by South Boston municipal councillor Louise Hicks, a leading figure
in the fight against school desegregation. A lawyer and elected member of the
city school board, she joined in actions protesting against busing. Most importantly, with her famous 1968 campaign slogan, "You know where I stand,"
she became the standard-bearer of a white population who sharply rejected
any active measures to fight racial segregation. During a session of the city
council devoted to the South End on November 2, 1974, she quoted the
Committee for a Balanced South End's survey of the public housing that had
been built, before turning to this Committee's demands, which she adopted
as her own: "The Committee of Citizens for a Balanced South End request
that the Boston Redevelopment Authority call an immediate moratorium on
all subsidized housing in the South End."

At a time when civil rights struggles were starting to restrict the space for
expressing racist views, and in a neighborhood to which many liberals had
now moved, a Committee that—unlike the Historical Society's official literature—explicitly described poor and black residents' presence in terms of a
"dumping ground" had become an embarrassment.[35] Another attitude was
emerging, which we see in well-off South End residents' use of South
Boston as a foil. Referring to the battles waged by racists in South Boston
allowed these particular South Enders to show off their own racial tolerance, by way of a contrast—though certainly they themselves were not

---

35   "No More! The Dumping Ground Is Full"—title of a column published by one
of the Committee's fourteen founding members in the *South End News* of August 21,
1976. See also Lukas, *Common Ground*, p. 434.

totally lacking in prejudice. This attitude prevailed within the Historical Society also. Its then-president was trying to integrate herself into the ranks of prominent Bostonians, by way of the connections linking her to the wealthy upper class. This could only strengthen her objections to the Committee historian's lack of self-restraint. Ultimately, what happened in the Historical Society and the Committee for a Balanced South End sheds light on the manner in which the most conservative element of the gentrifiers dealt with the specter of a radical redefinition of class and racial relations. So we can understand the Society's weak intellectual output, given that its potential writers were firmly situated in the "extremist" camp of the Committee. The fact that the extremists were unable to conform to the degree of "neutrality" necessary for any legitimate historical work combined with their lack of recognition in the academic world. They were thus shunned by the people who were now drawing closer to Boston's high culture scene; and this ostracism endures still today.

In the end, the Historical Society's output—other than its tour booklets and newsletter—barely went beyond the level of self-published photocopies. The resident who established himself as its historian in the late 1980s was the partner of the son of one of the first realtors. He became an active member of the Society in 1987 and put his name to several texts, including the tour booklets and a brief history of Union Park. However, even this was just a mimeographed document of fifteen pages, sold for $2 at the neighborhood association's annual picnic.

More "diverse" histories

For many South End residents, the Historical Society today appears as a conservative body too explicitly linked to a social elite. The transformations of the US historic preservation movement in the 1980s and 1990s and the efforts to integrate minorities' and working-class districts' history in the name of "cultural pluralism"[36] found little echo in the South End Historical Society. It was thus logical enough that it was within the most liberal wing of the local elite that an initiative emerged offering another vision of history based on very different practices, albeit one that did not openly compete with the Society. From the beginning of the 2000s, guided walks of the South End

---

36   Barthel, *Historic Preservation*.

were organized every month, except in winter. In contrast to the images put forward in the Historical Society's rituals, for example in its annual tours, the objective of these walks was to celebrate a "diverse" neighborhood, suiting what had by then become the local elite's catchphrase. Through the manner in which it is organized and the discourse that accompanies it, this walk—a particular relation to space—invokes, portrays and advances a certain vision of the neighborhood.

It was a neighborhood association that first organized these walks, on the initiative of my first ally. The South End community center is today responsible for running them. Publicized via the Internet and the local *South End News*, they are open to all South End residents, and in order to widen the spectrum of participants, the meal that follows is held in a moderately priced restaurant. Dogs are explicitly welcome ("Walks are pet friendly"), in a nod to a substantial group of gentrifiers. And this also sends another signal—for when dogs are present, we are getting away from historical discovery and entering into another urban practice, namely daily walks with a pet. In general around twenty residents usually take part in the walks, including three or four people with dogs.

The walking tour is not only about taking the dog out, however. While it is rather short—rarely more than an hour long—by way of the guide's comments it offers a certain narrative of the South End's history and, inextricably linked to this, a vision of its present. The neighborhood that these walks portray is the South End of diversity, far more than the South End of Victorian architecture. None of the walks that I attended, or of which I was made aware through the e-mail list, was devoted to architecture. Only one, inviting residents to discover the "literary South End," was centered on culture in the narrow sense. A concern for openness drove the choice of guides invited on each occasion. So the walks featured a mix of contrasting figures from the civic scene, some of them dating back to the 1970s—from my second ally, an activist now opposed to gentrification, to a conservative real estate developer specialized in transforming buildings into condos.

The preferred choices were individuals whose own biographies and anecdotes echoed the South End's rich diversity of experiences and populations. They resuscitated the past of the working class, immigrants and even crime. The walk guided by one colorful policeman, author of a column in the *South End News* in the 1980s, emphasized the dangers that people used to face on every street corner given the mix of hookers, thieves and mafiosi. Poverty, inevitably described in folkloristic terms, has entered into South End herit-age, the walk's discourse here marking its distance from the stigmatization that appeared in Historical Society literature. A certain relativization was also at work in a walk guided by my second ally, when she recounted her 1964 arrival in the neighborhood. Hair-raising anecdotes always finished with a wisecrack putting a different spin on the violence that took place. This violence was not minimized as much as posed in a different light, as one among many dimensions of a working-class neighborhood's trials and tribula-tions. Thus she adopted a humorous tone to describe the three days of rioting sparked by a beauty contest organized by Hispanic residents, the outcome of which angered another group in the neighborhood. Our guide's delivery of this anecdote made the attendees burst out laughing, even when she mentioned a group of youth attacking police cars.

The real estate developer's narrative took an exactly opposite approach, without anyone remarking on the contradiction: diversity, after all, implies the diversity of all points of view, which the rejection of conflict allows to coexist within one common heritage. While the previous guide had incorporated memories of her bohemian student years into her narrative, the developer's history recounted his professional success. He pointedly noted the price of a house bought in the early 1970s—$9,000—and the attendees exclaimed how they envied his instinct for a deal. He stuck to the approach of evoking a dangerous neighborhood, a foul-smelling South End populated by alcoholics and disturbed people "with illnesses." He explained that thirty years ago, if we had come to the place where we were now standing, three drunkards would already have come and hassled us. Insisting on the fact that this was once a very dangerous area, he emphasized the bravery of the "pioneers", himself included. Indeed, the presence of alcoholics was a recurrent theme in his narrative, in which he portrayed himself as having been active in the campaign against bars. Of course, this is not an entirely negative portrayal. But while the previous guide insisted on the terrible conditions in which immigrants lived, notably the Puerto Ricans, the developer reduced the poor to a series of devi-ant behaviors, except for a few worthy cases. Among these, he mentioned Charlie, a former alcoholic who was proud—according to our guide—of not having had a drink for several decades. He emphasized the wealth of social ties in the neighborhood and the ease of obtaining local insights (and from this we can detect the importance of such information to his professional activity). Having recounted a particularly profitable deal, he exclaimed, "There was always something going on!"

The walk appears to be one of the forms of socialization organized for the new inhabitants' benefit. The first time that I went along, a member of an association was handing out leaflets for John Kerry, who was at that time the Democrats' candidate for the 2004 presidential election. For my first ally, the organizer of these walks, they were clearly very much part of the effort to educate new arrivals, who were particularly encouraged to come and discover the neighborhood. After the walk guided by the real estate developer, we dined at a restaurant together with a couple who had just arrived in the South End. The objective was to help them become conscious of this social mix, evoking its most troubling aspects (but which for the most part belonged to the past), and above all, insisting on the possibility of overcoming any disagreements. Before a walk began, they announced fundraisers that participants were invited to support—for example, plugging the soirée organized by the social workers' association for which I volunteered. My first ally extolled this association's capacity to fight delinquency, thus emphasizing the virtues of a preventative rather than repressive approach.

The "spirit of place"[37] created during these walks thus had little to do with Victorian splendor. Here was a South End boasting of a capacity and a long-standing history of accepting and welcoming diversity. The group leader's attitude toward the Historical Society was telling: she had never joined, and even if she had friends among its members, she gently mocked the ball, its behavioral codes—which she thought outmoded—and the straitlacedness of its participants.

In 2000 the Historical Society still played a role in the local civic association scene, albeit on the margins. Participating in its events is a marker of socializing among the local elite, and its most active members generally live in the most prestigious part of the South End, on the "good" side of Tremont Street—proof that this frontier still holds, in their eyes. Moreover, on the streets where they live, reconversions of condo buildings into town

---

37 Pierre-Yves Saunier, "Le syndrome d'Aladin ou le génie des lieux comme objet pour les sciences sociales," in Dominique Poulot, *Patrimoine et modernité*, Paris: L'Harmattan, 1998, pp. 185–97.

houses—bought by very rich households—are frequent. At the same time, their advocacy of conservative positions and maintenance of an elitist attitude alienate them from many residents, with the oldest of the Society's members preventing it from adopting a less restrictive definition of local heritage. Others, like the eccentric historian in his house full of dust and improbable collectors' items, are relegated to a past in which real estate agents now take little interest. While he still goes to his neighborhood association picnics, he remains outside the sociability organized around the South End's restaurants. Having grown old, and hardly well turned out, he is conscious that he is now considered a "bum on the stoop," to use his own term. And he tells a revealing anecdote in this regard. A realtor was showing someone around the house next to his own, and through the window he heard the realtor tell the potential buyer—who was astonished by the old man's rather ravaged appearance—that "he won't live forever."

Besides, while the woman who today leads the Historical Society represents continuity between its founders and its current members, and allows for the transmission of resources constituted within the Society; however she also impedes its renewal, in terms of its rhetoric but also from a financial point of view. The financial resources that the tour and the ball provide are barely sufficient to pay the upkeep of its offices. The reduced participation in the Society—whose links to the real estate sector nonetheless remain solid—principally speaks to the fact that it has, in a sense, achieved its mission. The big firms that dominate the market can content themselves with drawing profits from the added value that the Society has created. The Society is still the site of a respectable sociability, but in spite of this, it has lost one of its principal attractive traits: offering a local elite a valorizing identity. From the 1990s, the label "artist" emerged as a more useful social marker for those residents who wanted to emphasize their attachment to diversity, now that they had become omnivorous in their relation to culture, and faced fewer social conflicts.

AN HISTORIC NEIGHBORHOOD OR AN ARTISTIC ONE?

In the early 2000s the Historical Society had to deal with a competing approach to valorizing the South End. Once it had acquired the label "historic," other interests pushed for a considerably different representation—and thus a different history—of the neighborhood. The interests at play were not incompatible. But the "historic" reference today represents just one form of distinction, mixed among other registers based on openness and modernity, the artistic and the trendy, ultimately constituting a hybrid cultural taste.

From SoHo to SoWa

In New York, the role of investors leveraging culture to valorize certain districts, notably the "artistic" Lower East Side of the 1990s, was of decisive importance. The South End was marked by a somewhat later progression that, unlike the cases of New York or Chicago, ultimately played out in opposition to the artistic community rather than with its support. This community, which was barely active or visible in the first decades of gentrification, developed only weak links with the mobilized gentrifiers and drew minimal profits from the revalorization of Washington Street. The role of artists—often identified with the "pioneers" of gentrification—eventually proved marginal here; yet the label "artistic" was of considerable importance. How can we explain this curious "marriage of 'gentrification' with the 'art market'"?[38]

While the effort to create a South End heritage took place in the northeastern area of the neighborhood, the "artistic" label was used in the area that did not entirely belong to the historic district: the southwestern portion. The renovation of Washington Street marked a decisive turning point, since the extent of the land that could now be valorized set considerable financial interests in motion. Washington Gateway's director estimated the development in the area as worth $5 billion in 2004. City mobilization had been decisive in the mid-1990s, but here the reference to history and the appeal to heritage were only very little utilized, despite the institutionalization of the Historical Society. The federal program supporting the renovation of Washington Street focused on so-called historic districts, but it gave priority to commercial development

---

38   Jean-Samuel Bordreuil, "SoHo ou comment le 'village' devint planétaire," in *Villes en parallèles* 20–21 (December 1994), p. 146; Christopher Mele, *Selling the Lower East Side: Culture, Real Estate, and Resistance in New York City*, Minneapolis: University of Minnesota Press, 2000; Richard Lloyd, *Neo-Bohemia: Art and Commerce in the Post-Industrial City*, New York: Routledge, 2006. On artists' marginal role in the gentrification process, see, Elsa Vivant and Éric Charmes, "La gentrification et ses pionniers: le rôle des artistes en question," in *Métropoles*, http://metropoles.revues.org/document1972.html.

without tackling the question of whether this approach was compatible with maintaining diversity. The city's website is particularly telling in this regard, when it refers to the capacity of these "historic commercial districts to compete in today's market. The Main Streets program helps the local districts to capitalize on their unique cultural and historical assets while focusing on the community's economic development needs." Though in 2005 Washington Gateway won the plaudits of the National Trust for Historic Preservation, it devoted little energy to protecting architecture. It was more concerned with applying the definition of "heritage" elaborated by the Historical Society to modern buildings. So for the construction programs of the 1990s, it developed "an image of town houses" similar to the brownstones in the area closer to the city center, picking up on "elements of the typology of the South End, with internal courtyards and the addition of brickwork."[39] This body's logo was a picture of Boston's famous streetlamps, as seen in Beacon Hill—and, from the 1970s, so too in the South End.

Promoting Washington Street by making reference to its history would have demanded a valorization of the neighborhood's working-class and industrial past. But how could this be done, without contradicting the official image of the South End—a Victorian neighborhood of brownstones? Would it not have been necessary to find a heritage interest in the old factories, and thus considerably open up the definition of what heritage means? The recomposition of South End economic actors doubtless played a determining role in the rupture that took place in symbolic investments in the neighborhood. Indeed, the interests associated with the Historical Society in the 1960s and 1970s— with its famous "kitchen brokers"—gave way in the 1980s to firms that were becoming significantly more concentrated. As in other gentrified districts, notably Manhattan's Lower East Side in the 1980s, we see in the South End the emergence of developers linked to the big firms, which given the boom in real estate prices were now the only ones able to invest in the neighborhood. These companies largely replaced the activities of residents who had previously devoted themselves to buying and renovating properties through their homemade businesses.[40]

---

39   Marie-Hélène Bacqué (ed.), *Projet urbain en quartier ancien. La Goutte d'Or, South End*, Paris: PUCA, 2005, p. 98

40   "Prior to the 1980s, landlords operating in the East Village were primarily petty

In the South End, Silvio Dante, the representative of one of these firms, led a campaign to attach the label "artistic" to the neighborhood—entirely in support of his commercial interests. He had owned a real estate agency since the 1970s, throwing himself into the buying and renovation of properties at the border between Back Bay and the South End. To this day, he controls dozens of South End buildings, particularly in the once-abandoned lot to the east of Washington Street, where he built up an impressive portfolio in the 1980s. At that time, he tried without success to expel the artists who were living there illegally. He allowed his holdings to grow in value before dedicating himself to renovating his properties in the mid-1990s. The crisis in the housing market having come and gone, Dante faced an advantageous economic situation, and it was also particularly favorable to the use of the "artistic" label. The US art market was booming, and the transformations of the southern part of Manhattan had proven how commercially lucrative this image could be. The undertaking needed in order to profit from this in the South End was thus quicker and easier than the Historical Society's efforts had proven. Silvio Dante, working in collaboration with Washington Gateway, was at the origin of this initiative. However, there was now a peculiar game developing among artists, public authorities and investors, with very different outcomes for each of them. Here we see a process very different from what happened in SoHo or in the Lower East Side, where "the transformation from subculture to mainstream was authored by the artists, musicians, designers and writers through active promotion of themselves, their work and their setting [providing] the developers the images, symbols and rhetoric to reinvent the neighborhood for middle-class consumers."[41] In the South End, the use of the "artistic" image responded to a desire

---

capitalists, rarely holding more than a few buildings and viewing their property as a supplemental source of income. As the costs (purchase price and tax costs) of entry into the neighborhood land market skyrocketed in the early 1980s, the form of ownership shifted heavily to mid-sized firms and corporations capable of paying exorbitant property costs. Small-scale of single 'mom and pop' owners began to drop out and brokerage firms, property management corporations and individuals with extensive property holdings within the neighborhood and in similar neighborhoods, such as Harlem, began to purchase and develop properties." Mele, *Selling the Lower East Side*, p. 244.

41   Ibid., p. 221.

to defuse the oppositional squatters' movement, and it would develop largely without their involvement.

For the real estate developer, the situation was perilous—this being a neighborhood that had seen strong tenants' movements. Silvio Dante found allies among some artists who collaborated with him in an attempt to escape their precarious situation. Such was the case of one very engaged member of the Washington Street neighborhood association, a former artist living in one of the developer's buildings who would keep her distance from the tenants in struggle. A theatre director, she was also one of the leading figures in the dog park association. In the early 2000s, the developer set up artist studios in a former textiles factory. Able to make use of a space amounting to two acres, he launched a planning operation—and, indeed, a business initiative—with a name coined on the model of New York's SoHo: SoWa, South of Washington Street. The renovation of "SoWa" thus extended regeneration beyond the first revalorized areas of the South End, namely the northeastern parts closer to the city center. While Silvio Dante had postponed the rehabilitation of his properties for some years, he had laid the basis for their commercial valorization by creating an "artistic" added value—and for this reason, in the end, his operation saw no drop in profits. His firm's website describes SoWa as "a lively commercial district serving artists, residences and creative business," now intended as a rival to Newbury Street, Boston's trendiest and most chic artery, located in Back Bay. Moreover, classified ads also make use of this vocabulary: for example, in the property supplement of the July 12, 2008 *Boston Courant* we read, "Spacious loft with built out bedroom area in boutique building in the rapidly emerging SOWA district."

The area has become "artistic" thanks to a number of initiatives: an "open studios" soirée takes place on the first Friday of every month, while SoWa Walks span one weekend per year. They attract a crowd of well-off residents from the South End and Boston as a whole. The usually deserted area is suddenly full of people, and it is impossible to find a table in any nearby restaurant before ten o'clock (late, for Boston). It also helps that the *First Fridays* have made a media splash: "It's a giant, arty block party, attracting hundreds of visitors who sip wine, view art, and then pop over to the Red Fez or Cafe Umbra for dinner."[42] Moreover, the promotion of SoWa's charms

---

42   Cate McQuaid, "The New Art Neighborhood: Open Studios Showcases SoWa

attributes great importance to what its restaurants have to offer — much more than to the artistic scene and the bohemia that attract less well-off gentrifiers in other neighborhoods. The artistic dimension almost disappears in favor of the explicit valorization of a certain population and clientele. Silvio Dante's commercial director openly expressed his desire to push undesirable elements away from this area. Asked about the homeless shelter situated nearby, he explained: "We're in the business of turning the lights on. You create a reason for people to come here, like the galleries or the restaurants. Then you have people walking around. For lack of more interesting metaphor, when you turn the lights on, the roaches scatter."[43] Indeed, as this implicit comparison of the Pine Street Inn homeless to insects suggests, commercial interests regard the situation in this part of the neighborhood as unfavorable to them. Unlike the South End as a whole, where whites form a majority of the population, the population of the district delimited by Washington Gateway is 31 percent white, 39 percent black, 20 percent Asian and 16 percent Hispanic.[44]

The commitment to diversity vaunted by Washington Gateway and its sponsors, the real estate developers, translates into little concrete action. They support mixed programs, notably those including accommodation for artists, and they advertise their desire to keep a few small shop owners in the area, like the grocery store that was in the neighborhood for twenty years, frequented by the poorest residents and notably Latinos — but which closed down in the end nonetheless. Their initiatives are ultimately largely symbolic, such as "convinc[ing] a new grocery store to offer products sought by the nearby public housing residents along with its gourmet foods and persuad[ing] a new high-end restaurant to offer nutrition classes at a local grammar school."[45]

Silvio Dante's firm is more oriented toward obscuring the socio-demographic and urban realities than recovering this social diversity. Indeed, in 2000 the businessman launched a major public relations campaign "to rechristen a blighted area of the South End in hopes of transforming it into

Gallery Boom," *Boston Globe*, December 9, 2003.

43   Linda Laban, "Call it 'Mario's Village,'" *Boston Globe*, June 3, 2007.

44   Karl Seidman, *Revitalizing Commerce for American Cities: A Practitioner's Guide to Urban Main Street Programs*, Washington: Fannie Mae Foundation, 2004.

45   Ibid., p. 85.

a trendy arts district. He flew SoWa flags from his buildings, published a
SoWa newsletter, established a shuttle to the subway with 'SoWa Express'
emblazoned on the side."[46] He did not hesitate to spend $250,000 a year in
order to set up a private security patrol employing twenty-four people.[47] The
establishment of an outdoor market and the opening of a gym and several
restaurants contributed to changing the image of this area, in spite of its
proximity to the homeless shelter and the predominantly black and Hispanic
men who frequent it. The opening of artist studios also had a certain effect,
with numerous galleries appearing—notably on Harrison Street, the road
on which the developer's holdings are concentrated. Among the twenty art
galleries surveyed in 2004, twelve had opened in the previous two years,
and only one had existed since the 1980s.[48] We can clearly see the extent of
the renewal of the art scene that the renting-out of galleries and the devotion of space to studios or lofts permitted.

Ultimately, it was the joint action of the public authorities (via Washington
Gateway) and the real estate developers that proved decisive in giving the
South End this new image. Another consideration was that Silvio Dante lent
offices to Washington Gateway for free, while also making generous contributions at its fundraisers. He financed the gates for the dog park, whose
creation marked an important stage in the renovation of Washington Street.
More generally, given the decisive importance of obtaining Washington
Gateway's support in order to enter the market, there was an active motivation for developers to help fund this body—under the cover of helping the
"community." Its director explains:

> The people who do development have to give community benefits to the
> neighborhoods and we've had so much development and this is the first
> community benefits that we've gotten. And so we got $25,000 this year
> from one of the developers, Walsh Companies . . . If we had gotten just one
> percent of what was going on here, we'd be rich.

---

46   Lisa Wangsness, "SoWa? EaBo? Boston Plays Name Game," *Boston Globe*,
September 5, 2005.

47   Suzanne Smalley, "A Force of Their Own. Neighborhood's Private Guards Help
Keep the Peace," *Boston Globe*, May 26, 2006.

48   McQuaid, "The New Art Neighborhood."

Today controlling many hundreds of apartments in Back Bay and the South End and managing a commercial space of almost 23 acres in SoWa, Silvio Dante is a force to be reckoned with. While he played a pioneering role, other developers from Boston would in turn adopt the "artistic" label he first promoted. One newly built block on Tremont Street—with thorough security at its entrance—was thus christened "Atelier."

A modernized history

In South End gentrifiers' relationship with housing, the taste for the architecture of yesteryear is thus mixed with other points of reference that have also appeared in New York, such as lofts.[49] Still, we ought to note that while such cultivated tastes remain a decisive social marker, they are not considered aestheticist or exclusive. Just as the watchword of diversity has become established even among the most conservative mobilized residents, the desire to be trendy and the quest to be modern and show off one's wealth seem to prevail over any aestheticist relationship to high culture. This ultimately results in a more hybrid approach to culture.

This relationship with culture has much to do with social positions. The people that I studied were endowed with a great degree of economic capital, and with the exception of the architects, they did not practice professions of an artistic, cultural or intellectual nature. I came across a single university professor (of law), while lawyers, city planners, business executives, realtors, consultants and accountants were legion. When I visited houses for interviews, not many books were on display. I saw few bookcases, and the works on display were a small number of coffee table art books. It is fashionable to frequent the exhibitions offered by the Museum of Fine Arts, but this occasions few discussions on the content of the artworks concerned. The relationship of these residents to the "beaux-arts" seemed more social than intellectual. The hybrid taste—somewhat removed from the most exclusive high culture—was particularly apparent in the decorative arts, which like the culinary arts discussed in Chapter 5, allow for a powerful marking of space.

The Historical Society's work on the symbolic revalorization of the South End, as well as real estate figures' promotion of these efforts, forged a widely

---

49 Sharon Zukin, *Loft Living: Culture and Capital in Urban Change*, London: Radius, 1988.

expressed interest in architecture. The discourses and practices of numerous interviewees were, however, distinct from those of the Society's founders, a certain number of whom did take a scholarly approach based on precise knowledge, reading and even personal research. By contrast, residents active in the neighborhood associations today rarely valorize Victorian architecture in terms of specific historical and material considerations, but rather through a singular, affective experience. Nonetheless, this does allow them to join the camp of those who had the intuition to pick out the marvels of the Victorian past from amidst the rubble. This attitude is encapsulated by the register in which they generally recall their encounter with the South End: being "head over heels" in the moment when they "fell in love" with architecture. While far from an objective urban reality, this memory of the buildings that captured their attentions has the virtue of hiding away any element of constraint in their migration to the South End, instead favoring a narrative of "a free choice," which is all the more noble on account of its aesthetic basis.

Decorative styles display the same distribution of tastes. Among many members of the Historical Society, a style prevails that is supposedly loyal to an epoch—the Victorian era—of which they claim to be the heirs. It combines Victorian wallpaper and furniture, paintings and sculptures, and is based on a room arrangement corresponding in whole or in part to the fashions of the second half of the nineteenth century. The first-floor parlor is generally kept clearly off-limits—designed for visitors going about relatively formal interactions, it marks a strict separation from the private space. The kitchen is often situated at the back of the ground floor, as in the upper-class houses of the Victorian period. In the nineteenth century this room was reserved for the domestic staff, the first floor was divided between the parlor and a lounge used by the family, and the bedrooms were spread across the other floors, with a top floor for the domestic staff. This arrangement echoes the family and moral norms that prevailed in the Victorian period, which a whole reform movement, including architects, was charged with promoting in its interior design efforts.[50] A strict separation between

---

50   "The Victorian crusade to improve the American family home was similar in many respects to the other waves of reform that swept across the nation in the middle decades of the 19th century. Energetic, aggressive, and intensely moral, architects, plan-book writers, journalists, and housing reformers fought to create a new standard for

the public and private spheres was then the norm, isolating the dining room and the parlor from the rest of the house. The parlor was dedicated to outside visitors, unlike what later became the living room, a space of conviviality shared by family members. Historical Society members' upkeep of the rooms in their homes, their antique furniture, as well as their large number of tables, dressers and small decorative items, express a certain attachment to these norms.

If these residents can mark in space both their fidelity to the Victorian past and their break with the more recent working-class history, they are able to do so because the inherited urban forms lend themselves to this—much as they were conducive to change in the 1870s and 1880s when this chic neighborhood became a district of immigrants. At this moment, the large upper-middle-class residences were broken up into apartments, and the smallest transformed into lodging houses. Slender partitions were erected to separate the lounge from the stairwell, and thus to form small apartments. The upper-floor rooms reserved for domestic staff were now combined into rented apartments. Lodging houses divided up the rooms, and placed rudimentary washing facilities—often simply a sink— in each room. The decorative elements now fell into ruin, or else, like the moldings, they were painted over. But in most places the repartition of the rooms was essentially the same, with often-minimal investment for the ever-poorer and more transient population coming into the South End in the late nineteenth century.

Naturally, while the 1960s and 1970s transformations of lodging houses into town houses and then into condos did require knocking through walls, this did not involve major restructuring projects. Nonetheless, there were notable differences in architectural and decorative practices among well-off South End residents. Far from the first Historical Society members' aestheticist approach, the later gentrifiers were more concerned with comfort, which made up part of middle-class housing norms from the beginning of the twentieth century onward. The modernization movement affecting both

---

single-family dwellings. The middle-class housing promoters and reformers wanted nothing less than the creation of a new national family ideal [and to this end] to stress the importance of private discipline and self-control in an ordered environment." Clifford Edward Clark, *The American Family Home, 1800–1960*, Chapel Hill: University of North Carolina Press, 1986.

interiors and the family had left its mark. Fussy decorating, the strict differentiation among rooms, the restricted use of the parlor—all this was the
object of sharp criticism at the end of the Victorian period. The houses built
in the first decades of the twentieth century offered a more informal lifestyle,
with fewer pieces of furniture. Lounges, available for all sorts of uses, now
prevailed, as comfort, functionality and economizing became established
norms. In the interiors of the South End's renovated houses, we see the
effects of the parallel movements of breaking down walls and asserting new
norms (informality as against formality), in compliance with the evolution
of the private and family sphere. From the 1960s, the vertical opening up of
space—made possible by the none-too-difficult purchase of whole houses—
allowed for the creation of open spaces encompassing two floors. Above all,
another recent architectural tendency allowed the new values prevalent
among the gentrifiers to express themselves in the residential space itself—
namely, the often-total opening between the kitchen and the lounge,
speaking to a desire to lessen the differences of role and status between men
and women. Interior design was thus charged with reflecting the most liberal
values, a desire for openness, and a refusal of hierarchy within the private
space. Unlike the Victorian home, whose designs and divisions were
intended to promote order and discipline in space—and thus over bodies—
the nooks and crannies of modern houses are meant to create more intimate
movements, revolving around relations that are not *a priori* defined by strict
familial and social norms.

For many South End residents, therefore, an attachment to history and the
architecture of yesteryear offers one of the ways in which they can valorize
their residential choices. Buying property gives them the opportunity for diligent revitalization of this past. Nonetheless, they generally do so in an ad hoc,
limited way, unlike the exhaustive preservationist impulse of some Historical
Society members, one of whom I heard lamenting the new residents' lack of
"purity." These latter often make use of the same elements, like exposed
brickwork, fireplaces and above all restored crown molding. But beyond the
beloved molding, these residents sometimes redesigned the layout of whole
rooms, in the context of wider changes. I often asked my interviewees if I
could visit their houses; many suggested this without prompting. They told
me at length about the renovations that they had undertaken, and a great
number of them drew particular attention to their "parlors"—reviving a

Victorian past, though now combined with modern comforts. Indeed, we often find that the parlor now features a TV, or even a vast home theater. This reveals a particularly ostentatious consumption pattern, revolving around expensive audiovisual equipment and household appliances far more than works of art.

CONCLUSION

Far from the institutional academic standards that regulate its European counterparts, the South End Historical Society has come to establish itself as a true "cultural entrepreneur." Its initiative in creating an architectural heritage valorized the neighborhood and contributed to accelerating migration toward the South End. Mobilizing a cultural tradition that is particularly strong in Boston, these amateurs, who are not part of the city elite, but many of whom are involved in real estate—an extremely market-oriented professional sector—invested in the register of history and art. Paradoxically, the spread of this highbrow taste among the middle classes combined with particularly exclusive processes of distinction. Indeed, the official history of the South End was modeled on a highly undemocratic conception of culture, which represented a useful tool for combating interventionist urban policies and ensuring that the legitimacy of private property prevailed over subsidized housing. Is this not proof of the always-inexhaustible resources that the most exclusive high culture offers for the drawing and redrawing of class boundaries, lending itself to infinite re-appropriations and transformations?

In focusing on a particular effort to resignify an area and the actors who brought it to fruition, this chapter shows in what conditions cultural distinction is still activated today, even among the segment of the upper middle class that has moved into working-class neighborhoods. It explains how a form of resistance to the shock provoked by the social movements of the 1960s played out within the upper-middle-class relationship to culture. This reaction would also mark the history of the US Left, as the role that high culture played in the identity of the group forming in the South End demonstrates. This commitment to diversity presents itself as an inheritance—and, certainly, a substantially reformulated one, partly relieved of its oppositional implications—of the protest movements of the 1960s, thus offering a fundamentally different view of the richest residents' philanthropic disposition. But it seems that along with this, the value of an elite cultural heritage was reaffirmed; after all, for the civil rights activists and more widely the groups mobilized in the South End from 1968 onward, the neighborhood was defined by values quite other than Victorian splendor.

As the last part of this chapter has shown, however, high culture's place among the upper middle classes must be understood by way of its uses of this culture. The fact that at a given moment of local political struggles this group was able to constitute a resource of decisive importance does not mean that the role of this resource could not subsequently be reviewed. Indeed, in the 1990s, "diversity" established itself as a point of reference, and the residents who asserted this value struggled to marry it with valorization of an architecture that was closely associated with an elite. Thus we understand the success of the "artistic" label that was promoted from the early 2000s onward. But at the same time, the role that the Historical Society played in the early years of gentrification sheds light on the limited scope of the "diversity" that later became the consensus. If "diversity" indicates a valorization of minorities, then, as we have seen, it implies coexistence without a local redistribution of positions of power.

Chapter 5

Conquering the Nooks and Crannies

As in numerous neighborhoods the upper middle class has returned to, the new restaurants and shops opening in the South End have contributed significantly to the transformation of the neighborhood's public spaces.[1] However, such a transformation was far from preordained. While the Great Depression of the 1930s and the city's purchase of abandoned lots during the urban renewal era did weaken commercial life in this Boston neighborhood, its public spaces continued to be marked by an intensive working-class sociability in the postwar period. The thousands of lodging-house tenants who ate their meals at neighborhood bars and cafeterias translated into a massive presence out in the streets and parks. The eventual transformation of these public spaces across the decades of gentrification was not just a matter of City Hall's encouragement or market forces. It was also the result of collective mobilizations, from the efforts in the 1970s to shut down area bars, to the campaign forty years later to remodel parks to accommodate dog owners. If, as this chapter will show, these battles were not already won in advance, these mobilizations do seem to have met with a certain success. We see this not only in

---

1 Sharon Zukin et al., "New Retail Capital and Neighborhood Change. Boutiques and Gentrification in New York City," *City and Community* 8: 1 (2009), pp. 47–64; Jason Hackworth and Josephine Rekers, "Ethnic Packaging and Gentrification: The Case of Four Neighborhoods in Toronto," *Urban Affairs Review* 41: 2 (2005), pp. 211–36.

the constant succession of new, extravagantly expensive restaurants opening in the South End, and in the eventual renovation of the parks, but also in the substantial retreat by the neighborhood's public housing residents into their own living spaces. Indeed, the gentrifiers' appropriation of public space remains one of the most important grievances that the earlier residents raise.[2] So what do these transformations tell us about the gentrifiers' pretentions of sharing and equitable exchange?

Beyond a simple refusal to exist in geographic proximity to "other" groups, the gentrifiers' relation to public space instead reveals their tight control of spatial coexistence. This operates by way of a strong distancing within larger shared space, as we see in the multiplication of the exclusive spaces reserved for the wealthiest residents. Here too we need to examine the dividing lines closely. Rather than retreating into the domestic sphere, these white homeowners have engaged heavily with public space; meanwhile the exotic cuisine of the neighborhood's new restaurants echo the diversity that these residents value so highly. The recently renovated Peters Park symbolizes the gentrifiers' ideal public space: next to the children playing baseball and not far from the handful of homeless people stretched across the park's benches, the dog run brings together wealthy residents, gay and straight, in a shared sociability. This chapter, devoted to public spaces, continues our description of a lifestyle structured by this singular taste for diversity.

CONTROLLING AND MARKING SPACE

The protection of the private sphere is a fundamental value of the US upper middle class, and it implies a scrupulous respect for personal space. Nonetheless, coexistence in the South End and the norms that regulate it have led to a redefinition of the boundaries between public and private. Valuing streets, pedestrian spaces and mingling is part of the lifestyle of this segment of the upper middle class, coupled with a strong critique of cloistered life in the suburban home and intensive car use. How are these tastes expressed? And above all, how were they implemented in a working-class neighborhood that, up until the 1980s, teemed with bars and liquor stores?

---

2   Japonica Brown-Saracino, *A Neighborhood that Never Changes: Gentrification, Social Preservation and the Search for Authenticity*, Chicago: Chicago University Press, 2010.

The drawbacks and delights of public spaces

The relative softening of the boundaries between public and private is one of the characteristic traits of upper-middle-class South End residents' lifestyle. The image of a lively, vibrant area where neighbors constantly cross paths is a strong means of legitimation for these residents' relationship to the neighborhood, standing in contrast to the "upper-middle-class suburbs."[3] They laud the habit of sitting in front of the house and greeting passersby—a practice associated with the working class and stigmatized as such in the world of the well-off residential suburbs—as a sign of the South End's diversity and the strength of its social bonds.

Asked what it is about the neighborhood that they like, many of my interviewees mentioned the "stoops." You access the brownstones by way of these high and wide external stairways, which mark a break with the compartmentalization of the domestic sphere and public space insofar as residents can sit out on the steps in good weather. One woman, an accountant who arrived in the South End a few years ago, enthused about this neighborhood tradition:

"What I want in the neighborhood? . . . I want to get to know my neighbors. I want to stay on my stoop on Saturday night with a glass of wine, and: 'How was your week, what's going on this weekend?'"

ST: "You wouldn't do that in a suburb?"

"Never, never, never. You would never do that . . . I grew up in a suburb. The suburban life is totally different. You plan to get together. And we're always joking, because it's very lonely in the suburbs. "

I came across her in the neighborhood on a number of occasions, but I never saw her on her stoop—nor any of the other association members whom I had interviewed. However, it used to be a widespread practice in this working-class neighborhood, which gets very hot in the summer. One German friend who has lived in the South End for several years helped me experience it for myself one day, phoning me to suggest "an authentic South End stooping."

---

3   David Halle, *Inside Culture: Art and Class in the American Home*, Chicago: University of Chicago Press, 1993, pp. 44–51.

Despite these numerous invocations of the practice, often linking it to the diversity of the neighborhood, in the span of a summer, I only once saw a black woman seated on a building's steps. A few times I did see gay white residents "stooping," but when my friend and I sat on the stairs with a bottle of wine (wrapped in a paper bag, since public drinking is not allowed), I got a few rather suspicious looks. Apparently even when whites are doing it, this practice is neither widespread nor totally accepted. And it is still liable to be associated—without doubt, depending on who's doing it—with loitering, which the neighborhood associations' members strictly forbid.

Engagement in the public space thus takes singular forms. It revolves around tightly circumscribed spaces: the businesses catering to a very homogenous clientele and the restaurant terraces, but also certain sections of the parks (some of which are officially delimited, such as the dog run). Nevertheless, with the number of dogs in the South End on the rise,[4] white homeowners now walk their pets down sidewalks covering the whole length of the neighborhood, sometimes stopping to chat at length when they see a neighbor. This desire to mingle stops when they reach the projects, especially when festivities are taking place there. Each July, Villa Victoria celebrates the successful mobilization that led to the construction of this development in 1968, a victory that gave the project its name—which has nothing to do with Victorian architecture. Hundreds of Puerto Ricans gather around immense food stands, concerts, majorette parades or even a greasy pole contest, in which teams compete to climb a mast covered in oil and hoist the Puerto Rican flag at the top. I attended in 2008, with the festivities taking place across an entire weekend; but during these two days I did not come across a single one of the neighborhood association members whom I saw so frequently in the street or in local cafés. My second ally—who brought me along—and I were almost the only whites present. Mario Small confirms that South End residents who do not live in the projects are absent from these events. He moreover tells us that across the whole weekend, except for one parade, the festival participants—that is, around 15,000 people—are strictly confined to the space of the Villa Victoria development itself. It is worth noting that 2008 was a special year, the fortieth anniversary of the successful tenants' mobilization. Yet even this did not bring down what Mario Small describes as an

---

4   See below.

"invisible fence, drawn neatly around the Villa that kept residents (and Latinos) in or nonresidents out."[5]

This combination of coexistence and exclusion in public spaces has a history. White homeowners' interest in public spaces reflects the values they brought with them when they moved to the South End: openness to the other, tolerance, the search for diversity and a more adventurous life. Nonetheless, from the 1960s onward this attraction to the outside world came up against major obstacles, linked to the density and working-class composition of the population occupying this space. Constructed a century and a half ago, the South End was laid out on a grid pattern, its central part composed of multi-story brownstones and crisscrossed by major arterial roads. It does not have the architectural density of certain working-class districts in Europe where the streets are narrow and the buildings do not take up much land area. However, at the end of the nineteenth century, the working classes easily succeeded in appropriating the neighborhood's urban form, originally conceived for upper-middle-class families. On the South End's major avenues, a multitude of businesses sprang up, the wide sidewalks allowing large numbers of people to hang around at length — and this was characteristic of a masculine working-class sociability, in which bars and taverns played a central role.[6] On Washington Street in the early twentieth century, a particularly intensive nightlife developed around the theaters, billiard rooms and all-night restaurants, attracting a nocturnal crowd under the elevated railway.

A municipal report appearing in 1962 listed the South End's businesses, whose large numbers city planners saw as one of the neighborhood's biggest problems. This list comprised dozens of liquor stores, 49 men's barbershops, 38 beauty salons, 199 restaurants and no less than 27 bars, not to mention the 86 grocers and countless other shops. The parks, around which the most chic blocks were built in the mid-nineteenth century, also drew in the local population. These spaces played host to practices that were deemed illegitimate in

---

5   Mario Small, *Villa Victoria: The Transformation of Social Capital in a Boston Barrio*, Chicago: University of Chicago Press, 2004, p. 98.

6   David Halle, *America's Working Man: Work, Home and Politics Among Blue-Collar Property Owners*, Chicago: University of Chicago Press, 1984; Richard Hoggart, *The Uses of Literacy: Changing Patterns in English Mass Culture*, Fair Lawn, NJ: Essential Books, 1957.

terms of both alcohol consumption and sexuality. Indeed, alleyways, remote streets and parks became centers of prostitution and cruising. But it was above all the dozens of bars that gave the South End its reputation in the early 1970s: while the clientele varied from bar to bar, certain establishments were frequented by sometimes sinister regulars. Booming unemployment during the Great Depression, but also the influx of jobless veterans after the Second World War, considerably increased the number of taverns and liquor stores.

For white homeowners moving into the South End, the shock of arriving in the neighborhood was aggravated by the contrast with the way of life that they were used to. Of course, not all of them were from the suburbs, with large numbers having come from Beacon Hill or Back Bay in order to buy a property in the South End. Nevertheless, in moving into the neighborhood they faced a social and racial diversity that was previously unknown to them. Moreover, while not all of the gentrifiers grew up in the suburbs, they still largely internalized the residential norms that have become widely established in the US: the primacy of the individual home, the valorization of the domestic space and outdoor activities centered on family life, the intensive use of cars and the stigmatization of the inner cities. Moving to more mixed spaces like Cambridge or less homogeneous inner-city areas—particularly when they were students—did not simply wipe away this socialization. Moreover, those who came directly from the suburbs saw their private space much diminished. They were leaving behind vast houses and more broadly environments in which public space is only very little occupied, to the point that any presence in the streets other than in a car is considered almost a deviant behavior.[7] Moving to the South End implied a different relationship to noise, or rather, to certain noises—the noise made by people in the streets, often late at night, but also that of cars and above all the much-unloved "Washington Street Elevated" train, taking populations

---

7 "Individuals who use the streets or other public places more than is customary, especially for socializing, are seen as deviants. Young people are the greatest offenders in this regard. Simply being in a public place at all can be offensive. Quiet residential streets, and the public parks scattered among them, are used on a day-by-day basis almost exclusively by neighborhood people. If outsiders appear in such locations, they are likely to arouse uneasiness or even alarm. People have been singled out as 'suspicious' while merely walking along residential streets." M.P. Baumgartner, *The Moral Order of a Suburb*, Oxford: Oxford University Press, 1988, pp. 103–4.

from the poor neighborhoods into the central business district. Indeed, until 1987 trains passed directly through the South End, making no stops in the neighborhood, just a deafening racket.

The crusade for everyday surveillance

The new inhabitants very quickly turned their energies toward public spaces, whose "undesirable" uses sparked significant mobilizations. The first initiatives that the white homeowners launched began in the first half of the 1970s. With the help of the mayor's office, some residents now took to the offensive against some of the neighborhood's bars: but the balance of power was far from favorable, given the great number of bars and patrons at the time.

Wiping out the stigma of a working-class neighborhood

The first mobilizations to get rid of the stigma of a "skid row" again demonstrate the little-known alliances that made the gentrification of the South End possible. Mobilized new homeowners and upwardly mobile "old" residents acted in concert. In 1974, Brian Hanson—a native South Ender of Irish origin—organized a neighborhood watch patrol on West Canton Street, where he himself lived, with the aim of combating crime. This initiative was of significant benefit to the good reputation of this street—which was part of the first wave of gentrification[8]—and to the expansion of the areas considered respectable or even desirable. Indeed, the creation of similar patrols by other neighborhood associations bears witness to this. Louise Fitzpatrick constantly publicized this patrol's activity. It is one of the subjects regularly addressed in her neighborhood association's minutes, and a good part of the documentation in her archive is devoted to this issue.

The presence of bars in the area was another matter of concern. Louise, the association president, devoted enormous energy to negotiating with the BRA to close some of them down. In 1968 her association vigorously opposed an attempt to transfer a bar license to the South End. In a three-page letter dated February 15, 1968, accompanied by a list of the nineteen "liquor outlets" already in existence, Louise Fitzpatrick contrasted the deleterious effects of the bars to the efforts that the "community" had made in conjunction with the BRA to improve the neighborhood: "For the past seven years, the South End

---

8   See Chapter 4 and the map on p. 155. See the section on Brian Hanson in Chapter 2.

community has worked for the improvement of the area and two years ago approved an urban renewal plan which promises rehabilitation and enhancement of the South End. This plan provides for the limitation of liquor licenses."

The association president's archives feature a number of letters addressed to doctors seeking their support for this campaign. But its main theme was the equivalence it drew between bars and crime. In the missive mentioned above, we read: "An excess of liquor establishments provides a breeding ground for alcoholics and other social misfits . . . Criminal elements flock to an area filled with liquor outlets and make the neighborhood unsafe for residents and visitors." The neighborhood's children, parishioners, hospital patients and finally the women at a nearby shelter were cited as potential victims of the bars' customers.

In 1975, a more imposing campaign was organized at neighborhood level, on the initiative of a "Bars Task Force." This campaign was jointly waged by the mayor's office, numerous neighborhood associations, influential members of the Historical Society and certain key figures among the lodging-house owners, including both Louise Fitzpatrick and another woman, of Lebanese descent, who lived in Union Park, was a member of SEPAC and would later be director of her local "little city hall." The SEPAC's March 1975 newsletter announced the creation of the task force as well as the BRA agency's support for closing down the Rainbow Lounge. This bar, like the majority of the establishments that this campaign targeted, was situated in the center of the neighborhood, on Tremont Street. Indeed, it was not far from the few streets to the west of this central artery that had begun to be rehabilitated: the stakes were significant.

This initiative was launched at the same time that the Pine Street Inn homeless shelter moved from nearby Chinatown to the South End. Angered residents mobilized, using the increased presence of homeless people as reason to demand that the BRA at least take into consideration their request to close down the bars. Indeed, 150 people had already signed a petition against what were considered the most disreputable establishments. Under pressure, a long-passive City Hall ultimately did give its support to the Bars Task Force. There were, however, significant obstacles to this campaign: even apart from the considerable number of the bars and their massive clientele, many of these establishments were Mafia-run. But at the same time the BRA was far from opposed to the task-force initiative, as the question of alcoholism was at the center of the city planners' diagnosis of the South End's problems. Indeed, we could even say that it was the main prism through which the 1962 BRA report described the neighborhood, with long passages devoted to the number and characteristics of its "alcoholics." It divided the skid row population into five groups, one of which was "chronic alcoholics— men who have passed beyond the excessive drinking stage and who cannot control their drinking enough to hold a job or care for themselves. These men are arrested repeatedly for drunkenness or disorderly conduct." In this period, public intoxication was a crime.

The task force called on City Hall to close down five other bars, with the neighborhood associations' members actively participating in the campaign. The infractions that they flagged to the authorities allowed the latter to take away the bar owners' licenses—in total, twenty-eight bars were shut down. This fight against working-class drinking echoed a long reformist tradition in the US around alcohol.[9] Nonetheless, the campaign waged in the South End marked a turning point in the public approach to alcoholism, involving not just outright repression but also rehabilitation. At the end of the 1960s, a movement developed in the US administrative, university and medical spheres that favored the decriminalization of alcoholism, seeking to transfer the management of this issue from police and judicial control to the medical arena. This shift took place at the same time that the definition of the "problem" changed from a moral question to a medical phenomenon.[10] The 1971 Alcoholism and Intoxication Treatment Act was an important landmark. At the same time, several states including Massachusetts began to open detox centers. In Boston, one active task force member, who was also the SEPAC president—and thus well-versed in negotiations with the BRA and closely acquainted with the public authorities—was asked to take charge of one of these establishments in 1971. The center opened up in the eastern part of the South End, far from the residential area that was being redefined. The center's stated objective was not to criminalize alcoholics but to offer them treatment.

---

9 Nicolas Beisel, "Class, Culture and Campaigns Against Vice in Three American Cities, 1872–1892," *American Sociological Review* 55 (1990), pp. 44–62.

10 Linda Bennett and Genevieve Ames, *The American Experience with Alcohol: Contrasting Cultural Perspective*, New York: Plenum Press, 1985, pp. 23–39.

Nonetheless, the fact that medical bodies were now addressing alcohol-ism did not spell the end of moralizing approaches to this question in the United States. Rather, the two ways of dealing with the problem coexisted, and this was all the more true in the South End given that economic inter-ests encouraged the stigmatization of alcoholism. The campaign in favor of decriminalization opened up a space of intervention for those residents who wanted to shut bars down and rid the streets of drunks whom they considered an impediment to reestablishing the neighborhood's value. This was clear in the comments of one real estate developer, who set up his business at a time when the South End attracted few investors, before throwing himself into converting lodging houses into condos in the 1980s. Born in 1941 to a middle-class Italian immigrant family, he grew up in a rather well-regarded part of Dorchester, a working-class neighborhood. Quick to mock liberal hypocrisy, he was deeply hostile to state intervention. During our interview, he expressed his hatred for civil servants so virulently that he suddenly cut himself off, realizing that he was probably speaking to a representative of this category. For him, the closing down of bars, as well as the implementation of waste management (which he describes as "a way for people to mark their territories") were key stages in the effort to redefine the neighborhood. He described at length the efforts to fight against "qual-ity-of-life crimes"—picking up on a term popularized in 1990s New York, within the framework of the repressive "broken windows" theory.[11] Asked about the transformation of the South End, he immediately focused on alcohol:

> As the area changed, it become very unwelcoming to people who would do things like that. Kind of dirty people. It wasn't a place for them anymore. We knocked them off. We forced these people out of the area. You have people saying: "Oh, that's gentrification and it's bad." No, it's not bad. It's very good. So we were glad, you know . . . cracking down on them . . . This was how the area changed. It has a lot to do with drink. Now, you know you can't drink. They started to make the area impossible to people who had bad habits. Like drinking.

---

11 Mitchell Duneier, *Sidewalk*, New York: Farrar, Straus and Giroux, 2001, pp. 158–9.

Creating a new commercial offering

This developer's wishes were realized. He put it to me as: "We lost the worst of liquor licenses. Now we have the best." His repeated references to the efforts made to bring this about bear witness to the fact that the substitution of one range of bars and restaurants for another cannot be explained by the simple interplay of supply and demand. Chapter 4 explained how the creation of demand for brownstones was the result of a long-term effort on the part of the Historical Society, and similarly, how demand in the restaurant sector was socially organized.[12] The emergence of a range of bars and restaurants catering to well-off residents was made possible first and foremost by the closing-down of the lowliest bars on Tremont Street and the gradual disappearance from public space of the populations that the upper middle class considered deviant. It thus seems as if the marking of public space first required the erasure of all traces of what had come before. The mobilization of residents in the Bars Task Force, working in collaboration with the BRA, played a decisive role. In the years that followed, the gradual departure of the lodging-house tenants—with these buildings now converted into condos— also caused a drop in the number of bars, while at the same time, many liquor licenses were bought up by business owners who wanted to set up shop outside of the South End. Finally the Mafia started to pull out of the neighborhood. While gambling—popular among the working classes—had been the stock in trade of organized crime, it was supplanted by drug trafficking in the 1980s. With the Mafia's departure, new space opened to other investors.

The second stage—creating the "best" commercial offering possible after having got rid of the "worst," to use the developer's expression—came with the renovation of Washington Street. At the beginning of the 1990s not only was the number of "problem" bars on Tremont Street much diminished following the task force's mobilization, but commercial activity on Washington Street had also significantly declined in the wake of urban renewal. Many plots bought by the BRA were left abandoned until the late 1980s. This major artery was peppered with vacant lots, and their number multiplied with each fire—accidental or otherwise. Indeed, a number of property owners living

---

12   Here we see how classical economic doctrines can only unsatisfactorily account for the social logics at the foundations of economic relations. Pierre Bourdieu, *The Social Structures of the Economy*, Cambridge: Polity, 2005.

outside the South End preferred to cash in their insurance policies rather than wait for meager and uncertain rent payments. Again, the former task-force president played an important role here. In the mid-1990s, after a career as a consultant, he converted the social capital that he had built up in the South End into an economic activity within the neighborhood space itself. He obtained one of a limited number of professional licenses allowing him to deal in commercial realty and to earn commissions on the sales. He then worked as a realtor for Betty Gibson's agency, helping twelve new restaurants setting up in the South End. His first contract was signed with the chef Gordon Hamersley. After having previously worked on the French Riviera, Hamersley arrived from Los Angeles at the beginning of the 1980s and opened a bistro that became the neighborhood's most expensive restaurant, a window into the "new South End."

The election of a new mayor in 1993 took place in a context in which local authorities were increasingly dependent on private investors. Boston had to transform its image in order to attract investors, shaking off memories of the anti-busing protests of the 1970s and the photos that circulated around the world of white residents greeting black children with volleys of stones.[13] The objective was to make Boston an open and international city, capable of attracting high-level professionals and enterprises and, to this end, importing the traits associated with New York's real estate and finance boom, such as new "cosmopolitan" restaurants, the fashion for fusion food and other world cuisines. The director of the Washington Gateway organization very much conceived of commercial development in the South End as a prelude to changing the neighborhood's image.

> We believe that the commercial districts define the neighborhood. So if your commercial district looks very bad, people think it's a bad neighbor-hood. If it looks very good, people think that the bad housing around it is a mistake. They say, "How could this bad housing be in this nice neighbor-hood?" So it really is the first thing people see. And it really defines your neighborhood, so it was very important for us to work on that.

---

13   A photo showing a white man taking part in the mobilization against the Boston school desegregation project, swinging a pole with an American flag at a black activist, won the Pulitzer Prize in 1977.

By the end of the 1970s some more expensive businesses had already appeared on Tremont Street—a restaurant that doubled as a gourmet store and an Italian place a little more costly than the neighborhood's traditional Lebanese establishments. Yet it was only in the mid-1990s that these "new" businesses seem to have overtaken the "old" ones, first on Tremont Street. Up until this point an old-style liquor store was still operating not far from Union Park, and Amy, the consultant profiled in Chapter 3, still remembers it:

> When I moved [in 1994], there was an old-style liquor store. Drunks hanging around. That was awful. Drunks hanging around. You came in to the liquor store. You couldn't even touch the liquor. You had a big table like this, with the liquor merchant, behind the table . . . like the communist countries! And you'd say, "A bottle of that, and a bottle of that." And the guy would take it and package it for you, which is a very old fashion way and a very down-market way.

A few years later, the liquor store had been bought out and transformed into a café-restaurant particularly popular among the white residents. Its owners, moreover, were board members in their neighborhood association, and made generous donations to its coffers. I conducted many interviews in this café. But it was the Washington Street development operation that gave the South End a new commercial face, its restaurants raising it to the ranks of the neighborhoods showcased by guides and the papers' dining pages. In 2004 this operation led to the construction of 1,571 new or renovated dwellings and the creation of a commercial area of just over three acres.[14] Indeed, Washington Gateway gave the greater part of the subsidies it distributed to businesses. The Red Fez, a long-standing Lebanese restaurant that has today been renovated to welcome a wealthier clientele, received $14,000. Flour, an establishment serving various kinds of coffees, sandwiches and pastries, enjoyed subsidized rent and credit from the BRA upon its opening. Since 1995, seven new restaurants, a bar (called Bank) and a café have appeared on Washington Street, which runs the length of a dozen South End city blocks. These businesses are not chosen at random. Some—such as cafés, chic

---

14   Karl Seidman, *Revitalizing Commerce for American Cities: A Practitioner's Guide to Urban Main Street Programs*, Washington: Fannie Mae Foundation, 2004, p. 87.

restaurants, furniture and decor shops and pet supply stores—are favored over others like inexpensive barbershops and pawnbrokers.

These subsidies concerned not only the type of businesses but also their appearance and more particularly their storefront windows, which are powerful social markers. The transformation of the liquor stores was accompanied by the disappearance of Plexiglas and window gratings. At the South End's new alcohol vendors, the products sold (almost entirely wine), their spacious interiors and their wide windows, distinguish them from the traditional somber liquor stores surrounded by metal grids. Indeed, a front window improvement program encouraged this development: $75,000 of the $9 million subsidies that Washington Gateway handed out in 2004 were devoted to this. Commenting on the importance of external appearance and the virtues of large windows, this organization's director explained that its objective was indeed to encourage businesses to attract a new clientele. Here she talked about one grocer's store:

> We worked particularly with the Don Quixote market. It's an example of a business that had no windows, and we were able to work with them to expand, get windows, get a lease, improve their market, so that these businesses—we try to help the existing businesses that primarily serve the lower income people who are here, that primarily populated the district when it started, to not only retain their customers but also to bring in new customers. So a good example is the storefront improvement program, where if the businesses look better, the newer residents are likely to come in . . . The big thrust is to eliminate those metal roll-down grates that make the neighborhood look bad.

Windows thus replaced iron curtains and metal gratings. Transparency was now extolled as reassuring for new residents arriving in an unknown space, who saw bars that had no windows onto the street as the domain of the neighborhood's pre-existing populations. The South End's restaurants were thus called on to wipe away Boston's provincial and outdated image and give it a more international aspect. "No Chowdah Here," proclaimed one 2006 article appearing in the *New York Times*, which touted Boston's renaissance, though certainly with some circumspection and a dose of irony and condescension. "Boston, while still not quite an avatar of cool, is showing plenty of new signs, for better or worse, of hipness." So in the South End there was to be no more chowder—New England's signature dish—but a Venezuelan restaurant where the wine-loving journalist could taste "malbec from Argentina [and] carmenères from Chile."[15]

Keeping the neighbors in check

The bars and the campaign to shut them down make up part of the neighborhood's memory, transmitted to the residents who arrived since the 1970s. The episode often comes up in interviews, and my interlocutors mentioned it with implicit approbation. Thirty years later, the question of alcohol—posed in terms of liquor licenses and restaurant opening hours, supermarket wine sales and even liquor stores opening—remains one of the most discussed subjects. This issue drives some people into entrenched positions and mostly hostile, even vehement, reactions. The specter of seeing drunk people in the street haunts many, and not just the most conservative ones. During one of my stays, three associations animatedly discussed a plan to open a wine store, as put forward by the owner of one chic South End restaurant. A small committee meeting was called, and I managed to get myself invited to it. It took place in a fancy bar on Tremont Street, and apart from the many glasses of wine consumed during the meeting, the liveliness of the exchanges and the seriousness with which the matter was discussed, I was astonished by their active mobilization and meticulous examination of this issue. One of the participants explicitly expressed her fear that this would attract some of the "not-so-nice people" characteristic of an era when the South End was populated by these "not-so-nice bars." I later discovered that one of the most renowned figures of the local civic scene, who was engaged in numerous groups, had a serious alcohol problem; her socioeconomic status and thus her capacity to be one of the "nice people" despite her drinking problem allowed her to escape falling into the stigmatized category of "alcoholics."

One of the associations' requirements was that establishments must not sell small bottles of strong alcohol, which they associated with working-class drinking in public spaces. The visibility of these practices in the street, at all hours of the day, is still a concern for these residents. For example, in response to the petition against the Pine Street Inn project, one of the leaders of the

---

15   Ann Marie Gardner, "36 Hours in the South End of Boston: Row Houses on Union Park in Boston's South End," *New York Times*, June 30, 2006.

committee advocating for the project insisted on the fact that its residents had nothing to do with those who frequented the homeless shelter: "We are not dealing with the people who are walking into the shelter, who have the cheap wine in the brown paper bag. These are people who have gone through the Pine Street's programs, who have straightened themselves out and who have conquered their substance abuse issues."

All the same, the fervent tone of these debates does not hide the fact that there are no longer collective campaigns around drinking, even if it is a subject that arouses strong reactions. First, it suits powerful business interests for bars and restaurants to open up. Added to this, the number of drunk people in the street has significantly diminished—or else such people are a better-off clientele and students, whose abuse of alcohol is more widely tolerated. Finally, the discussions concerning restaurants and other businesses, or even housing development initiatives, do not only have the purpose of directly intervening in this or that project. They are also a matter, quite simply, of the neighborhood associations reasserting their power and, in so doing, reactivating belief in their authority. At the same time, this institutes a strong moral boundary between themselves and populations whom few of these wealthy white residents would overtly stigmatize on account of class or race.

These criteria do however arise in discussions of restaurant licenses and sites of alcohol sales—when it comes to designating what populations could be a potential nuisance. Indeed, when these mobilized residents turn their gaze to drinking and smoking, they explicitly categorize other populations, in a discourse that blends moral reprobation and a preoccupation with health. After a public campaign and sweeping legislation that was introduced in the United States in the 1990s, smoking has become the object of heavy opprobrium. The complaint that one neighborhood association president received from a resident bears witness to this. The complaint, directed against an association offering detox programs for former prisoners, referred to the presence of men who regularly stood together on the street corner smoking after they were forbidden from doing so within the association's own buildings. While distancing himself from the stigmatization of these men, this neighborhood association president told me that the resident's annoyance quite clearly derived from the color of their skin—black. He explained that he went to exchange a few words with the reintegration program's director, who had implemented strict rules to prevent loitering outside of the association's buildings. And the former president of another neighborhood association related a similarly revealing example of how the criteria for describing undesirable populations were blended together. A few years earlier, she had watched approvingly as another reintegration program for former prisoners moved out of the area. In her discussion of this organization and her delight at its departure, it was striking how she mixed a racial and economic characterization of these undesirable individuals together with references to their deviant behavior in regard to hygiene and relations among the sexes. In her sixties, a graduate of the prestigious Wellesley College and daughter of a wealthy New York businessman, she has owned an entire house not far from Back Bay since 1990. She told me:

> The ex-prisoners would stand on the window and whistle at the girls . . . And then, no smoking in the building. The men got permission to walk around the block, to have a cigarette. And these guys, often black guys, but not always, two by two, would walk slowly around the neighborhood smoking. People didn't like that.

We thus see that race is still a criterion of the boundaries that the privileged groups establish, but simultaneously that it is entangled with the question of gender—whether in terms of relations among the sexes or homosexuality. Indeed, some of the Pine Street Inn project's most fierce opponents emphasized the former prisoners' supposedly disparaging attitude toward gays. Such was the case with the couple whose comments on black people I referred to earlier, and who figured among the most conservative gentrifiers I met during my study.

The arrival of more wealthy residents in the last twenty years—with the incomes of the richest on the rise in the United States in general[16]—has allowed a strengthening of the links between property owners and charity organizations. It has thus become easier for the former to avoid, or at least to control, undesirable behaviors. In the 1990s, the poorest populations of the South End—their numbers having fallen drastically, with increased rents and the near-disappearance of the lodging houses—were mostly accommodated

---

16   L. Michel, J. Bernstein and S. Allegretto, *The State of Working America*, 2008–2009, New York: ILR Press, 2009.

in public housing projects, retirement homes and semi-shared lodgings run by charities.[17] The outcome of the fight over Pine Street Inn provided ample demonstration of this new control: white residents mobilized in neighborhood associations ultimately decided—naturally, at the cost of some conflict in their ranks—that poor residents would have access to housing, but the white homeowners also set the terms on which this would take place. The relations between the neighborhood association and the charity selling its three row houses to Pine Street Inn illustrate the control established over the course of the 1990s. The surveillance of the manner in which these "others" occupy public space is not based on making them totally invisible, but rather on integrating them by assigning them certain well-defined and generally subordinate places and positions.[18] As such, the homeowners invited the residents of one shelter to participate in their annual picnic—and as I saw at first hand, they came and cooked hamburgers with enthusiasm and good humor. Meanwhile a dozen of them carry out the cleanup operation that the neighborhood associations organize each spring, under the watchful eye of one or two association members. The gentrifiers champion this "community" goodwill (a community that they identify with themselves), although this zeal in fact contrasts with their own more spotty engagement. On the day of one such cleanup, I was walking through the neighborhood and passed several of my interviewees. But I also saw city employees who had come to bring spades and rakes. They waited all morning for the residents who were meant to come and pick them up for the cleanup. No one came.

Diversity on a plate

In encouraging new restaurants catering to a well-off clientele, the South End's gentrifiers have not simply worked to bring in more exclusive establishments; in this field also, they have continued to express their attachment to a certain social mixing. Yet they valorize diversity by way of significant detours. In the South End as in other neighborhoods, gentrification and culinary tastes are

17   In a few decades, the number of low-cost dwellings (notably Single Room Occupancy units) has fallen spectacularly in major urban areas like Boston, particularly in the South End. In 1950 there were 25,000, and just 3,000 by 1986. *Rooms for Rent: A Study of Lodging Houses in Boston*, Boston: City of Boston, Commission on Affairs of the Elderly, 1986.

18   On the links between neighborhood associations and charities, see Chapter 3.

closely related: and if frequenting exotic restaurants provides an echo of the diversity that the gentrifiers so value, their consumption of the food offered in these establishments also creates significant distance from other populations.

The uses of the "French" label

Drinks—those that the gentrifiers consume and those of which they disapprove—play an important role in the definition of social boundaries. Wine is a powerful social marker among the white property owners of the South End. Their taste for wine has a specific meaning that is not reducible to price differentials alone; instead it needs to be understood in relation to other drinks that they like much less: namely the beer of the working-class bars or the liquor sold in small bottles, often consumed on the sidewalk. The early 1970s campaign against bars and liquor stores targeted what these establishments symbolized: working-class, male alcohol consumption, implying a visible and often noisy occupation of space. Thanks to the wine cellars that opened up in the 2000s, wine overtook beer; tasting evenings focused on a particular type of wine or wine-growing region now make for widely appreciated rituals. Only two relatively cheap bars, whose interior decoration has barely changed, have managed to hold on—one of them situated on the edge of the neighborhood, not far from the homeless shelter. All the others have disappeared in favor of chic establishments offering sumptuous *cartes de vin* prepared by restaurateurs. The rather expensive Japanese place that has opened on Washington Street calls itself a "sushi wine shop" and offers weekly wine-tasting nights. Its website boasts that it is "an innovative combination of sushi restaurant and purveyor of fine wines."

This division of alcoholic drinks into the vulgar and the chic is matched by a division among the places in which they are sold. Similarly, the opposition between regular coffee and espressos or lattes traces the boundaries dividing the South End's populations into different spaces. Unlike the bars, the fast-food places where you can get a "regular coffee"—relatively low in caffeine and served in large quantities—have not disappeared, but they have been relegated to the arteries surrounding the neighborhood: Massachusetts Avenue and the areas to the north and south of Washington Street. By contrast, Starbucks as well as two further establishments serving a variety of coffees, sandwiches and pastries stand opposite one another on Tremont Street. Another, a little further away on Union Park—and whose owner is a neighborhood association member—attracts a similar clientele, while a fourth establishment has opened up on Washington Street, subsidized by the Washington Gateway group that guided the renovation of this major thoroughfare. The type of businesses changes as one moves further southeast. On Tremont Street, not far from Massachusetts Avenue, we find two pizza takeout joints, but since 2007 Upper Crust has catered to a wealthier clientele. Only at the approach to Massachusetts Avenue, the frontier beyond which we arrive in Roxbury—the city's black neighborhood—do we begin to find the series of Dunkin' Donuts, pizza places and small fast-food establishments. Here, hamburgers are one of the principal offerings, and the amount of vegetables in the sandwiches drops by half along with the choices of bread and additional ingredients.

French cuisine plays a non-negligible role in the South End's culinary scene. In addition to a "pâtissier-chocolatier," seven restaurants offer food associated with the country. "Petit Robert Bistro offers a taste of France and romance at 480 Columbus Avenue," we read in a *South End News* article devoted to one such establishment, easy to find thanks to the miniature Eiffel Tower set in front of the door.[19] Its decorative features—"the brick walls, the mirrors, and the golden bar that runs along the side"—are of obvious significance: "It looks like a real bistro … like it would look in Paris." Gaslight Brasserie du Coin, the last restaurant to open in the Washington Street area, organized a party for Bastille Day—while for the same occasion, a jazz club distributed postcards across the neighborhood showing Brigitte Bardot against a *tricolore* background. French words are scattered across the menus of many other restaurants, or even on their front windows. Gaslight is decorated with white ceramics, and vintage French advertising posters are attached to the walls above the banquettes. The menu includes dishes less well-known than the habitual steak-frites; a "pissalardiere grille" is a pizza, the waitress assures me. All the writing in the restaurant, from the menu to the restrooms, is in French. The website even goes as far as saying that the walls have tobacco stains. The old and the dirty, held up as signs of authenticity, are clearly valorized here.[20] But the path to authenticity goes by

19   Aviva Gat, "France & Romance: Petit Robert Bistro," *South End News*, February 12, 2009. Also read Emily Gelsomin, "A Slice of Parisian Life," *South End News*, November 10, 2010.

20   Sharon Zukin, "Consuming Authenticity. From Outposts of Difference to Means of Exclusion," *Cultural Studies* 22: 5 (2008), pp. 724–48.

way of the Old Continent rather than the working-class history of the South End itself, which is absent from these restaurants' menus as from their decor. In the former abandoned areas that have now been regenerated, only the restaurant Rocca preserves some trace of the neighborhood's industrial past: "A secluded patio to the rear retains the reclaimed factory's tall coal-fired chimney, lovingly preserved as an architectural feature."[21]

There are sometimes distortions in this attempt to affect a distinction imported from the Old Continent. One of the most chic bar-restaurants is called The Butcher Shop. The allusion to small businesses so dear to Jane Jacobs, the French words in the front window and the menus offering plates of "charcuterie" all allow the meat stands by the tables to be transformed into decorative features, even though since the birth of "good manners" and European "haute cuisine," these have traditionally been relegated to the back kitchen.[22] Pork has suddenly become a distinguished meat—though as we shall see, there is no space here for the pork of Southern cuisine.

We can see the opposition between "form" and "substance" in the small portions that the new restaurants serve.[23] It is also expressed in the assertion of "authenticity," whose mark we can see in the opening up of an organic food store and a particularly expensive produce market whose front windows exhibit a constantly changing mix of sophistication and frugality. However, abundance can sometimes be placed in service of distinction. In a line of thinking which would speak to a certain bad taste in France—where nothing signals chicness as clearly as minimalism—upper-middle-class Americans seem to augment cachet by adding together different flavors. The caterers hired for fundraisers are sure to provide contrasting tastes, not only through the coexistence of elements drawn from different cultural and culinary traditions—such as fusion food offers—but also by pairing base elements (shrimp, turkey) with sauces of very pronounced flavor (pineapple, curry, sesame) to dip them in. This type of dish could not be more different from the fried chicken and large plates of pasta served during a campaign event I attended

---

21   Linda Laban, "Call it 'Mario's Village,'" *Boston Globe*, June 3, 2007.

22   Norbert Elias, *The Court Society*, New York: Pantheon Books, 1983.

23   Pierre Bourdieu counterposes the popular classes' emphasis on substance to the middle-class focus on form, notably in their relation to food, in order to deny and distance themselves from material realities.

in working-class Roxbury one evening, organized for a black candidate. This accumulation of flavors is precisely what irritates Richie O'Brien, the "old" resident profiled in Chapter 3, whose culinary practices underscore the specificity of his trajectory. As he puts it, he prefers the simplicity of something starchy with some roast chicken to:

> fifty flavors on one plate. I need plain rice once in a while. Plain mash potatoes once in a while. Plus, there are reduction sauces, and their sauces . . . they're too harsh, they're too strong. It's too much. I'd rather eat healthy. I'm still a meat and potatoes guy, you know. I'm not in all this vegetarian . . . I like a roast chicken, you can't get a damned roast chicken anywhere!

Distinguished omnivores

French cuisine became a social marker in the US in the 1960s when Julia Child's television programs and cookbooks achieved major success. But other points of reference have appeared since then, as we see in the proliferation of restaurants of different origins in the great US cities—influences ranging from Northern Italy to Shanghai, Sichuan, Hunan and other Chinese regions, Greece, India, Indonesia and even the Middle East. Though to a much lesser extent than in New York, many such restaurants opened in the South End in the 1990s and above all the 2000s. Here the exoticism of the peasant dishes of the Third World satisfied a certain "culinary populism," to pick up on Pierre Bourdieu's expression.[24] We can see the crisscrossing of cultures in one South End restaurant that is labeled both "Asian" and "French," or indeed at Myers + Chang, named after its two owners, who offer their "personal" and "free" reinterpretation of "Taiwanese soul food" and "Southeast Asian street food." The much-vaunted hybrid element of this cuisine redoubles its tempered exoticism, which is now at the center of the culinary tastes of this segment of the upper middle classes.

Nonetheless, as Josée Johnston and Shyon Baumann aptly demonstrated in an article on restaurant critics, shaking the supremacy of "haute cuisine" does not mean putting an end to culinary distinction; rather it makes it more

---

24 Pierre Bourdieu, *Distinction: A Social Critique of the Judgement of Taste*, Cambridge, MA: Harvard University Press, p. 185.

complex, allowing the assertion of democratic values and an attachment to multiculturalism, all the while excluding those who lack the means to access this "authenticity."[25] In the South End, the restaurants whose virtue is in their openness to foreign and working-class cultures contrast—in what they offer but also in their geographic location—with the pizza places and fast-food joints of the neighborhood's peripheral arteries. While Johnston and Baumann could read articles devoted to "hamburgers, hot dogs, meatloafs, macaroni and cheese," we find none of these foods in the South End's most sought-after restaurants.[26] They are consigned to the category of illegitimate food, directly emerging as they do from a working-class past that the South End's white property owners have worked to bury, rewriting the neighborhood's history by way of the Historical Society. Mike's, a traditional diner situated not far from Massachusetts Avenue, still attracts a sizeable number of customers, particularly on Sundays when it serves pancakes and breakfasts with generous helpings of bacon and eggs. Many Tremont Street restaurants offer sophisticated dishes for brunch, with a few fruits invariably added to an omelet that customers like to enjoy together with a bellini or a mimosa—drinks made with prosecco and fruit juice.

My interview with one South End resident, a commercial executive at a major newspaper, spoke to the subtle forms of distinction at work in "omnivore" tastes.[27] When I asked him about his favorite restaurants, he mentioned Delux, thus immediately establishing a distance between himself and the legitimacy of haute cuisine. This former bar, which used to play host to drag nights and was once owned by the Mafia, has kept its classic interior and attracts many students. Here they serve various sandwiches, chicken tacos

---

25   Josée Johnston and Shyon Baumann, "Democracy versus Distinction. A Study of Omnivorousness in Gourmet Food Writing," *American Journal of Sociology* 113 (2007), pp. 165–204.

26   Levenstein speaks of a "rediscovery" of the US culinary tradition: "Perhaps this is the last major foreign lode to be mined, at least for the moment, for it has been followed by a 'rediscovery' of the American culinary tradition. Now well-heeled lawyers and bankers pay outrageous prices for the very catfish and hush puppies Riverbottom people had rejected" as too lowly. Harvey A. Levenstein, *Revolution at the Table: The Transformation of the American Diet*, Oxford: Oxford University Press, 1988, p. 207.

27   On theories of "omnivorism," see Chapter 4.

and even sides of pork. More than the locale itself, it is the "simple" food that attracts this executive, who immediately emphasizes that its cooking is impeccable: "I like hamburgers, and hotdogs and things like that, but also very high-end, it just has to be cooked well. That's why I think the Delux, they do very good grilled sandwiches. You don't go for very high-end food, but you go for basic food. But they do a very good job cooking."

He combines this "simple" taste with gastronomic practices—mentioned in the same breath—that he acquired during his stay in Europe, as he likes to emphasize. In his travels he developed a taste for good quality basic ingredients, and he enjoys cooking together with his wife at home, with a preference for seasonal produce. "We basically like to cook whatever looks good for ingredients. In the summer, we go vegetables. In the winter, stews." This cuisine valorizes simple—but also high-quality—basic ingredients. The French reference point is always present—here, starkly opposed to the food of the US Southwest. He can recognize the merits of this latter, but on condition that it is made with the right "technique," satisfying the aesthetic dispositions characteristic of these diversity devotees.

> We actually like Masa. The food is excellent, it's basically very classical, almost French technique, but using spices that are more Latin American, and Southwest American. So Steak Frites will be chili-rubbed-steak. I am not a big fan of Southwestern food per se—burritos—but what they do, by using real cooking technique.

Above all the Southern food—so-called "soul food"—associated with African Americans provides a powerful foil for South End culinary tastes. Until 2009, a restaurant on a block on the far side of Massachusetts Avenue, near Roxbury, served this food—the only establishment (other than a jazz club not far from there) where I saw as many black as white customers. In the restaurant that has now opened on the same site, all reference to soul food has disappeared, prices have gone up, and while you can still see jazz concerts there, on the evening when I went with three friends—one of them an African-American woman—I saw only one other black customer. However, fried dishes are still prevalent, despite the efforts to soften the "Southern" feel. "When Settles took over Bob's nineteen years ago, he transitioned the restaurant from cooking with lard to cooking with canola oil.

In an effort to become more health conscious, Bob's also phased out pork on its menu in favor of smoked turkey."[28]

When it comes to the dishes that the gentrifiers most appreciate, overly fried or heavy food is off the menu—for example, the kind of food served at the Villa Victoria festival—with no whites present—which Mario Small humorously describes as "fried, greasy and delicious!" This cuisine echoes the greasy pole contest's displays of physical strength and taste for danger, in which men have to climb a mast covered in grease. There is also fat on the gentrifiers' plates, certainly, but the highly caloric concoctions offered at the beginning of the meal are christened with the French word *hors d'oeuvres*. And you dip into them with little sliced carrots and sticks of celery, a token of a cuisine conceived as healthy for both the body and the planet. We see this in the taste for organic produce and the new restaurants' menus' emphasis on their "fresh" ingredients from "local" providers.

Manners in the absence of manners

These residents' socially distinctive relation to gastronomic practices is not only apparent in their rejection of huge portion sizes. These practices also involve a form of rationalization that implies a regulated relation to time. As we have seen, such a relation is also present in the neighborhood associations' modus operandi, as well as in other practices like sport, especially that practiced by the subjects of our study: jogging and exercise at the gym, organized around a meticulous counting of time, weight and speed, and entirely bound up with self-discipline and aesthetic work on the body.[29]

Their approach to frequenting restaurants bears the mark of this same control. They make appointments by phone or online, the serving staff diligently orchestrate proceedings, and the meals are served in short order. Spatial proximity allows them to experience the restaurant scene in an informal way, contrasting—according to my interviewees—with the long journeys

---

28   Lou Manzo, "Last Call for Bob's Southern Bistro," *South End News*, October 31, 2007.

29   These thus being far from the displays of strength and risk seeking—or even search for suffering—characteristic of working-class sports but also of the "free and disinterested" activities of the late-nineteenth century's aristocratic elite. Monique de Saint Martin, "La noblesse et les 'sports' nobles," *Actes de la recherche en sciences sociales* 80 (1989), pp. 22–32.

that suburb residents have to put up with. It encourages encounters between neighbors and acquaintances, who greet each other across the tables, without this at all challenging the rationalization of space and its division through the waiters' arrangement of the tables, each of them constituting "a separate, appropriated territory."[30] In the organization of the dinners we find a similar combination of control and leeway, of manners and the rejection of etiquette. We can see this rejection of "social ceremony" in the restaurants' interiors. Open cooking areas are now part of the eating space, with kitchen islands around which people cook, eat and chat, perched on high stools on which they are neither fully seated nor entirely standing. This new arrangement does not erase the traditional boundaries between the woman who cooks and the man who sits chatting and gets served, or even between those who cook and those who eat, but it does soften or mask them. This management of time and organization of space is markedly different from the carefully orchestrated dinners that the traditional elites organized. The moments preceding the meal are no longer so clearly distinct from the meal itself, thanks to the "hors d'oeuvres," which moreover allow restaurant-goers to satisfy their appetites before displaying distinguished reserve as they consume a main dish of limited portion size.

Nights out at restaurants make up part of the practices by which new arrivals are socialized in living in a "mixed" area: by virtue of the "exotic" food there on offer, but also on account of the significance of these outings for the research subjects, with whom I socialized over the course of several months. Indeed, "[the gentrifiers'] attachment to the neighborhood-village in large part operates by way of the commercial scene."[31] In the South End, where restaurants are constantly opening for business, particularly in the renovated area of Washington Street, each new establishment can count on getting an article in the local paper, the *South End News*. That becomes the object of constant discussion. Thus each time I returned to the field, I was invited to discover a new restaurant that had opened up, and—as a French

---

30   Bourdieu, *Distinction*, p. 183.

31   Sonia Lehman-Frisch and Guénola Capron, "Le sentiment de quartire en milieu gentrifié: de San Francisco à Bogotà," in *Le Quartier. Enjeux scientifiques, actions politiques et pratiques sociales*, ed. Jean-Yves Authier, Marie-Hélène Bacqué and France Guérin-Pace, Paris: La Découverte, 2007, pp. 116–26.

woman whose (good) culinary taste seemed to be taken for granted—to comment on its charms.

Thus we see how a group of wealthy inhabitants has managed to appropriate and mark a space for itself, by way of the commercial scene. Their arrival in this mixed neighborhood very much looks like a conquest of space, made possible by the most well-off residents' mobilization. Still, here we ought to distinguish between two periods. After earlier efforts that overtly sought to close down disreputable establishments, the new resident organized the later conquest not so much through the eviction of the poorest populations but rather through the distancing and control of their material and symbolic presence. And "culinary diversity" is also part of this process. Another phenomenon that has been less studied in the literature on gentrification, but which is characteristic of the new way of life developing in a certain segment of the upper middle class, has also encouraged the appropriation of space: the craze for dogs.

SOCIAL DIVERSITY, ANIMAL DIVERSITY

Among the surprises that a number of large US urban areas hold in store for the European visitor, doubtless one of the most unexpected relates to dogs and the place that they occupy in the city. From my very first stays in the South End, I was struck by the number of dogs and the businesses devoted to them, like the Shawmut Avenue dog bakery and the Washington Street dog spa, as well as by the announcement of a yoga class for dogs. Animals roam the streets, but they do not much resemble the strays that we see in some other metropoles—in Eastern Europe, for example. They are carefully kept on a leash, the object of endless affection and attention from their owners. I came across few pit bulls or German shepherds, but a number of breeds whose names I gradually learned: poodles, Labradors, greyhounds, so-called "French" bulldogs and even labradoodles. However, only in 2007, when the conflicts over the creation of a dog park reached fever pitch, did I understand the true stakes of pet ownership. The extent of the mobilization showed not only an intense love for these animals—which I found slightly ridiculous, having come from a country where dogs do not spark similar outpourings of emotion, and having never myself owned any pets. It also revealed the hidden or euphemized struggles over the appropriation of space. It became clear that the dogs of the South End—whose owners contrasted their gentleness and

good manners to the violence of the pit bulls, the so-called "ghetto dogs"[32] —
were not just companions but also "conquerors" of territory.

Indeed, in November 2007 a 13,000-square-foot space designed by a landscape architect opened in Peters Park. Divided in two—one area for little
dogs, another for larger ones—the Peters Park dog run is decorated with a
fountain allowing them to take a drink or splash around in the water. Together
with a small space not far from Back Bay and the lawns of Blackstone Square,
this is one of the places where residents regularly walk their dogs and take
them off their leashes. But the homogeneity of the dog owners is striking. The
questionnaire that I gave to around sixty people at the dog run provided
objective evidence of what I could already tell just by looking at the people
using it. Half of my respondents had an income of over $100,000 a year, thus
belonging to the richest 15 percent of the US population. 65 percent earned
more than $70,000, thus belonging to the richest quartile. 90 percent were
white, and among these, one-third were gay, including one woman.[33] The
strength of the social norms connected to dog ownership was also strikingly
apparent: these animals have indeed become powerful social markers, and
the in-group mentality of the miniscule dog park demonstrates their social
function even more clearly.[34]

Nonetheless, the constant promotion of diversity during the pro–dog run

32   Hillary Twining, Arnold Arluke and Gary Patronkek, "Managing the Stigma of
Outlaw Breeds: A Case Study of Pit Bull Owners," *Society and Animals* 8: 1 (2000), pp. 25–52.

33   Other than the low numbers of lesbians in the South End, their relatively lesser
presence is also explained by the logics of gender. Women are, indeed, more vulnerable
in public space, and more confronted by violence. Their less numerous outdoor presence
is also explained by their lower economic wealth and the constraints linked to schooling
children. Sy Adler and Johanna Brenner, "Gender and Space. Lesbians and Gay Men in
the City," *International Journal of Urban and Regional Research*, 16: 1, (1992), pp. 24–34.
In the survey my questions addressed the dog's age, breed and name as well as the owner's
profession, income level (in various grades), race (white, Hispanic, African American,
Asian or other), marital status, number of children and sexual orientation.

34   Many works on gentrification have noted this phenomenon, albeit without analyz-
ing it in detail. See Elijah Anderson, *Streetwise: Race, Class and Change in an Urban
Community*, Chicago: University of Chicago Press, 1990, pp. 222–8; Brown-Sarancino, *A
Neighborhood that Never Changes*, p. 91. See also Duneier, *Sidewalk*, pp. 202–12.

campaign did pose further questions. The dog park was, certainly, part of the conquest of space, but this operation also served to promote a certain representation of space and social relations. The fences separating the dog run from the rest of the park did not materially prevent people coming and going, but they did mark its distance from the poorest and to ethnic minorities, while including well-off gay whites.

Conquering green spaces

Only a handful of residents came to let their dogs off the leash in a corner of Peters Park in the 1990s, marking off a separate space for this purpose. This was an illegal practice erecting what were initially only flimsy barriers— particularly in a material sense, because it would be a number of years before fences were finally put up around this area. Gradually, however, separations did establish themselves—spatial ones, but also divisions among groups and in the minds of residents. In order to understand this phenomenon, we need to resituate the dog park's creation within the context of a longer history: the history of the new homeowners' interest in public gardens.

The "community" of community gardens

A number of parks saw the formation of eponymous neighborhood associations—Union Park, Chester Square, Worcester Square—many of whose members would later engage in the battle over the dog run. Such names point not only to the presence of parks in these areas but also to the role that these parks play in the associations' activities. Union Park devotes an important part of its budget to the upkeep of its garden, closed to the public, and periodically pays for repairs to the fountain as its center, the pride of the local residents. During my study, the association also collected funds to pay for the replacement of the park, considered long overdue. Indeed, the power that the associations have gained owes much to the fact that they compensate for diminished public funding: the municipal parks budget amounts to $250,000 while the annual costs are $475,000.[35] Homeowners have sometimes created ad hoc bodies, like the Friends of Hayes Park on West Canton Street, in order to find the necessary funds for renovation work. Four interviewees active in

---

35   Marie-Hélène Bacqué (ed.), *Projet urbain en quartier ancien. La Goutte d'Or, South End*, Paris: PUCA, 2005, p. 146.

other local groups like the Historical Society were also involved in the renovation and upkeep of this small park.

The semi-private management of gardens, implemented by way of the
civic sector, gives rise to forms of control that rest on certain residents' strong
sense of legitimacy in regulating who is present in these spaces. I became
aware of this when I was transcribing an interview that I conducted in Hayes
Park, which was punctuated by a number of interruptions. The interruptions
corresponded to each of the times that my interlocutor—who lives not far
from the park and is a key figure in the Historical Society and Friends of
Hayes Park—greeted one of her acquaintances. There were many such interruptions, on account of her position and long-standing involvement in the
local network of civic associations. "How are you? How are the children?" she
asked. But while at first sight these seemed like friendly greetings, sometimes
she also gave these people a suspicious look. When a dog wandered near to
the bushes, she sighed, "Lots of trouble with dogs." She herself has two dogs,
but sees herself as a model owner. More generally, those individuals who do
not play by the rules are put back on the straight and narrow. One weekday
summer morning, passing close by Union Park, I saw a young man sit on the
grass playing the guitar. It was a fine day and the music was not bad
either . . . But I was surprised by his presence and stopped to watch him. Not
fifteen minutes passed before someone came to tell him that outside access to
the park was forbidden. The associations thus set themselves up as the legitimate regulators of everyday interactions in public spaces. This engagement
expresses the particular norms of the US upper middle class, inducing
considerate behavior, a rejection of overt confrontation, and keeping a very
close eye on any potential transgressors.[36] Public spaces are of considerable
importance to learning how to be a "good neighbor" and how to be "nice"—
which is crucial for this segment of the upper middle class, determined to
establish a well-adjusted relation to "others" living nearby.

The way in which spaces are occupied changed as these residents established control. The mixed housing construction programs and then the
renovation of Washington Street in the second half of the 1990s played a
decisively important role in this. This period saw the green light being given

---

36   Michèle Lamont, *La Morale et l'argent. Les valeurs des cadres en France et aux
États-Unis*, Paris: Métailié, 1995.

for the conversion of empty plots into community gardens—spaces that have today almost all become socially homogeneous. The trailblazers for this movement can be found among the most liberal of the new homeowners: indeed, the current president of the community gardens association, who arrived in the South End in the 1970s, is a member of the League of Women Voters and actively supported Pine Street Inn.

At the end of the 1980s residents informally occupied a number of plots; often Chinese immigrants or black people from the South used them to grow the plants of their regions of origin. The mobilization around gardens developed simultaneously in interaction with and in opposition to City Hall. The gardeners judged the 1976 municipal program seeking to arrange new gardens to be insufficient, and they instead created their own association. This association today runs ten gardens and four small parks, bringing together some 450 gardeners. Nonetheless, the manner in which this project became institutionalized only strengthened the white homeowners' grip. Indeed, the negotiations with the mayor's office gave the white homeowners the opportunity to take the lead, mobilizing their connections. The neighborhood association bringing together the inhabitants of Washington Street—and a future Washington Gateway employee—played a prominent role in this regard. Compromises were reached that consecrated and institutionalized once more the homeowners' right to decide how land should be used.

A guided tour of the community gardens—one of the walks mentioned in the previous chapter—allowed me to see what transformations they had undergone. The association president led the walk, while two other white, gay members also spoke during the tour. Almost all of the participants, as well as the gardeners whom we met, were white. For sure, diversity has not disappeared completely: one garden is predominantly frequented by black residents of the neighborhood, and another by Chinese residents—the latter having recently been targeted by other residents hostile to what they consider disorderly plant beds. In other green spaces, a white and wealthy population today predominates. There, strict rules have been established in order to regulate the use of the small lots. They forbid any negligence and demand the diligent use of space. Those who do not fall into line are quickly labeled lazy, deviant or even criminal, and can soon see their patch of land revoked.

Gardening has become one of the most popular collective practices among the white residents, who have to sign up on a waiting list in order to obtain a lot of their own. The association organizes a fundraiser each June, the gardens tour. Today's gardeners no longer plant vegetables as black migrants from the South once did, but mostly flowers, herbs and some tomatoes. These were in any case the plants that I watered one summer on behalf of a vacationing neighborhood association president, having been given the code that allowed me to unlock the bolt that kept the gate closed. This president's emphasis on diversity points not only to her nostalgia, impotent in the face of the forces of the real estate market and the commercial developments of the 1990s and 2000s, but also to the reforming function of these spaces— this time for the upper middle class, and no longer for the working class. Like the neighborhood associations, they promote a set of behaviors among the white homeowners—notably including a taste for diversity, which implies respect for the few remaining low-income and nonwhite residents. That one of the neighborhood walks organized by my first ally would be devoted to gardens, with the association president serving as its guide, makes sense: as we saw in the previous chapter, the objective of these tours is precisely to allow new arrivals to see the charms of the "diverse" South End.

Friends of parks, friends of dogs

Some twenty years after the creation of the community gardens, debates over Peters Park led to a mobilization of similar intensity to the one around Pine Street Inn. I chose to analyze it in detail, first because it allows us to focus on an improbable object of sociological inquiry—dogs—and also because it allows us to measure what resistance to gentrification still existed in the 2000s.

The Friends of Peters Park is an association founded in 1998 with the specific objective of creating an official public space in the part of the park where some residents already used to walk their dogs. The majority of its members belonged to the upper middle class. The four leaders of this association from 1998 to 2007 were all property owners, and two of them consultants. As of 2004 the board included a doctor, the vice president of a real estate investment firm, a woman who was a senior administrator at Harvard University, an architect (who had built the loft facing the park, where he lived with his partner, and who had also outlined the plans for the dog run) and a theater director. A large majority of the board's members were white: 9 out of

11, as of 2000. Finally, half are gay.[37] Since its creation this group has been run in an extremely professional manner, deploying its members' expertise and benefiting from donations. The political context in which this mobilization took place also encouraged such methods. After having initiated the development of Washington Street in 1995, Boston City Hall devoted $1.3 million to the renovation of Peters Park. This project offered the Friends of Peters Park the opportunity to carry out the changes dearest to their hearts: fences surrounding the dog run, a new surface adapted for animal use, fountains, large rocks and a barrier dividing it into two areas for different sized dogs. However, the mayor's office approved these measures only on condition of the association's financial contribution. For this reason, collecting funds was a priority, and some particularly mobilized individuals took charge of the networking effort that this required. The mayor's office has also indirectly supported the dog owners' cause through the intermediary of Washington Gateway. In 2004, for example, this latter organized a "Doggy Fashion Parade," an initiative led by a designer living in the neighborhood and sponsored by the Animal Rescue League. A few years later, in 2008, this same body gave a $958 grant to the new dog grooming salon on Washington Street. It put the subsidy toward making a sign for the storefront.[38]

In order to collect the necessary funds, the Friends of Peters Park obtained 501(c)(3) nonprofit status, exempting it from taxation and allowing donors to deduct contributions from their taxes. It created an advisory committee composed of figures renowned for their status and political connections. Silvio Dante, the developer who controls large areas around Washington Street, financed the fences, on which his name is engraved. The Animal Rescue League, a prestigious Massachusetts foundation established in 1899 and headquartered in the South End, was the second main contributor, donating $50,000. A significant reservoir of social capital allowed the association to establish links with city councillors, one of whom—a fierce champion of the dog run—was the initiator of the 2005 decree creating an official label,

---

37   All these figures were gathered from interviews, and sometimes joined together with information found on the Internet.

38   On the parade, see the Washington Gateway website post of November 6, 2004. On the subsidy for the Espeso Pawtique store, see Aviva Gat, "Grant is a good sign for Pawtique," *South End News*, September 25, 2008.

"Dog Recreation Space," which was applied first to Peters Park in the South End and then to other parks across the city. It also made connections with the charity sector—enlisting a learning center for the homeless, very strongly supported by City Hall, to clean the dog run once a week. The association particularly focused on attracting the very wealthiest donors. The name of each dog owner who gave more than $1,000, as well as the name of the owner's pet, were reproduced on a brick walkway inside the dog park, and a list of the most generous donors is on display at the entrance. They include a former Union Park association president who owns a Labrador and whose spacious home played host to one of the Friends of Peters Park's main fundraisers. I attended this event myself on the invitation of my first ally. Upon entering we were invited to write our own names and those of our dogs on a nametag. There, I came across a dozen people whom I had already met during my study, as well as almost all of the candidates for the municipal by-elections due to take place the following month. The owners of the canine bakery offered treats for the dogs that had to stay at home.

Other than the resources of the most connected residents, the Friends of Peters Park also used force of numbers in order to get the green light from City Hall. In 2006 they launched a petition, managing to get 1,000 residents' signatures in three weeks. On account of their everyday encounters in the street or at the dog run, the dog owners form a very close-knit network, and a particularly effective one. That said, financial imperatives forced the organization to concentrate its efforts on the business world. In an association document listing the petition's signatories, it distinguished among individuals, local businesses (eighteen of them) and real estate agents (numbering twenty-nine)—the latter appearing to offer particularly important support.

By 2007 this mobilization had achieved total financial and political success. However, in the first half of the decade, the initiative taken by the Friends of Peters Park had caused a hard-fought battle, whose outcome was initially far from certain. Ever since the 1960s, strict rules had forbidden the presence of dogs off their leashes in public places, and sometimes of any animals at all in communal living environments, shops and offices. Moreover, the restructuring of public spaces and their usages was a complex process when it involved the redefinition of existing social norms. The city councillor for the South End's electoral district came from South Boston—an "Irish" bastion bearing particularly significant political influence in municipal affairs—and he provided only superficial support to the Friends of Peters Park.

It was after the erection of the first fences that a particularly strong opposition developed locally—initiated by a real estate developer who had in the late 1990s engaged in the construction of a block of 158 luxury apartments looking out onto the park, which at that time sold for between $440,000 and $1.7 million. He was one of the first developers to invest in the still-disreputable Washington Street area. In his mind, the presence of dogs and a muddy space near his development would create a nuisance putting off buyers who were already sensitive to the area's bad reputation. His perception of dogs was not entirely out of place. In 1979 a study commissioned by the BRA on inhabitants' image of the neighborhood posed questions on the following topics: "Too many alcoholics, derelicts;" "Dirty streets, uncollected garbage;" "Noise, streets too noisy;" "Too many dogs, dog litter."[39] Here, dogs were synonymous with urban decline.

The developer's opposition was of some importance. He was a member of a neighborhood association situated just beside the park, whose president—himself not lacking in resources—also put up active resistance. A gay man, and a South End inhabitant since 1992, he had held the reins of his association for many years, and he was moreover a member of the Washington Gateway board. He had established significant links with certain city councillors—including the one for South End–South Boston mentioned above—and more generally with the mayor's office, where his husband worked. He contacted City Hall protesting the illegality of the dog run and brandished the threat of court proceedings. A Chinese property owner living near the park also joined this mobilization. He was one of the few Chinese residents still present in a city block that had once been home to many Asians. He circulated a petition that picked up some 200 signatures. Three papers—the *South End News*, the *Boston Courant* and even the city's *Boston Globe* reported on the conflicts now under way. But ultimately, the submission made to the mayor's office holding that the South End dog run should be labeled a Dog Recreation Space was accepted on February 6, 2007. How can we explain the success of

---

39   Consensus, *Marketing Public Opinion: Communication Research Report of Findings, 1978 Urban Renewal Survey of the South End*, Boston: Boston Redevelopment Authority, 1979.

the Friends of Peters Park, despite the fierce opposition they faced, not only in opening the dog run but in making what had been a symbol of urban decay into the ultimate proof of the neighborhood's "mixed" character?

Creating a new public space

Between 1997 and 2007 the municipal department charged with animal control recorded a fourfold increase in the number of dogs in the South End. There were 841 dogs for a human population of 28,000, placing the neighborhood second in Boston in the number of dogs per person.[40] Going beyond this quantitative phenomenon, we also need to analyze the visibility of dogs in relation to animals' role in the workings of social distinction in the US.

Pets as a means of social distinction

Numerous studies, and even books, have focused on the fashion for owning dogs and the astronomical sums of money, time and affection invested in them.[41] The price of a pedigree dog is around $1,000, and can rise to around $2,000 for a French bulldog. Meanwhile expenditures connected to dog food, dog walkers and veterinarian bills have exploded. Between 2000 and 2004, spending on pets rose by 18 percent: a 17 percent increase for pet food, 18 percent for services and 38 percent for the initial outlay. Naturally this expenditure rises in tandem with the owners' income.[42] The average sum that each of my sixty dog-run questionnaire respondents spent on their dogs was $225 a month, reaching as much as $800 for multiple interviewees. Some respondents reacted to the question with a vaguely embarrassed grin and exclamations along the lines of "Too much!" albeit in a rather amused tone. Linda, a South End resident and TV journalist, explained during our interview:

---

40   Cristina Silva, "South End Dogs Lapping Up Luxuries," *Boston Sunday Globe*, June 11, 2006.

41   For example, Diane Brady and Christopher Palmieri, "The Pet Economy: Americans Spend an Astonishing $41 Billion a Year on Their Furry Friends," *Business Week*, August 6, 2007; James Vlahos, "Pill-Popping Pets," *New York Times*, July 13, 2008.

42   New Strategist Publications, *Who's Buying for Pets*, Ithaca, NY: New Strategist Publications, 2004; American Veterinary Medical Association, *U.S. Pet Ownership & Demographics Sourcebook*, Schaumburg, IL: Membership & Field Services, 2006.

I probably spend about 600 dollars per month on them or so. A dog walker for two dogs daily, food, cookies, treats, toys, etc . . . It adds up, but—well, once you fall in love with them, you do what you have to do.

As of 2008, there were five speciality shops offering pet food, accessories and services in the South End. One of them, the Polka Dog Bakery, is set out over two stories. At first glance, nothing suggests anything out of the ordinary about this bakery, except for the flavors—carrot, tuna or liver—and the bone-shaped form of the biscuits presented in thirty large bowls near the counter. Cakes and (reconstituted) animal bones arranged in large baskets are just some of the many handcrafted treats that the bakery invites owners to buy for their pets. It also offers numerous collars and other accessories. In 2008 the South End's yoga center offered a class called "doga"—a practice that has now spread to other US cities.[43]

The breed of the dog and potentially their numbers, the accessories they are dressed in, the activities and practices associated with pet ownership, and even the owner's body language and affective and moral relations with the animal, can all be analyzed as an indicator of the owner's social position—an aspect of a particular habitus. A dog is one of the objects displayed close to the body—like clothes and other accessories—that act as a powerful marker of status. But not to be confused with the exhibition this distinction functions to distance dog owners from primal needs and base animal natures, and through this, from the "vulgar who give into these desires without restraint."[44] You might think that having to deal with animals' basic needs would put these privileged groups off keeping pets in the home, following the civilizing process described by Norbert Elias.[45] In fact, the practices relating to dogs that have developed in recent years are intended precisely to obscure or euphemize this animal nature. Upper-middle-class residents have thus managed to inscribe social distinction in something as "natural" as the bodies of dogs.

They do so by way of accessories, often with high-end branding, as in the case of a Gucci collar or a Chanel dog bag. There is also a hierarchy of dog breeds. Nobility is defined by the "purity" of the dog's breeding which comes

---

43   "Tips for Doing Doga," *Washington Post*, April 1, 2008.

44   Bourdieu, *Distinction*, p. 196.

45   Norbert Elias, *The Civilizing Process: Sociogenetic and Psychogenetic Investigations*, Oxford: Blackwell, 2000.

at a price, but also by the dog's corporeal *hexis*. Such aspirations to ostentatious elegance are echoed in the appearance of greyhounds or of Great Danes (large, svelte dogs that have long legs and ambling strides), in the sophisticated eccentricity of some poodles and airedales (great plumes of fur and long noses), or even so-called "French" bulldogs and pugs (stocky bodies, flat faces). Miniscule pets with long fur like chihuahuas, Yorkshire terriers, and Malteses denote a minimalist chic, as well as evoking the most tender feelings. For their part, Labradors, Great Pyrenees, Eskimos and golden retrievers exhibit beauty norms based on a distinguished simplicity. The dog's pedigree, or cross-breeding,[46] but also the number of dogs that the owner has, are social markers that are directly visible in public space. When two dogs of the same breed walk ahead of their owner, the social distinction effect is redoubled.

The profile of the South End dog owners directly benefited the Friends of Peters Park. This is a well-off clientele, ever ready to set the powerful but now renewed stakes of social distinction in play. This population contributed generously to the association in several rounds of donations, allowing it to collect $363,000 in total. For example, tickets to attend one of its fundraisers cost $120 apiece. The dog owners' arrival in the South End was accompanied by the emergence of businesses that gave their financial backing to the association's battle. Many dog-walking companies were now operating in the area, each employing between five and ten people, while dog-related boutiques had become flourishing enterprises. The daily receipts of the dog bakery situated on a city block by Peters Park were around $2,500, with major peaks in activity at certain times of year, such as Christmas, that lent themselves to buying gifts. Meanwhile, a factory making the "handmade" products sold in the boutique employed six or seven people. One of its owners was on the Friends of Peters Park board, and lent the association his premises for one of the fundraisers.

Certain residents were all the more disposed to supporting the dog park campaign because it offered the opportunity to cash in on their local networks through related businesses. The dog-bakery owners—artists, but struggling to live off their art alone—found the bakery was a lucrative service to offer. One dog walker I spoke to had also understood this. A gay man and university graduate, he lost his editorial post at a Boston newspaper and began working

---

46   Recently coming into fashion are labradoodles, crossing a Labrador and a poodle, or even pugoodles, crossing a pug and a poodle.

for a friend who had been the first to establish a dog-walking company in the South End. He then put to use the numerous contacts he had made in the neighborhood since arriving in 1995, and set up his own company. Since then he has moved to invest in the dog market emerging in Somerville, a town near Cambridge undergoing gentrification, and where a dog run has recently been created. He also uses his own yard as a park for clients' dogs. As a sign of the roots he still has in the South End (where he gladly came one morning to answer my questions), as we sat on a bench during our interview he continually greeted people passing in the street.

The arrival of new, wealthy residents—which as we have seen owed much to City Hall's approach in the mid-1990s and the development of Washington Street—contributed to the explosion in this market. In turn, real estate agents have taken dog owners' requirements into consideration. The dog run quickly became a selling point. Signaling this adaptation is the fact that one block of lofts on Washington Street—a center of some of my research subjects' socializing—is promoted as being "dog friendly." It attracts numerous dog owners who face difficulties buying an apartment in a building that allows pets. The renowned developer of Washington Street immediately understood what benefit he might draw from the dog run, and he contributed to financing it, meanwhile, his initially hostile counterpart also eventually changed his tune. Indeed, the real estate developers who could have provided robust opposition to the dog run eventually became the Friends of Peters Park's greatest allies.

Public space and canine socialization

Insofar as it makes public space into a central issue, dog ownership also has an impact on the way in which social distinction plays out. Distinction through pet ownership is particularly visible and thus particularly effective, especially outdoors where the dogs' presence is very apparent. This is one of the central characteristics of dogs, which need walking more than other pets do. The principal arteries of the South End see a virtual canine parade, particularly on the weekend.[47] Added to this are the long periods dogs and

---

47   Costumed dog parades are organized for Halloween. In 2007, 250 to 275 dogs and 600 people participated. "A parade of pooches wearing outlandish costumes will make their way through the streets of the South End at the Divas Unleashed pet parade." Aviva Gat, "South End Gets Spooky," *South End News*, October 23, 2008.

their owners spend sitting out on the neighborhood's terraces, with a bowl of water generally set on the floor for the dog. In some places there are even little hooks where dog leashes can be tied. A kennel that offers a spa and "bed and breakfast" service, and organizes excursions for pets, offers pickup service in the South End every morning. The bus arranged for the dogs — each of them attached to its seat by a little seatbelt — then returns in the evening. Residents gather on the corner of Union Park for this purpose twice a day, waiting for their dogs and often discussing them among themselves in great detail.

But the dog run is the central site for deploying a social status in which the assertion of openness and the taste for diversity now play an important role. The stakes for defining this new social distinction doubtless arise from the fairly improbable function of the dog park space. This struck me from my first visit to the dog run. The unpleasant effect on certain senses — with the very strong smell of urine, and dust everywhere — is here combined with the spectacle of highly sophisticated rituals. It is striking how the animals fulfill their basic needs in the very space where their owners are able to distance themselves from such base urges. Indeed, in the dog park the owners do not just let their pets off the leash; they are also very much occupied with watching other dogs, throwing them balls, stroking their fur and collectively discussing their pets' behavior and appearance. As the animals urinate, defecate and sniff each other — and sometimes mount each other — the owners concentrate on how they run, jump and interact.[48] In the summer shade of the park's trees, before heading to a café or restaurant, the owners strike up conversations and flirt, allowing them to forget for a moment the dust and the smell, the saliva and the excrement. We thus see how these pets' presence at the dog run plays a role in shaping and displaying very particular social norms — norms that are visible at the dog run, but which daily walks also extend across the neighborhood as a whole.

Another factor adding to the importance of this public space and its highly exclusive character is the profound change, over the course of the 1990s, in the norms regulating the relationship to animals in the home. Not only did domestic pets rise in the US during this period, but above all there was an

---

48   On the masking of the "obscene," see Bourdieu's comments on nudity in opera in *Distinction*, p. 6.

increased investment in them—and this is not only a matter of money or of the affection expressed within the private sphere. The dog is no longer, or no longer only, considered an element of the family sphere distinct from parents and children—nor even its master's loyal pet who is trained accordingly. One marker of this changed view is that the vocabulary itself has shifted: once known as pets, dogs are now "companion animals."[49] Judging by the terms that the Friends of Peters Park officially used, dog owners now prefer to call themselves "dog guardians."

The animal thus becomes the object of a socialization effort—many of whose features are borrowed from child-rearing, in particular the fact that this socialization, reinforced by formal training, also entails a collective dimension. Linda, the television journalist mentioned above, strongly insists on this point. She took her young Labrador to a puppy training class, where he learned a few "basic rules."

> I brought my youngest lab to a puppy training class and it was great. I highly recommend it. The puppies are all so cute and they teach you a lot about basics, potty training, how important socializing your dog is with people and other pooches and just what to expect with a puppy. They can be a handful!

As for her second Labrador, which she chose to adopt rather than buy: "I brought him to a dog trainer a couple of times just to refresh the basics with him." She then concluded:

> I think constant dog socialization and interaction is key to a well-behaved and adjusted dog. The more scenarios you can bring them to, the more places, people and pooches, the better.

---

49 "Something remarkable has been happening in post-industrial contexts across the world since the 1990s: a shift from considering pets (especially dogs) as a species apart, to a reconsideration of pets (especially dogs) as profoundly appropriate objects of human affection and love." Heidi J. Nast, "Critical Pet Studies?," *Antipode* 38: 5 (2006), pp. 894–906. See also Leslie Irvine, *If You Tame Me: Understanding Our Connection with Animals*, Philadelphia: Temple University Press, 2004.

Often, the same businesses involved in the kennels and dog-walking markets offer these classes. The new norms of socialization are also spread by other channels, from popular books to magazines.[50] One turning point was the best-selling *The Hidden Life of Dogs*, published in 1993. On the website of the well-known publishers Simon & Schuster, which reprinted a paperback edition in 1995, we can read that the author offers "the simple and surprising answer to the question 'What do dogs want most?' Not food, not sex, but other dogs."[51]

This compulsory socialization requires collective organization, and no longer just a one-to-one relation between the animal and its master. It is collective in the sense that it relies on specialists' support—their competence validated by professional training and established in their written works—but above all insofar as their socialization proceeds by way of integration into a group of dogs and dog owners. The dog must not only learn behaviors based on obedience, but also acquire the capacity to evolve alongside both its canine counterparts and other human beings, in an interaction that is at once both dynamic and controlled. I could also see negative proof of this in the dog that I looked after, whose eccentricity seemed to echo her owner's. Other than the fact that she was of totally unknown breeding, her profound indifference to the other animals and the climbinbg rocks at the dog run contrasted with the other dogs' attitude.

From this point of view, Linda's comments were of considerable interest, showing the extent to which owners have internalized this imperative. In her mind, learning is conceived as a collective process, but it is also a singular one in that it is adapted to each particular dog and its own "personality." This personality moreover leads the animal toward particular relations with other animals and human beings. The owners' doting words on their dogs when they release them at the dog run often refer to the friends they are going to make. Moreover, the difficulties that they may face in this socialization process are the object of a section in the local paper, the *South End News*. Like the readers' letters column in women's magazines, "Lady Dog" answers questions and offers advice for problems that are not only practical or medical

---

50   See for example *The Bark*, "a magazine about modern dog culture."

51   Elizabeth M. Thomas, *The Hidden Life of Dogs*, Boston: Houghton Mifflin, 1993.

but above all affective and relational.[52] Even more importantly for our study, these relations with dogs involve places where people meet to organize this socialization — training and classes for puppies, outings organized by professional dog walkers, but also more everyday sites of apprenticeship like public parks. Dogs are brought here several times a day not only to give them some exercise and return home in a calmer state, but also to allow them to socialize and make friends, and to let their owners do the same.

Homeowners and dogowners

The dog owners' demand for public space is particularly strong in the South End. This is a result of the growing number of upper-middle and even upper-class residents. All the same, the craze for dogs and the dog run is also explained by factors linked to family and sexual orientation. Indeed, one part of this population is not only financially able but also particularly well disposed to adherence to the norms that now regulate people's relations with animals. For a certain number of gay people, whether singles or couples, dogs play a role in filling in for offspring of their own, as having children remains an arduous process in spite of Massachusetts's liberal legislation that legalized same-sex marriage in 2004. Meanwhile, dogs seem to be much more present in the company of gay men than gay women, doubtless because the former are better positioned to take to public spaces. Indeed, out of sixty survey respondents at the dog run I found just one lesbian.

While we find many dog owners among the South End's gay population, they are also popular among young heterosexual couples who make their homes in the South End for a few years before moving to raise children in the suburbs. This is also the case of early retirees who, having brought up their children in these same suburbs, now wish to savor the pleasures of city-center urban living. Animals thus compensate for the absence of children, without involving any of the constraints associated with putting kids through school. For these households as for gays, nonetheless, the dog cannot be understood only as a default option connected to some desire to conform to

---

52 One South End resident who was worried about having to share his new girl-friend's bed with her dog wrote in to Lady Dog. She advised him to put up with this at the girlfriend's house, while reserving the right to make the dog sleep on the floor at his own place.

a hegemonic marital and family norm. Indeed, the owners' strong connection with the animal also expresses the fact that they are taking some distance from traditional norms. We also find this logic among the divorced or separated women discussed in Chapter 3. A certain number of these women around fifty or sixty years of age turn to a sociability that is disconnected from the family sphere—as the South End's civic life allows them to do—as they (re)construct their affective and domestic life around short-term or non-cohabiting romantic attachments and a privileged connection to an animal.

For this population of singles, and more generally for all inhabitants in search of partners and socializing in the context of steeply rising divorce rates, the dog run offers a space to meet people. It is renowned for providing this function, facilitated by the relatively similar basic scenario facing all those who frequent it: upon arriving they let the dog off the leash and vaguely keep an eye on it, then their gaze turns to the center where a number of animals are usually playing around the boulders. The spectacle that this offers those in attendance encourages commentary. Their gaze may then turn to the edges of the dog run, where other human beings are standing. The dogs' own behaviors spark interactions, as I learned unexpectedly during my week of dog sitting during one research visit. Though I recoiled from the animals' friendly but overbearing—and all too wet—displays of affection, for the sake of playing along with the game of participant observation, I did go so far as to stroke the dogs' heads and throw them balls. I also tried as best as I could to spark casual conversation. The other dog owners, who were certainly much more at ease than I was, were brimming with jocular comments and smiles. During my week observing the dog run I thus came to see this space as a site of intense sociability, playing host to animated conversations. It is difficult to judge the closeness of the friendships established (according to the dog park's defenders) thanks to these animals.[53] That said, I did see a few instances of flirting, and I also came across a number of the residents whom I had already interviewed during my study. Moreover, it was here that Linda met her husband.

---

53   Douglas Robins, Clinton Sanders and Spencer Cahill, "Dogs and Their People: Pet Facilitated Interaction in a Public Setting," *Journal of Contemporary Ethnography* 20: 1 (1991), pp. 3–25.

The mobilization around the dog run not only benefited from the large number of dog lovers. It also owed much to the contacts and resources that built up within local groups. The majority of active members of the Friends of Peters Park were also members of these other organizations, including one woman whose husband was a mainstay of the neighborhood association. Furthermore, the mobilization in favor of the dog run strengthened the alliance between dog owners and gay and straight residents from the middle classes. This alliance rested on the links that homeowners had forged with one another in the neighborhood associations from the late 1960s onward. The association situated on Washington Street had, on the basis of just such ties, actively participated in this thoroughfare's renovation by driving the creation of Washington Gateway—and now it, too, signed the Friends of Peters Park's petition. The dog run offered the prospect of an influx of residents who could drive the frontier of the "bad" part of the South End further to the east. While not so long ago this boundary was located along Tremont Street, what was now at stake was to remove the stigma associated with Washington Street by making it a space that brought together residents from across the whole neighborhood. The people championing the dog run devoted a significant amount of energy to strengthening existing connections with local groups, notably in going to association meetings with maps and promotional materials and presenting the plans for the park. I came across one of the group's leaders at these meetings on two occasions.

The mobilization in favor of the dog park thus stood in continuity with the renovation of the neighborhood and of its infrastructure, which proceeded over the decades by appropriating public spaces and exercising control over those populations considered "deviant." It presented the dog run as a further step in clearing Peters Park of drug dealers, prostitutes and the homeless, and it also offered the prospect of an exclusive space. At the same time, the park appears to be the perfect illustration of "diversity" considered as the simultaneous presence of different populations in the same location. Ultimately, this collective action strengthened the bonds whose genesis in the 1960s we have already described: the connections among homeowners engaged in civic life, but also, within this context, the connections that gays and heterosexuals had forged. The dog run furthermore provided a demonstration of the values that have gradually developed fostering these rapprochements: a taste for diversity and a gay-friendly attitude.

From the Dogs' Cause to the Children's Cause
"Diversity" in School

Founded in the mid-1980s, the Neighborhood Parents for the Hurley School is another local group whose members maintain close ties with one another. Its history as well as the profile of those engaged in it also reflects the history of gentrification itself. Its founder, born in 1944, grew up in an inner-city neighborhood not too far from the South End, and he moved there as a student in 1969. He quickly abandoned his studies to go into real estate, before working for mayor Kevin White and the BRA, redeploying social capital and knowledge of the neighborhood that he had acquired during his extensive meetings with buyers and sellers. "Because I was in real estate, I knew people on every single street. I knew every building." Later returning to real estate, he fell victim to the crash at the end of the 1980s. His financial situation led him to send his children to the public school located on the street where he lived, and he created the school's first parents' association. This group sought to improve both the functioning and reputation of a public school that had been deserted by many middle-class parents, who opted for private schooling or else left the neighborhood entirely.

But only at the beginning of the 2000s, when the improvement in the South End's reputation made the prospect of raising children in this neighborhood less frightening, did the association really take off. It used the same fundraising techniques that we saw earlier, with the help of the same neighborhood restaurants. The association's efforts were met with major success, collecting $300,000 to build shiny new sports facilities for the school. Association members continued seeking donations outside the neighborhood, and managed to get Ikea to replace the school's furniture.

Today, the former leader of the dog-park group pours her energy into the parents' association. This consultant, born in 1964 and holders of an MBA, works from home and is mother to two children. Her efforts regarding the Hurley School are clearly based on the promotion of diversity—both in relation to her own children, vaunting the benefits they will draw from a mixed urban environment, and for working-class children, maintaining that the solution to public schools' problems is the presence of a 20 percent proportion of middle-class children. After showing some reluctance toward the gentrifier parents' initiatives, the Hurley School principal was soon replaced. The parents' association's founder took a step back after the conflicts in the school, but in our interview he summarized what they had achieved: "We took power."

The South End: A Victorian, mixed, artistic, gay-friendly and dog-friendly neighborhood

At the beginning of the 2000s, the mobilization in favor of the dog park was growing, winning valuable allies. Just as valuable as social or economic capital, the rhetorical resources the movement developed helped establish the legitimacy of this initiative. The organization's need to make itself a "moral entrepreneur" led it to promote a "good" way of being a dogowner. The Friends of Peters Park actively engaged in this campaign, with a note to group members on July 22, 2004, mentioning the growing opposition to the dog run and exhorting pet owners and walkers to respect and enforce the rules: "Peer pressure works, please use it." Another document listing the association's activities reflected the priority it gave to promoting certain types of behavior. A section entitled "Education" listed six points: "Rules Posted; Dog Run Users Guide; Emphasis on Self-Policing; Letter to Commercial Dog Walkers; Meeting with Neighborhood Associations; Website Launch."

For the purposes of establishing these norms, the Friends of Peters Park naturally enough drew on the behavioral codes that had taken shape in recent years, sanctioned by magazines and books. This was not a neutral enterprise, and valorized practices pointing to a certain level of income. Other than banning barking and obliging owners to pick up dog litter and to respect the posted park hours, it explicitly invited dog owners to donate money. All the more important, these norms supposed the owners' willingness to submit to collective rules rather than restrict themselves to a relation centered on their own pet. They presupposed a feeling of belonging to a community of dog owners that was very strongly established and made itself highly visible among the gentrifier group.

Adding to the implicit forms of exclusion that this type of attitude favored was a more explicit desire for distance from deviant populations. During one neighborhood association meeting, a member of the Friends of Peters Park was asked about the potential use of fountains by individuals other than the dog owners. She replied, "We don't want people who are not here for the dogs." Responding to concerns of this kind, the campaign in favor of the dog run became increasingly colored by a persistent suspicion toward individuals who did not live in the neighborhood. This disdain was fed by the knowledge that there was no chance of these people giving money. One of the association's leaders told me:

> It's a continuous education process, because you always have new people coming from other places, Dorchester . . . One Sunday there was a group of punks who'd met on the Internet . . . Well, it's a public park. You just have to try to educate them. We ask them for money . . . It is a privilege, not a right, to have this dog run. We have to repeat that constantly . . . You should contribute with good behaviors, with money, with time in order to make this thing work. . . . We do all kind of things. We go up there on Saturday morning, talk to people. We went to a meeting for the dog walkers to make sure they don't bring more than three dogs at a time.

This distancing from other populations is also expressed in these residents' attitude to pit bulls, a widely publicized phenomenon in the US that is closely associated with the black working class. In 2004, the city decree making the dog run official mentioned an incident that had taken place in the South End, in which a very wealthy couple living in the neighborhood was embroiled: "In August 2003, a pit bull mauled and killed Lucy, the family dog (a Maltese) of Superintendent of Boston Public Schools Thomas Payzant while his wife, Ellen Payzant, was walking in the neighborhood." I was repeatedly told the story of the death of this tiny dog, almost swallowed whole by a pit bull. The fact that this unhappy event became part of the historical epic related by the dog run's champions tells us a great deal about the boundaries they established with regard to the "other" dog owners in the area, dividing lines which accompanied the decline of pit bulls in the South End. As one of the group's leaders explained:

> When we first lived here, there were a lot of people around Peters Park and there were people, owners would bring them, not necessarily in the park,

but to train them to fight. You would see it a lot. People with pit bulls. And I don't see that anymore. Maybe it's the pit bull . . . We had incidents . . . But it's been a long time since . . .

The norms on display during the campaign echoed the rhetoric of the residents backing the project. This symbiosis can be found in various documents, including emails sent by residents who signed the petition. While only a limited number of the signatories mentioned their profession, fifteen out of eighty-three could be identified as members of the upper middle class (consultant, executive, doctor). Six others whom I had been able to interview or whom I had met at other moments during my study were of similar socioeconomic status. In general, the style of their letters was clear and well argued, and their tone serious rather than emotional. Only one of them, evoking a small puppy picked up from an animal shelter, fell into the sentimental. As in the association's own documents, three main themes recurred: the dog run suits the neighborhood's image, offers a source of increased safety and encourages commercial development.

The neighborhood's image was evoked using the following terms: community, sense of community, diversity, neighbors, a vibrant and diverse community, close-knit community, and socialize. The reference to community first and foremost allowed dog-run advocates to claim to represent a general cause and avoid appearing to be special interest group. The appeal to general interest—even if it is conceived as the aggregation of particular interests—was explicitly touted here. During my interviews, some residents explained to me that they paid taxes and thus ought to be able to enjoy the park as suited their own needs. They even drew parallels with parents' use of sandboxes that everyone has to pay for, whether or not they have children.

The reference to diversity spoke to another, slightly different line of argument. A letter to the city parks department in May 2003 evoked diversity, here defined as the peaceable coexistence of different groups:

Our park . . . is probably the most diverse pocket of activity you will ever see: Gay men walking their dogs, Hispanic kids playing baseball, Asian women practicing tai chi, white refugees from the suburbs planting flowers, African American toddlers tumbling about the playground, yuppie adults playing basketball, and homeless residents snoozing under the trees.

The intensity of social bonds and the ease of meeting one's neighbors and making friends in the South End are well-known themes: they are part of the arguments that residents mobilized in order to vaunt the neighborhood's diversity. The association's prospectus thus lists "Connecting People" as one of the space's positive attributes. A number of the emails repeat this anecdote, reproduced in the prospectus:

> As a new South End resident put it, "To our delight we discovered Peters Park right across the street. There, not only did we find a convenient spot for our dog to run, but a wonderful arena to meet our neighbors and feel a part of what we discovered was not merely a neighborhood, but rather a vibrant community in the richest sense of that word. Within a few weeks . . . we met more people than we had in the last five years we lived in Brookline."

We ought to emphasize that a "new resident" related this anecdote. The promotion of diversity by way of dogs is very much the work of a particular group in the South End. Class boundaries are drawn based on this centrally important value. It seems as if "diversity" here means that low-income residents can indeed use the park, but on condition that there is also a space reserved for the upper middle class. Here as well, love of diversity goes hand in hand with its strict limitation and control. This ambivalent relation also translates into a particular vigilance with regard to populations considered deviant. This is one of the main planks of the second theme that the residents writing in support of the dog park addressed—"safety." They mobilized this theme in a rather euphemized way, when it came to speaking of the individuals whose presence they considered undesirable. However, the manner in which they had conceived of and publicized the dog run did imply that homeless people ought to be kept at bay.[54] In one document written for the Friends of Peters Park, the first point reads: "Dog parks promote public safety." Responding to the question of "why the Peters Park dog run is the South End's best friend," it explained, "The Peters Park dog run makes Peters Park

---

54   Nevertheless, this stance took much less violent or more euphemized forms than the repression to which gentrification is often reduced. See Neil Smith, *The New Urban Frontier: Gentrification and the Revanchist City*, London: Routledge, 1996.

safer," because "Peters Park has historically been a magnet for crime and unsafe activity." Closely interlinked with the question of safety, the topic of homeless people and "illegal behavior" recurs throughout these emails. A retired engineer wrote:

> Over the fifteen years that I have lived here, that area of the park has been transformed from one that was dangerous, neglected, and infested with weeds, debris and illegal behavior, into one that is popular, safe, much cleaner, planted with flowers and filled with people enjoying themselves.

Three other messages explicitly refer to this question. One of them emphasizes the fact that the park "could be very easily lost to a criminal element." Another letter, in a rejoinder to those who complained about the smell of urine, wrote that it "may very well be caused by some of the human residents of the Park rather than its canine visitors." The couple whose dog was devoured by a pit bull evoked "a decrease in undesirable activity."

After addressing the closeness of social bonds and safety, the third theme instead stuck to a more commercial register. "Investing in Growth" was another benefit of the dog park that the prospectus listed, with one paragraph specifying the existence of a "lucrative market for a wide range of products and services generated by the dog-owning community." These three themes were far from being considered and deployed in contradiction with one another. Rather, they combined and mutually reinforced one another: after all, the upper middle class has never considered "being a good citizen" to be incompatible with a high socioeconomic status. As the prospectus makes clear in one sentence combining these three themes (community, safety and commerce), the dog park is the space "where friendships among dog guardians, regardless of age, income, or race, have been created, where couples have met, and where real estate and business deals have had their start."

The campaign mobilized these social norms *in vivo* in order to delegitimize the dog run's opponents and more specifically the Chinese resident at the origin of one petition, who was quick to vent his anger publicly. During one neighborhood association meeting, I saw how much the other participants didn't care for his sharp tone but also his strong accent and his body language as he stood up and approached the Friends of Peters Park representative in order to question her. This was perceived as being particularly inappropriate—even among those who had no prior sympathy for the dog run—in that it contravened the upper middle class' prevalent norms of conflict-avoidance and search for compromise. One of those present stormed out of the meeting complaining of having been taken hostage, despite the association's representative having assured him that she would take into account his point of view. The Chinese resident's stance was also discredited during another meeting where he rejected the idea of putting "Asian plants" in the park, since this had been proposed precisely in order to win his support. The champions of the dog run emphasized his "difficult" personality and inability to "compromise." Explaining that he was afraid of dogs, or even that he hated them, many association members stressed the psychological and emotional bases of his opposition, as opposed to there being any question of social divisions. Barely veiled allusions to Chinese cultural practices emerged in some conversations—indeed, with more than a whiff of racial stigmatization, as certain people who had attended meetings organized by the Friends of Peters Park were able to tell me.

The campaign's ultimate success was also possible thanks to the lack of countermobilization. Certainly resentment against gentrification does exist in the South End, and dogs have come to symbolize the arrival of the "new" inhabitants appropriating territory from the "old." This latter category includes a number of lower or middle-income residents, both gay and straight. The *South End is Over* blog railed against the yuppies' arrogance, the hold that families and their strollers exert, and, at the same time, the craze for dogs.[55] However, other than that site and a few articles occasionally appearing in the papers, hostility to gentrification—or even, "doggie yuppification"[56]— has little collective expression. This can largely be attributed to the decline of the protest movements of the 1960s and 1970s. The Chinese resident, who works in a Castle Square hardware store, did find support among his own community, but it did not mobilize in any great numbers. Their opposition was all the less likely given that the Friends of Peters Park generally made an effort to avoid any explicitly racist discourse, and indeed never ceased extolling the virtues of diversity. No other group—whether the Chinese, the black

---

55   On this site, see Chapter 3.
56   Wesley Morris, "I hate your dog," *Boston Globe*, July 13, 2008.

community or the Puerto Rican community at Villa Victoria whose declining civic engagement Mario Small explained—set itself up as an oppositional force of any consequence.

CONCLUSION

In delving into the upper middle class' relationship with public space, this chapter has shed light on debates over the logics of privatization and repression in the "neoliberal city."[57] Many works devoted to gated communities or commercial centers have brought to light some of the extreme forms of controlling undesirable populations. Exclusion mechanisms have also been introduced in inner-city neighborhoods, deliberately limiting access to previously more-open places like parks: indeed more effectively than the simple play of the market could.[58] But what about gentrified neighborhoods where a remaining working-class presence effectively compels residents to interact with different groups constantly? Logics of control are, certainly, at work here, but they are based on means that are both more unexpected and less violent. The conquest takes place not in wide-open spaces but rather in nooks and crannies, in the stoops, street crossings, little parks and community gardens. Animals have provided a resource of some importance in the gentrifiers' appropriation of spaces, allowing the initially-illegal presence of pets to be transformed into an engagement upholding the general interest—with City Hall's backing. Further still, animals contributed to the creation of institutionalized norms concerning both the transformation of space and, simultaneously, the relations among social groups. These animals, which cost so much and yet have also become "priceless," can only remind us of the "priceless child"

---

57   Jason Hackworth, *The Neoliberal City: Governance, Ideology, and Development in American Urbanism*, Ithaca, NY: Cornell University Press, 2007; Margaret Kohn, *Brave New Neighborhoods: The Privatization of Public Space*, New York: Routledge, 2004.

58   Setha Low, *The Politics of Public Space and Culture: On the Plaza*, Austin: University of Texas Press, 2000; Setha Low and Neil Smith (eds.), *The Politics of Public Space*, New York: Routledge, 2006; Mike Davis, *City of Quartz? Excavating the Future in Los Angeles*, New York: Verso, 1990.

that Viviana Zelizer described.[59] So after the legitimization of babies in the sand boxes and of children in the playgrounds, next came the legitimization of dogs' presence in public spaces. The heterosexual and family norms that marked the public parks created in the nineteenth century thus seem to have become less important. These parks' dark recesses are no longer the privileged, and stigmatized, cruising sites of decades past. Chance friendships or even the beginnings of dates grow out of conversations about dogs, whatever their owners' sexual orientation. The animals bring together both gays and heterosexuals in everyday practices like dog walking and frequenting the dog run and the dog boutiques, but also conversations and a wider sociability revolving around the Friends of Peters Park's events. Yet this relation to animals not only excludes less affluent gays, but simultaneously sets boundaries on gay visibility.

However much of a "success" this appropriation of space may be in terms of the control and exclusivity that the gentrifiers have established, it is neither total nor asserted openly. Not all deviant populations have been excluded from the neighborhood—a fraction of them remains present, evolving to adapt to specific locations and moments. The distancing of these "different" populations has proceeded on the basis of greater tolerance and in a different form than we see in the homogenization established through the creation of suburbs. The changing face of public space in the United States is not reducible, therefore, to the logics of repression and "war on the poor." Rather, this study brings to light the subtle way in which microsegregations are recomposed even as diversity is celebrated. We have seen that public spaces are sites where forces that are simultaneously both powerful and contradictory crystallize first because gentrifiers want to elaborate a way of life different from that of the suburbs, translating certain liberal ideas into action. At the same time, they still have a deep-rooted fear of the "ghettos" and of "the other" especially as embodied by black men." Neighborhood associations as well as groups like the Friends of Peters Park allow for the management of this contradiction, organizing forms of diversity made

---

59   Viviana Zelizer's work *Pricing the Priceless Child* (Princeton, NJ: Princeton University Press, 1994) draws out the phenomena that contributed to redefining the place of childhood in contemporary societies, such as emotional investment and the end of their economic use.

possible by the maintenance of strong barriers. The effect of this is that engagement in and control over public spaces can go hand in hand, producing the mixing that the gentrifiers seek; even if some of them would like to reduce this sharing of space even further.

Conclusion

The Making of the Liberal Upper Middle Class

This book has studied the way in which a space has been rehabilitated and appropriated by a group of inhabitants much wealthier than those who initially occupied it—without reducing gentrification to the contemporary logics of capitalism or to the repressive impulses of a privileged group. In a context marked by the political legacy of the 1960s—deindustrialization and the retreat of the state—the transformation of slums of Boston and other cities into trendy neighborhoods has required engagements taking many forms, involving the classic domains of local political life and culture, but also more surprisingly, food and pets. But this book's objective is not only to explain, avoiding simplistic schema, the metamorphosis of the inner city. Starting from the practices of the inhabitants of a major US city, it has also sought to bring to light the transformations of the social structure itself, through the emergence of a specific group within the privileged classes.

A MOBILIZED CLASS

Historians and sociologists of social classes have, for several decades now, questioned the strictly economic character of certain Marxist readings that obscure the long and nonlinear processes of forming social groups. Whatever the objective economic conditions may be, "it is not often that social groups appear suddenly out of nowhere or disappear bag and baggage from the social scene," as Luc Boltanski notes.[1] As the introduction underscored, the question of gentrification has led to numerous critical analyses, focused on the new populations considered "gentrifiers," "hipsters" or other parts of the "new middle classes." But these discussions would benefit from incorporating the precept that classes and their subsections are formed through the political work of mobilization, which also operates by way of everyday experiences that ought to be documented in detail. As the historian E.P. Thompson put it, "the working class did not rise like the sun at an appointed time."[2] As capitalism did not mechanistically generate the working class, neoliberalism does not make the gentrifier spring to life. Historians sharing this approach have delved, at the other end of the social hierarchy, into the recompositions of the upper classes, whose boundaries and cultural identities cannot be assumed in advance.[3] Proceeding along an analogous trajectory, this monograph on Boston has allowed us to retrace the stages of one group's formation. Though this group does not belong to the more widely studied upper fringes of the elite, today it shapes the landscape of major contemporary cities through the phenomenon of gentrification — even if not the 'rising sun' of the working class, still a central star in the constellation of contemporary social classes, and one whose rise we have been able to track over decades.

The South End inhabitants I studied are not part of the "upper class" in the sense that contemporary English usage implies, with the highest income levels and longer-standing wealth. The new residents do not have the same resources that the "old money" can use to live in the most desirable and

---

1   Luc Boltanski, *The Making of a Class: Cadres in French Society*, Cambridge: Cambridge University Press, 1987, p. 35. See also Pierre Bourdieu, "The Social Space and the Genesis of Groups," *Theory and Society* 14: 6 (November 1985), pp. 723–44.

2   Edward P. Thompson, *The Making of the English Working Class*, London: Penguin, 1991, p. 8.

3   Sven Beckert, *The Monied Metropolis, New York City and the Consolidation of the American Bourgeoisie, 1850–1896*, Cambridge: Cambridge University Press, 2001 ; Pierre-Paul Zalio, *Grandes familles de Marseille au XXe siècle: enquête sur l'identité économique d'un territoire portuaire*, Paris: Belin, 1999.

homogeneous parts of the city.[4] Situated slightly lower on the social scale, the group in question is nonetheless very much part of the privileged class. These high-level professionals and managers, the vast majority of whom earn salaries in the top fifth of US incomes, occupy powerful positions in fields such as consulting, law, management and finance. This group has grown considerably as the number of independent entrepreneurs has fallen in the past decades.[5] As their rising income in this period demonstrates, these professionals have emerged as the winners of the transformation of finance capitalism and the neoliberal reforms of the 1980s and 1990s. In the US context, they benefited from the Reagan-era tax cuts, growing salaries, and above all, the explosion of bonuses in large corporations.[6]

Beyond this obviously advantageous financial situation, another facet of their power can be identified when we turn our gaze away from the strictly economic sphere. They exercise power first and foremost over the city because urban renewal policies and gentrification favored the unceasing extension of bourgeois neighborhoods through city centers and then to the areas bordering them. More important still, the urban migration of these professionals, once restricted to the affluent suburbs, particularly in the United States, allowed a new social group to form and consolidate around a language, lifestyle and morality. That process is at the center of this book. The monographic study of a single neighborhood allows us to follow this development step by step, gradually seeing the boundaries of a group take shape—a group whose class culture structures the urban environment, but

---

4   Michel Pinçon and Monique Pinçon-Charlot, *Dans les beaux quartiers*, Paris: Seuil, 1989; Edward Digby Baltzell, *Philadelphia Gentlemen: The Making of a National Upper Class*, New Brunswick: London, 1992.

5   The proportion of self-employed managers has fallen from half of managers in the 1950s to 8% fifty years later. Dennis Gilbert, *The American Class Structure in an Age of Growing Inequality*, Belmont, CA: Wadsworth, pp. 61–2; Steven Brint, "Upper Professionals. A High Command of Commerce, Culture and Civic Regulation," in *Dual City: Restructuring New York*, ed. John Mollenkopf and Manuel Castells, New York: Russell Sage Foundation, 1991, pp. 155–76.

6   Robert Perrucci, *The New Class Society: Goodbye American Dream?* Lanham, MD: Rowman & Littlefield, 2008; L. Michel, J. Bernstein and S. Allegretto, *The State of Working America, 2008–2009*, New York: ILR Press, 2009.

also contributes to determining the fate of other social groups. Because gentrification is accompanied by a collective mobilization seeking to appro priate a terra incognita previously occupied by the working classes and racial minorities, the process also raises other, little-studied stakes: the recomposition of the privileged class.

This study has followed the formation of a group, not limiting itself to investigation of the group's economic resources and the influence over space that these allow. More precisely, this ever-greater spatial control has its origin in processes first of a political character, when the participatory turn opened up the municipal field of play. Mobilizations against the authoritarian remodeling of cities, often connected to the social movements of the 1960s, forced government authorities to retreat, and ultimately to consult the public in the rehabilitation of run-down inner cities. Nonetheless, "participation" was implemented in a manner that relied on the wealthiest residents' support, giving rise to a real co-management of urban space that continues today in control over real estate and commercial operations, and, above all, over public spaces. This new local politics allowed a group of wealthy residents to impose their preferred manner of rehabilitating the city. It also opened up sites for them to organize themselves, and to create a common culture and particular lifestyle—in sum, to constitute themselves as a legitimate group.

Indeed, South End inhabitants were only able to anchor their power in the city because they constructed this authority on the basis of a particular legitimacy, sanctioning themselves as a local elite authorized to make its voice heard in community affairs. The power of this group did not solely result from whatever preexisting resources they may have brought into the neighborhood. While the South End's gentrifiers clearly were well-equipped financially and culturally to begin with, they also accumulated wider and more diverse resources that now form the basis of their authority and ultimately made their appropriation of space possible. Following Max Weber, Pierre Bourdieu emphasized these legitimation processes; he saw the privileged relation to high culture and the relegation of the working classes to "vulgarity" as the linchpin of the upper classes' power.[7] Our study confirms

---

7   Pierre Bourdieu, *Distinction: A Social Critique of the Judgement of Taste*, Cambridge, MA: Harvard University Press.

this direct relationship between cultural tastes and social authority, even though gentrifiers are generally seen as eclectic consumers.[8]

South End Bostonians have proven their inventiveness. Though constantly signaling their distance from typical upper-middle-class neighborhoods, they have in fact used the most elite resources of high culture in order to impose themselves. In the 1970s, they mounted an effort to redesignate the neighborhood entirely, which, beyond their symbolic takeover of South End history, operated by way of promoting Victorian architecture as desirable and "in good taste." Residents who became real estate agents fashioned a new image of the neighborhood, erasing the poverty of the working-class lodgings and foregrounding the beauty of crown molding and high ceilings. Certainly the promotion of brownstones from the 1960s onward was a phenomenon that spread across the United States, but our study of the South End shows that it was not a matter of rediscovering an objectively valuable architectural reality. Rather, it was a cultural *and* political enterprise, and moreover one that contrasted with the postwar popularity of modern architecture. In Boston as elsewhere, the construction of this new sensibility was accompanied by particularly hard-fought battles whose stakes also included halting the construction of public housing projects and promoting the legitimacy of property owners to decide the fate of the neighborhood.

So this is far from a "new middle class" making a clean break with the old means of legitimation. Certainly, these residents have developed novel resources, but they have done so on the basis of the old means of domination; to bring all of these to light, we need to "avoid both the illusion of timelessness and the fascination with what is new."[9] It was only in the 1990s, once gentrification was already well advanced, that the watchword of "diversity" became so prevalent, and along with it, a specific mode of managing the neighborhood. Still, it remains true that the taste for brownstones—today widespread among the inhabitants of "mixed" neighborhoods—continues to encourage migration into working-class areas, where new inhabitants propose to restore the neighborhood's "former grace."

The multiple facets of this local power, which cannot be reduced to economic factors alone, outline the traits of a specific and novel class culture.

---

8   See Chapter 4.

9   Boltanski, *The Making of a Class*, p. 35.

In addition to their similar social characteristics and residential trajectories, it is a collective project that knit together this group of "good neighbors": the construction of a rehabilitated neighborhood, through which this group also constructed itself. This study traveled through the specific locations where this new authority was established (parks, streets or street corners, restaurants or living rooms), the groups who institutionalized it (neighborhood associations, the Historical Society, the municipal advisory boards), the practices through which it became routinized, and the events that punctuate these inhabitants' lives, from local meetings to restaurant dinners, from visits to artist studios on "open days" to charity soirées—without forgetting walks at the dog park. This lifestyle has the specificity of unfolding in a way somewhat distanced from the family unit, where not just working-class culture typically asserts itself,[10] but also the traditions of the aristocracy and upper class. Instead, local spheres, particularly the closely-tied civic and commercial dimensions, constitute the crucibles for this culture. Indeed, consumption is at the heart of these upper-middle-class residents' lifestyle, with each new restaurant—expression of both their standard of living and their residential project—becoming the object of endless commentary and debate. These practices are an expression of classed and class-defining tastes, speaking to this clientele's love for cosmopolitanism but also to their distaste —indissociably culinary and also social—for racial minorities. Effectively, blacks and Latinos remain stigmatized groups, and their "overly" visible presence—the expression of their culture in public space, as well as any demands they might make—awaken a great deal of worry for the new elite.

There is nothing new about this racialized fear, but white homeowners in these "mixed" neighborhoods have invented novel ways of managing it. Indeed, the residential project that they carried forth, at some remove from a certain style of upper-middle-class life, rapidly transformed into a moral quest. The ethic uniting these "good neighbors" involves a stigmatization of the closed, in-group mentality of the residential suburbs, replaced by a controlled proximity to poorer residents; distancing from conjugal and family norms in favor of a gay friendly attitude that nonetheless excludes any

---

10   See Norbert Elias, *The Established and the Outsiders*, Dublin: UCD Press, 2008; Richard Hoggart, *The Uses of Literacy: Changing Patterns in English Mass Culture*, Fair Lawn, NJ: Essential Books, 1957.

identitarian assertions of gay community; a way of life revolving around consumption but disdaining the accumulation of economic wealth if it is not accompanied by engagement in the "community"; and finally a rejection of racial segregation and celebration of multiculturalism that has not, however, eliminated the still-powerful fear of the black population and its culture. In sum, a genuine ethos of diversity came to shape the practices that also formed boundaries separating this group from the "others."

Diversity's New Elites

The upper-middle-class residents who speak of their taste for diversity parsimoniously organize their interactions with the preexisting populations. Urban sociology has already established this finding: conflicts linked to each social group's norms do not magically disappear as these groups imprint their aspirations and lifestyles on space.[11] Consequently, since spatial proximity does not erase social distance, coexistence produces singular forms of distinction among those confronting that proximity. This is the case for this privileged social group. Facilitated by the migration that postwar city planning policies encouraged, and by the economic transformations of the 1970s, this group also constituted itself in reaction to the earth-shaking social upheaval provoked by the protest movements of the 1960s. Indeed, these movements were not without consequence, speaking to the role that conflict and the mobilization of subordinated groups play in social change. The recomposition of the urban landscape allows us to see exactly how the relations of domination were reorganized by the revolt of workers, students, the colonized, women, gays and racialized people. While the asymmetries in these relations did persist, they were now accompanied by the greater integration — in certain places, on certain conditions — of social groups previously despised and removed from visibility, habitually relegated to cultural disdain and geographic distance.

In effect, a specific form of managing the relation to the "other" was instituted, based on the strong local power that wealthy residents, extolling the virtues of local democracy, were able to construct through the civic

---

11   Jean-Claude Chamboredon et Madeleine Lemaire, "Proximité spatiale et distance sociale dans les grands ensembles," *Revue française de sociologie* 11: 1 (1970), pp. 3–33

sector as they moved into the neighborhood. The South End gives us the chance to see the influence of a group of white homeowners, who though divided over the proper definition of "social mixing" could come to an agreement when it came to organizing and controlling that mixing. In order to understand the forms of coexistence in this neighborhood— whether they permitted social exchange, or reinforced the exclusion of the least well-off—this book returned to the battles that coexistence occasioned, in order to understand the forms of coexistence at work in these neighborhoods. In Boston, the symbolic erasure of the poorest residents, removed from visibility, as well as the fight against the mass construction of public housing, together formed an essential step in paving the way for lucrative real estate projects, the opening of new restaurants and an influx of households who had previously been more frightened by the "ghetto" than attracted by its Victorian architecture. As we have emphasized, the watchword "diversity"—implying that "others" be recognized, but in restricted places and numbers—only emerged later. This power allowed for a tight control of coexistence, though this coexistence was nevertheless strongly valorized. As such, the South End's new inhabitants were also capable of fighting to keep poor residents in the area, and they proclaimed themselves gay friendly in a neighborhood to which a number of gays have moved since the 1960s. Nonetheless, all this was possible only on the condition that this diversity existed in "reasonable proportions" and that its presence, especially in public space, did not contravene the norms that this group succeeded in imposing.

The defense of diversity is not, however, just window dressing, a mere pretense masking exclusionary practices. It entails a singular attitude that demands a certain openness, while at the same time undertaking to organize the openness with caution. Moving into a poor neighborhood—which could have meant a drop in their class status—in fact allowed these residents to maintain their position as white property owners. Even so, while critics might be tempted to speak of the "revanchist city,"[12] these residents have not emerged unchanged from their adventure. Whether they have been compelled to revisit their principles (for the most liberal among them) or to

---

12   See Neil Smith, *The New Urban Frontier: Gentrification and the Revanchist City*, London: Routledge, 1996.

euphemize their prejudices (for the most conservative), their relationships to other groups have not strictly obeyed market forces or economic interests. Instead, they have also conformed to the logic of a collective project: constructing a socially diverse South End. The taste for diversity thus proves to be more than just for display purposes, more than just lipservice paid to win both moral prestige and social domination. In reality, it both constrains their practices and reveals the reworking of class divisions. The mobilizations that we have seen take hold in the South End do not seek purely and simply to displace populations, but, more subtly, to structure their presence. This group founded its authority on a legitimacy that these residents had to construct—not that of racial superiority or even the privilege of wealth whitewashed by philanthropy, but rather that of respect for "diversity." This principle implies symbolic recognition of the dominated groups and acceptance of their presence in the residential space, though, certainly, only in limited numbers and without this leading to any sort of redistribution of resources.

The repudiation of exclusion and the valorization of openness—breaking with the social rejection of the poorest and with spatial segregation—have reworked the manner in which social distinction operates, as well as redefining class relations. Far from the kind of property owners' "Bolshevism"[13] reigning in some neighborhood associations—and more generally, straightforward contempt for other classes—the relation to the other that this lower section of the upper class maintains is, furthermore, distinct from middle-class mimicry of the elites.[14] Instead, it is characterized by a skillful mix of weakening divisions in some instances and reconstructing boundaries in others. In the 1960s the civil rights, gay rights and women's movements—and even the New Left—profoundly challenged the foundations of central divisions in US society. They put an end to de jure racial segregation, the exclusive power exerted by the white and Protestant elite, the strict division of professions and gender roles between men and women, and even police repression of homosexuality. Of course the neoliberalism and neoconservatism that took hold in the 1980s did pose a powerful

---

13   Mike Davis, *City of Quartz? Excavating the Future in Los Angeles*, New York: Verso, 1990.

14   Bourdieu, *Distinction*.

backlash against these emancipation movements.[15] But equally significantly, diversity became an established motif in the worlds of business, universities and political parties—one of the many ways of safely managing the conflicts of the 1960s and the disturbance of social domination.[16] This historic innovation—the love of "diversity"—was also taken up by a particular social group (which in turn would be structured by this value). This we can see at the neighborhood level, as well as in the relations between groups spreading across this space. Here the promotion of diversity does not erase the still-deep divisions underpinned by violent inequalities. Territorial segregation has not disappeared—far from it—and nor have racial discrimination and economic exploitation. Nonetheless, residents sing the praises of mixed neighborhoods, even as this posture is accompanied by the conquest of working-class neighborhoods (rather than opening up middle-class ones) and a strongly asserted control over the residential population. The paradigm of "diversity," such as it exists in the political and economic world, does legitimize the presence of certain representatives of dominated groups. Of course, it does so in only certain places and on certain conditions, and amidst an overall situation of persistent inequality. But nevertheless this has undermined a certain conception of social exclusivity, based on a brutally closed-off, in-group mentality and uncompromising geographical segregation; in order for such class boundaries to endure, they had to be remade.

The spatial dimension of power

In contrast to analyses that show a naïve optimism toward commitments to diversity—while also avoiding falling into the critical schema of "same old, same old"—this book has not set itself the objective of evaluating what progress this new governance of diversity has made. Rather, it aims to describe the logics by which this regime functions. Seeking to understand the specific forms by which a space is controlled, this study has focused on collective

---

15   Michael Omi and Howard Winant, *Racial Formation in the United States: From the 1960s to the 1990s*, London: Routledge, 1994.

16   Frank Dobbin, *Inventing Equal Opportunity*, Princeton, NJ: Princeton University Press, 2009; Sara Ahmed, *On Being Included: Racism and Diversity in Institutional Life*, Durham, NC: Duke University Press, 2012.

mobilizations, and observed, by way of its spokesmen from the civic sector, a group in the process of formation. The question of space proved central here—first because the city provides a valuable terrain for observing social and symbolic boundaries in the process of being reconfigured. A monographic work on a neighborhood that has undergone a gentrification process lasting many decades allows us to follow the remodeling of a space. But while the brownstones were being reconstructed and infrastructure renovated, and as the commercial scene was recomposed and public spaces occupied in a different manner, the designations for the neighborhood also changed; its administrative designation (a neighborhood in need of regeneration), its journalistic designation (a neighborhood of trendy restaurants), and its cultural designation (a historic district to preserve). As this book has shown, the erection of these symbolic boundaries is a decisively important dimension in redefining the neighborhood. At the same time, this interplay of representations and material space also introduces a third level of analysis, namely, of the agents and social groups engaged in the redefinition of the neighborhood; and—if these are not one and the same—the group of residents who mobilize to bring about the "good" South End at the same time that they defined themselves as a coherent group, tracing the boundaries that distinguish them from the "others."

As such, an analysis of the formation of these groups also benefits from introducing the question of space. Thus these inhabitants love the historic South End, and reject those who would prefer the construction of public housing to the preservation of the brownstones. In their attachment to diversity—contrary to the suburban denizens they criticize—they define this term as the peaceable and non-conflictual coexistence of a multitude of social groups, rather than in terms of the right of others to advance their own cultures and demands. Thus, there are close ties between the social boundaries that form a group, the symbolic boundaries between categories of social standing, norms and cultures, and finally the geographic boundaries through which a neighborhood is fashioned.[17]

As such, while certain readings today hold the city to be the central site of

---

17 On the interaction of these three levels, see Pierre Bourdieu, "Site Effects," in *The Weight of the World: Social Suffering in Contemporary Society*, Stanford, CA: Stanford University Press, 1999, pp. 123–9.

capitalist exploitation,[18] there also exist other, more complex means of thinking about the links between the spatial dimension and social structure. The first deals with the manner in which the mobilization of privileged groups operates through local space. Next to the professional sphere, which in large part defines social status, the liberal upper middle class has organized itself through the local neighborhood associations in which they engage. It is here, in the space of a few city blocks, at dinners among neighbors or in the public gardens where they cross paths, that Bostonians have come together to bring about the "diverse South End." Through the proximity of their homes, through their conversations—by appearances, trivial—about houses to be renovated and parks to be maintained, they formed and circulated ideas on transforming the neighborhood, ways of seeing the world, and, consequently, the manner of treating other social groups.

Class identities are thus constructed by way of a relationship with space, which, for the rich, is not restricted to maintaining residential segregation or to a generalized globalization. Indeed, these residents' attachment to the "good neighbor" ethos shatters clichés about "globalized elites" traveling from one fancy hotel to another, indifferently finding their bearings in the international spaces created for them. Instead, wealthy residents of these mixed neighborhoods are willing to spend not just money but also considerable amounts of time and energy to maintain "autochthonous capital,"[19] patiently constructed at the intersection of the philanthropic, commercial and political spheres. This involves controlling comings and goings in public spaces and taking to these spaces together with their pets; plunging into the past in order to write an official history of the neighborhood; evaluating all real estate projects in great detail; putting their generosity on display at charity soirées; and relentless surveillance of restaurant hours of operation. Control of the neighborhood thus demands a considerable investment. Not only does this moral enterprise confront those inhabitants who bear quite different norms and interests, but it also involves socializing new homeowners to the dangers and virtues of diversity, inculcating them with *de rigueur* social tolerance—as well as its limits.

---

18   David Harvey, *Rebel Cities: From the Right to the City to the Urban Revolution*, London: Verso, 2013.

19   See Chapter 1.

Of course, this group's capacity to regulate the residential space does not only operate by way of local engagement. It requires the support of City Hall, and combines with practices deployed on many levels. As has already been shown, the wealthiest residents pair intensive use of the neighborhood with significant mobility. Indeed, a number of active South End residents travel frequently, whether to the great cities of the East Coast, to Europe or to Central America in order to escape the rigors of the Boston winter. Moreover, while all of them emphasize their rich local sociability, extolling the community and singing the praises of running errands on foot, their uses of the neighborhood involve very specific practices: the closed in-group of the civic associations and careful avoidance of the public housing projects, the frequenting of certain parks and their preferred neighborhood restaurants. The cuisine that these establishments offer provides what these inhabitants see as an appealing experience of multiculturalism: the exoticism of Third World peasant food nourishes these prominent residents' "cosmopolitan habitus,"[20] at prices prohibitive to a large portion of the neighborhood population. Putting an autochthonous multiculturalism on display thus strengthens the microgestures of distancing from others, even if in an imperceptible way and under the cover of openness. But paradoxically, it has been in this mixed local space, whose culinary scene has been restructured, that a cosmopolitan habitus has been able to assert itself, more so than in traditional middle-class areas. It seems as if these residents' detour through the neighborhood has allowed for the affirmation of an international identity. The Bostonians living in the South End thus show that, far from being incompatible, the "local" and "cosmopolitan" influences described by Robert Merton can be merged into one figure.[21] Parochial attachments can participate, without contradiction, in an assertion of openness to the universalism of cultures.

This group's relation to space entails one last dimension. Significantly, a strong civic engagement has not erased the boundary between public and private that has been at the center of the middle-class ethos since the nineteenth century. The "good neighbor" is kind, respectful of his environment,

---

20   David Ley, *The New Middle Class and the Remaking of the Central City*, Oxford: Oxford University Press, 1996, pp. 307–9.

21   Robert K. Merton, "Patterns of Influence: Local and Cosmopolitan Influentials," in *Social Theory and Social Structure*, New York: Free Press, 1957, Chapter 12.

engaged in his neighborhood and ready to lend a hand—but does not trespass on other people's private space. The location of this boundary has shifted, however. This group of residents, faced with a demographic mix which it had never before experienced, particularly in public space—and which was more difficult to control than houses, businesses or even the associative sphere— succeeded in the course of appropriating this space in turning the object of their anxiety instead into a point of pride. Once exclusively the source of fear, public urban space became for these new arrivals the focus of rapt attention: it is the site where diversity is now put on display and where these inhabitants signal their liberal lifestyles. And just as was the case with bourgeoisie of a century ago, the redefinition of the boundaries between public and private also entailed a recomposition of the norms of gender and sexuality.[22]

Sex, city and class

One more particularity marks the formation of this social group: not only does it display a particular mix of exclusion and inclusion in its relation to others, and not only is it heavily engaged in local public spaces, but gender and sexuality are also directly involved in the redefinition of this class identity. For these populations, a commitment to the principle of equality between men and women was closely associated with a rejection of the previous generation's social codes—but also, more recently, with a rejection of what they presumed to be the social codes of the working class. Indeed, the South End's good neighbors are quick to assert the sexism of "other" populations, particularly the lowest-income men who are the clients of the neighborhood's charitable associations. The control over these men is not explicitly framed in terms of the color of their skin, and wealthy residents instead point to behaviors they considered deviant, such as smoking, drinking and these men's attitude toward women, often described as insulting. Yet even as these gender-based logics of distinction contribute to subtle forms of exclusion, they do also have effects on those who deploy them. Civic engagement, which, as we have seen, has allowed a new elite to emerge, also saw a weakening—certainly, a relative one—of differentiated gender roles. This facilitated access for women to positions of authority, beyond just in those clubs traditionally

---

22   Leonore Davidoff and Catherine Hall, *Family Fortunes: Men and Women of the English Middle Class, 1780–1850*, Chicago: University of Chicago Press, 1987.

reserved for them; meanwhile, the management of local political affairs has ceased to be an all-male affair; and restaurants and cafés are also no longer exclusively occupied by men.

All the same, the egalitarian discourse widespread among the privileged class translates only imperfectly into practice.[23] Their measured, cautious reorganization of heteronormativity can be seen also in the relationship to homosexuality. Exclusion—whether in terms of sexism or homophobia—is always exoticized as something that "other" people do, something from which good neighbors—necessarily open and gay-friendly—differentiate themselves carefully. Indeed, the diversity now promoted by part of the elite does not only concern populations defined by race and class, but also includes sexual orientation. Residential migrations have had some effect on this, in the extent to which they have facilitated the recomposition of sexual norms through which class divisions are also constructed. Ethnographic immersion in South End sociability reveals a certain relaxation of the marital, familial and heterosexual imperative. This can be explained in connection to this group's departure from the residential suburbs, even if there, too, there have been important changes. The presence of gays in city-center neighborhoods also entails a transformation of sociability, closely connected to civic engagement. For numerous heterosexual women, family life is no longer a strict condition of social integration, which now develops also on the basis of close friendships with gay men. Through their relatively increased integration of gay men (and to a much lesser degree, lesbians), the upper middle classes who love diversity thus reshape heterosexual domination. Vaunting their gay-friendly credentials, these members of the upper middle class share in a sociability that does not rest exclusively on heteronormativity. However, when gays and non-gays meet, they do so in practices anchored in their common socioeconomic status and in norms that still strongly emphasize the couple and the family, thus to some degree erasing the role that "sexual politics" have played in gay culture and gay movements.

While gender hierarchies are far from shattered, and the acceptance of homosexuality does not stop sexuality itself being held at arm's length, gay friendliness nevertheless now structures this group's social identity. Far from

---

23   Kathleen Gerson, *The Unfinished Revolution: How a New Generation is Reshaping Family, Work, and Gender in America*, Oxford: Oxford University Press, 2010.

constituting a linear process inevitably leading toward greater acceptance, this attitude has specific characteristics and strict limits. In the name of "diversity," all the old divisions have been shaken up, from the middle class's respectable homophobia, to the central roles of marriage and sex difference, or even the strict application of social and racial boundaries onto space. However, on each occasion these openings have been measured and required tight control, at once of gay populations, and even more so of low-income and black populations. The other gays—less wealthy, nonwhite or less attracted by marriage and children—remain largely excluded from this celebration of diversity.

Index

Note: All neighborhoods are in Boston, unless otherwise noted in parentheses